DATE DUE

Th
Community   nsider

Lawrence W. Tyree, I   *de los Santos*

FOR INNOVATION
IN THE COMMUNITY COLLEGE

League for Innovation in the Community College
with support from

University of Florida

378.111
L434

The League for Innovation in the Community College is an international organization dedicated to catalyzing the community college movement. The League hosts conferences and institutes, develops web resources, conducts research, produces publications, provides services, and leads projects and initiatives with more than 750 member colleges, 100 corporate partners, and a host of other government and nonprofit agencies in a continuing effort to make a positive difference for students and communities. Information about the League and its activities is available at www.league.org.

Copies of this publication are available through the League's website at www.league.org, or by calling (480) 705-8200. The publication is also available in digital form through iStream, www.league.org/istream.

Printed in the United States of America

ISBN 1-931300-40-2

Table of Contents

Acknowledgments

The editors wish to thank the dozens of community college leaders who stepped forward to share their edifying and enriching experiences for this work, which will undoubtedly be a guide and great resource for those who will follow in their path. Inspirational and instructive, sometimes wrenching and sometimes wry, these contributions shine a bright light on the corridor to community college leadership.

We also wish to thank the University of Florida for its support and encouragement in this project.

Larry W. Tyree
Mark David Milliron
Gerardo E. de los Santos

League for Innovation in the Community College

The Leadership Dialogues:
Community College Case Studies to Consider

An Introduction: Advancing the Art of Leadership

> *The process of learning an art can be divided conveniently into two parts: one, the mastery of the theory; the other, the mastery of the practice. If I want to learn the art of medicine, I must first know the facts about the human body, and about various diseases. When I have all this theoretical knowledge, I am by no means competent in the art of medicine. I shall become a master in this art only after a great deal of practice, until eventually the results of my theoretical knowledge and the results of my practice are blended into one – my intuition, the essence of the mastery of any art.*
>
> Eric Fromm (1956, p. 5)

Theory is a vital part of framing decisions, sizing up situations, and analyzing contexts. In the world of leadership theory, we explore the mechanistic, bureaucratic, and humanistic models. Others challenge us to move beyond simple management actions to more nuanced and higher-order leadership strategies. The virtues of mission, vision, and goal setting are extolled and argued to be essential to any effort to lead an organization down the road ahead. Deming and other advocates of continuous quality improvement and re-engineering argue we have to look deeply at the systems and processes that define our work and target our outcomes – and involve all levels of the organization in that endeavor (Walton & Deming, 1988).

Culture and climate theorists push us to examine more closely the social systems that weave a web of complicated and vital interrelationships – a web that can either empower and strengthen us, or trap and confound us. Peter Senge (1990) wants us to master the Fifth Discipline, while Jim Collins (2001) wants us to move from Good to Great by leveraging level-five leadership. Still others advocate that we get in better tune with our organizational energy systems, develop leader and team maturity, or look to our authentic selves and organizational souls. Making learning about leadership even more problematic, chaos theory advocates sometimes argue that the mix of variables is so out of our control that we have to release ourselves to this delicate art, which requires a light touch rather than a driving force. Margaret Wheatley (1999) would encourage more awareness of "butterfly wings" and less dogged driving toward strategic plans.

Make no mistake: We feel that these theoretical examinations and perspectives are useful. However, as Fromm (1956) notes in the opening quote, to truly advance the art of leadership, we need to test our formal theories and informal assumptions against the hard and sometimes cold realities of practice. And with this in mind, we began our initial conversations about this volume – a book dedicated to showcasing the ups and downs, ins and outs, and joys and pains of leadership.

But it was not just leadership in the abstract in which we were interested. It was leadership in the community college – this amazingly inspiring and sometimes confounding context in which we work. We wanted real-life examples of cases involving community college governance; executive leadership; administration and finance; instructional programs and services; student life; legal issues, politics, and policy; fundraising; media; technology; and workforce, partnerships, and outreach. And we wanted a special category for those stories out of the ordinary. Of course, these categories are limited in their scope; and we hope to expand them in later versions of this book. Indeed, we see this volume as the base of an ongoing project to feature community college cases for use in graduate programs, leadership institutes, and administrative retreats. It is meant to be beginning fodder for in-depth conversations about the art of leadership in the community college.

Why focus only on community colleges? Put simply, all too often we are lumped into discussions of K-12 or university models without sufficient and in-depth exploration of the distinctive nature of our context. We argue that there are substantially different twists to the art of leadership in a community college; so much so that we deserve a dedicated dais for our dialogues. We invite you to sample the twists and turns of leadership in the community college and begin your dialogues.

References

Collins, J. (2001). *Good to Great: Why Some Companies Make the Leap and Others Don't.* New York: HarperCollins.

Fromm, E. (1989). *The Art of Loving.* New York: HarperCollins/Perennial.

Senge, P. (1990). *The Fifth Discipline: The Art and Practice of the Learning Organization.* New York: Currency Doubleday.

Walton, M., & Deming, W. E. (1986). *The Deming Management Method.* New York: Perigree.

Wheatley, M. J. (1999). *Leadership and the New Science: Discovering Order in a Chaotic World.* San Francisco: Berrett-Koehler Publishers.

Part I

Governance

1. Jumping In With Both Feet

Mary Ellen Duncan

Context

Nirvana Community College is located between two major eastern U.S. cities, in an affluent community of about 260,000 residents. Because a planned community is part of the service area, community leaders are used to creating new institutions and setting high expectations.

The college serves about 6,000 credit (headcount) students and 12,000 noncredit students. The board of trustees is appointed by the governor upon recommendation of state senators in the college's service area.

Summary of the Case

In 1997, the board of trustees made a decision to encourage the college's second president, who was completing his 16th year as president, to retire. This action was taken rather suddenly and based primarily on the initiative of one board member who had a myriad of concerns about the "freewheeling" nature of the president and key staff.

The board had not been included in the innovative culture of the college and were surprised about a number of entrepreneurial projects undertaken there. An interim president was hired through ACCT, but the board began in earnest to run the college themselves, starting with the premise that everything was suspect and should be fully investigated.

The board hired a consultant, a neighbor of one of the board members, who was an accounting professor on sabbatical from a small liberal arts college. This person was charged with writing policy governance for the board, along with acting as an internal auditor. When he spoke to staff, he spoke with the authority of the board. Another consultant was hired to prepare for Y2K, the upgrading of the administrative software system, and the restructuring of computer services. This project was the prime interest of another board member. A third board member decided to devise a detailed planning process, and conducted workshops with staff. A fourth member set the number of projects that should be undertaken by faculty on learning outcomes.

And so on. There was nothing that occurred at the college that did not raise the eyebrows of the board members and precipitate intervention, *e.g.*, the making of a television course for public television or the transfer of any funds of any amount to any other account, even within a unit budget.

The board was particularly suspicious of the relationship the college had with a contractor who ran the administrative hardware and developed a one-of-a-kind home-grown administrative software system. The college was this contractor's only client. The contractor was a colleague at a college where the former president had worked. This person was also the initiator of a computer product to facilitate communication between a desktop computer and the print shop. College funds were used for the development of this product, which was eventually abandoned.

The board embarked on a participative process to choose new administrative software from an experienced vendor, and Datatel was selected. The board decided a fast-track implementation was necessary to be ready in time for Y2K. Yet they were afraid to sever the relationship with the contractor, because those people were the only administrative computing staff and were needed to implement the new administrative software – and on a rapid schedule.

Additionally, the contractor's contract was coming to an end in June 1998. The board hired an attorney to draw up a contract to keep the contractor for an additional 18 months, even though they were very concerned about how committed the contractor would be to the new product, and they wanted to be sure to terminate the relationship.

Simultaneously, the college was involved in a process to hire a new president. All constituents were represented in the process, and the board made a choice for its new president by March 1998. The new contract for the IT contractor had to be signed prior to July 1, 1998. The new president was scheduled to begin on July 1, 1998.

Questions to Consider

1. If you were the new president, what would you do, knowing the disdain the board has for the IT contractor and knowing their fear about moving to a new administrative software?
2. Would you make any contact with the IT contractor or the employees of the contractor?
3. What resources do you need to make a decision as to what you might do about managing administrative computing?
4. Should you take action now, or ride out the 18-month term of the board's proposed contract extension, as advised by their attorney?

Thoughts and Analysis

The board chair has given you copies of the contract, of the consultant's recommendation, and other information. The consultant recommended the 18-month transition and a national search for a new director. Datatel provided an on-site manager to help with the rapid nine-month implementation schedule.

The board did not know the salaries of the contractor's employees. They did not know if the employees would stay at Nirvana if they were asked.

In this process, the board never spoke directly with the contractor. They only speculated about what he might do and what his reaction might be.

Outcomes

The new president requested moving the start date two days prior to July 1, 1998 so that the contractor's contract would be in the president's hands before the due date. The president also obtained permission from the board to hire an interim IT executive on a one-year-only contract to help assess the situation. As soon as permission was granted, in May, a review of the available materials began.

Upon arrival on June 29, the president and the interim IT director assessed the qualifications of the existing staff and spoke directly to the contractor. The contractor agreed that he would rather not work under the existing conditions, and a buy-out was discussed. The interim IT director calculated that most of the employees of the contractor would choose to work for the college if asked, but no one even knew what their salaries were and what the cost of the assimilation of the employees would be.

The president asked the contractor for this information, and the contractor gladly provided it. A buy-out amount was negotiated. The contractor proposed $250,000. The president gave a maximum counter offer of $100,000. While technically, no buy-out was necessary, good relations with the contractor and his employees were necessary for a smooth transition. However, the contractor and employees expected a new agreement to be signed. The negotiations were conducted in a nonconfrontational manner.

On the second day of employment, the president invited the board chair to the college to discuss the proposed buy-out and get board approval. At first, board members were very concerned about the risks. All members were called. By the end of the day, all members agreed to leave the decision in the hands of the president.

The relationship with the contractor was severed at the end of Day 2, saving the college $500,000 over 18 months, in addition to the $100,000 buy-out. All of the employees (except for the contractor himself) agreed to work for the college and were hired at a 10 percent increase. A search for a new IT vice president began, and he was appointed at the end of the one-year temporary contract for the interim director.

In the meantime, everyone was ready to work on Datatel rapid implementation. And the work began.

The board started to develop confidence in the new president and began a return to its normal role.

Mary Ellen Duncan is President of Howard Community College in Columbia, Maryland.

2. The Florida Council of Presidents

Susan M. Lehr

Context

Florida's Community College System is comprised of 28 community colleges and serves approximately one million students in credit and noncredit programs, with over 300,000 FTEs in the system. The governance structure for the system consists of the Council of Presidents (COP) and the Florida Department of Education (DOE), Division of Community Colleges and Workforce. The DOE is an agency of the Executive Office of the Governor, whereas the COP is a stand-alone body that determines policy and budget requests and submits them through the DOE to the legislature for the 28 colleges. The COP prides itself in acting on behalf of all community colleges and sets forth policies and budget requests as a comprehensive community college system (CCS).

Summary of the Case

In 1997, the Workforce Development Education Fund was created by the legislature to provide a new way of funding workforce programs for community colleges and school-district vocational technical schools. It created common definitions, standard program lengths, a common database and common fee structures. It was performance based and included postsecondary adult vocational programs, adult general education, and the associate in science programs. While colleges embraced performance-based funding, this legislation created controversy and dissension among the colleges.

For the first time in the history of Florida's CCS, colleges' budgets were split into two categories at the individual college level within the Appropriations Act; part was in the Workforce Development Fund (WDF) and part was in the CCS budget commonly referred to as the Community College Program Fund (CCPF). The CCPF is the primary operating budget for a college, providing salaries and other ongoing expenditures.

Colleges ranged from 9 to 66 percent of their budgets in the WDF, while other colleges had between 34 to 90 percent of their budgets in the CCPF. On the whole, 35 percent of the system's FTE was in Workforce, and 65 percent of the CCS' FTE was in traditional associate of arts transfer programs, which constituted the CCPF.

The split of the colleges' budgets caused a change in the way presidents viewed their budgets. Those with very large CCPF programs were primarily interested in CCPF funding increases, while those with large workforce programs had that as an emphasis. Much effort was put into making the WDF and performance-based budgeting work. And though workforce performance outcomes continued to rise dramatically, the legislative promise of additional performance incentive funds was never realized. In fact, between 1998 and 2004, the WDF lost $57 million through legislative action, a decrease of 6 percent, while the CCPF increased by 33 percent during the same time period.

Over several years, there were numerous campaigns by the colleges to obtain funds for workforce education. A major problem was that while the colleges lobbied for workforce funding, the vocational technical schools did not; the vocational technical schools report to their district school superintendents, and the superintendents would only lobby for their K-12 funding. This left the colleges alone lobbying for not one but two budget issues (CCPF and WDF). Furthermore, any funding obtained for community college workforce programs went equally to the vocational technical schools. Additional funding was acquired only one year (2000), and in most years, the funding for WDF was reduced.

The colleges' primary increases each year came through the CCPF, which meant that only a portion of a college's budget obtained an increase. Each year, the CCPF received an increase and the WDF did not, leaving colleges with large workforce programs achieving increases on only half of their college's budget. The college presidents concluded that it was counterproductive to lobby for two budget items.

So in 2001, the COP developed a new strategy for the CCS. They abandoned efforts to obtain new money for the WDF and instead tried persuading the legislature to dissolve the WDF and reintegrate the colleges' workforce budgets back into the CCPF. The colleges collaborated on the development of a new CCPF formula, which included workforce. Though not all colleges benefited equally, all 28 college presidents formally endorsed the new model, which distributed by formula any new funds the CCS might receive from the legislature. This was presented as legislation endorsed by all 28 colleges; the legislature passed the new CCPF formula in 2001. However, they did not dissolve the WDF, which still left two statutory formulas.

In 2001, the World Trade Center terrorist attacks wreaked havoc on the state's tourist economy. In December, the legislature was called into special session to cut the budget because of shortfalls in state revenues. The WDF budget was cut by $24.3 million and the CCPF was cut $55 million.

During the regular 2002 legislative session, many cuts were restored. However, only $800,000 in workforce funds was restored (of the $24.3 million cut), whereas the CCPF budget was restored with all $55 million, plus it saw an increase of $9 million, for a total of $64 million. This left the colleges with large workforce programs at a severe disadvantage.

Questions to Consider

Issue 1: In preparing the 2003 budget, the COP discussed whether it should support the restoration of funds for the colleges that lost money from the WDF budget cuts during the previous special session. Keeping in mind that there is only a finite amount of money given to the CCS, a yes vote by college presidents with minimal workforce programs would mean there would be less money in the CCPF for their own college.

1. Should the president vote for what benefits the college most?
2. Is the president's duty greater to the COP and the system or to the president's own college?

3. Should colleges abandon their workforce programs because of lack of support from the legislature and only offer A.A. transfer programs?
4. What are the ramifications of every college voting for what benefits its college most financially?
5. How do these decisions affect the board members' perception of the president?
6. What are potential solutions for this dilemma?

Issue 2: The 2003 Legislative Session was another disappointment. The legislature did not provide any new money for the CCS and, in fact, there were more cuts totaling $5.2 million. Following that dismal budget year, the COP began discussions in preparation for the next legislative budget request for 2004. Presidents were again faced with the same proposition of renewing the deal of splitting 50-50 any new money that might be given to the CCS between workforce and CCPF. This time, the deal would be in effect until the $22.1 million (revised figure) was restored, no matter how many sessions it took. Taking into consideration that enrollments in the CCS were up 23 percent over the previous three years, and state funding per FTE had declined by 10 percent, all colleges were in great need of funding. Presidents with small workforce programs (budgets were mainly CCPF) were hard pressed to support this initiative, as it would mean even less money for their own colleges.

1. How would you vote? Would it depend on your college's program mix?
2. At what point does supporting the system's goals become too burdensome for the president's individual college?
3. What is to be gained by retaining the cohesive system approach?
4. What are the consequences of abandoning the system approach?
5. Once a policy is agreed upon, what are the ethics of changing positions to benefit one's own institution?
6. What are the policy implications for the future as others look upon the actions of colleges within the COP?

Thoughts and Analysis

Decisions based on equity and concern for all colleges enable the COP to stand apart from other education groups. The COP's reputation for debating the issues internally and then speaking with one united voice continues to make the system strong and highly regarded by legislative leaders.

Outcomes

Issue 1: The COP voted to request that the legislature split any new funds given to the colleges 50-50 between workforce and the CCPF, up to the amount needed for the WDF restoration. This was in recognition that workforce funding had never been restored from the 2001 Special Session. This was to be a one-year deal that would expire at the end of the legislative session. There was much dissension and discussion, but the vote was unanimous.

Issue 2: The presidents again voted unanimously to support the restoration of workforce funds. This consistent one-system message has to date produced extraordinary results. The 2004 governor's budget provides the largest increase in the last 14 years, with $114.4 million in state support for community colleges, and reintegrates the workforce fund into the CCPF. Also for the first time, the governor released the CCS section of his budget in a special news conference prior to the release of the entire budget. This priority emphasis generated statewide news coverage and positions the CCS to be first in line for funding during the 2004 session.

Susan M. Lehr is Vice President for Government Relations at Florida Community College in Jacksonville, Florida.

3. Strengthening Community Colleges to Meet Public Needs

Kay M. McClenney

Context

In the mid-1990s, the Commonwealth of Kentucky took a close look at its status with regard to the educational attainment level of the state's population – and many people across the business, political, and educational communities were concerned about what they saw. A statewide postsecondary education task force determined, in a nutshell, that the future economic viability and quality of life in the commonwealth would depend on strengthening the state's community colleges, regional universities, and research universities and promoting significantly increased college participation and attainment rates for Kentucky's citizens. The task force made a number of bold recommendations that were converted into proposed legislation.

The proposals for postsecondary education reform included a number of significant provisions related to the organization, mission, governance, and funding of the state's colleges and universities. But by far the most controversial measure was the proposal to separate the community colleges from the governance and control of the University of Kentucky (UK). Prior to 1997, the state's 14 community colleges were part of the university system, and another state agency oversaw the work of 15 technical schools. University leaders saw that arrangement as beneficial, because it provided political outposts for UK across the state. On the other hand, the governor and other reform advocates argued both that the community colleges were seriously limited by the university control and that the university's priority should be on development of its research mission. The reform legislation would combine the community college and technical schools into a single system with its own governing board.

A pitched political battle ensued, pitting the university president against the governor and featuring substantial expenditures of money to mobilize student and public opinion in opposition to reform. While debate occurred across the state, the real struggle was in a closely divided legislature, where the ultimate decisions would be made. The governor understood that losing the debate over the community colleges might torpedo the entire reform package – and could also seriously jeopardize his chances for re-election to a second term.

Summary of the Case

Data documented that the state had an unacceptably low educational attainment level across its population, and the rate at which associate degrees were awarded was too low for the state's workforce to be competitive. Furthermore, the adult illiteracy rate hovered at about 40 percent. The community colleges were doing good work, particularly with regard to the transfer mission, but there were significant constraints on their workforce and economic development roles, as well as on their contributions to adult basic-skills development. Large numbers of the state's citizens, therefore, were not being served by the community colleges and technical schools at the level required by their communities and state. This was the backdrop against which the political struggle for a separate new system of community and technical colleges was waged.

Questions to Consider

1. What are appropriate and effective strategies to make the case for strengthening the community and technical colleges in a state?
2. How should advocates of change in higher education deal with their powerful adversaries?
3. What are fundamental principles of effective public policymaking for postsecondary education?
4. What are important design principles for a strong statewide community and technical college system that should be considered in developing and proposing state policy?

Thoughts and Analysis

The Kentucky experience highlights a number of important elements of leadership, political debate, and policymaking that will hold true in many other settings, both at the state level and on the campus.

Political Courage. The governor's political future was clearly at stake. Perhaps the most important thing to recognize in this and similar situations is the sheer courage that is required to do the right thing. Advocating significant change, even when that change is in the public interest, is risky business.

Using Data to Make a Case. To paraphrase President Lyndon Baines Johnson, it may often be less difficult to *do the right thing* than to *know the right thing to do*. Too seldom seen in public policymaking is the use of clear and credible data that defines the public interest. Early in discussion of the role and future of community colleges in Kentucky, the crucial strategy lay in taking the time to document where the state was in terms of economic viability, workforce development, adult literacy, research capacity, educational access, and educational attainment. Once the facts were clearly laid out, the debate quickly moved from *whether* change was needed to *which* changes would most likely produce the desired results. The use of credible data in that debate proved crucial as well, and leaders from the media and business community became informed advocates for reform.

Clear Public Policy Objectives and Accountability. Another essential element in the development of reform legislation – and in the ensuing work as well – was the definition of clear public-policy objectives. The Kentucky Postsecondary Education Improvement Act of 1997 includes the following language:

(1) The General Assembly hereby finds that:

    (a) The general welfare and material well-being of citizens of the Commonwealth depend in large measure upon the development of a well-educated and highly-trained workforce...

(2) The General Assembly declares on behalf of the people of the Commonwealth the following goals to be achieved by the year 2020:

    (a) A seamless, integrated system of postsecondary education strategically planned and adequately funded to enhance economic development and quality of life;

    (b) A major comprehensive research institution ranked nationally in the top twenty (20) public universities at the University of Kentucky;

    (c) A premier, nationally-recognized metropolitan research university at the University of Louisville;

    (d) Regional universities, with at least one (1) nationally-recognized program of distinction or one (1) nationally-recognized applied research program, working cooperatively with other postsecondary institutions to assure statewide access to baccalaureate and master's degrees of a quality at or above the national average;

    (e) A comprehensive community and technical college system with a mission that assures, in conjunction with other postsecondary institutions, access throughout the Commonwealth to a two (2) year course of general studies designed for transfer to a baccalaureate program, the training necessary to develop a workforce with the skills to meet the needs of new and existing industries, and remedial and continuing education to improve the employability of citizens; and

    (f) An efficient, responsive, and coordinated system of autonomous institutions that delivers educational services to citizens in quantities and of a quality that is comparable to the national average.

(3) The achievement of these goals will lead to the development of a society with a standard of living and quality of life that meets or exceeds the national average.

(4) The achievement of these goals will only be accomplished through increased educational attainment at all levels, and contributions to the quality of elementary and secondary education shall be a central responsibility of Kentucky's postsecondary institutions.

(5) The furtherance of these goals is a lawful public purpose that can best be accomplished by a comprehensive system of postsecondary education with single points of accountability that ensure the coordination of programs and efficient use of resources.

The Kentucky Council on Postsecondary Education subsequently established five "key indicators of progress toward postsecondary reform." The indicators were created to answer these central questions about how the state's colleges and universities are contributing to the overall well-being of the state and its citizens, and they form the basis for annual accountability reports:

1. Are more Kentuckians ready for postsecondary education?
2. Are more students enrolling?
3. Are more students advancing through the system?

4. Are we preparing Kentuckians for life and work?
5. Are Kentucky's communities and economy benefiting?

Purposive efforts were made to change the nature of the higher education debate in Kentucky. Advocates of reform argued not that the central concern should be the welfare of institutions, but that the central concerns were the needs of the state and the welfare of its people. This change in the lens used for examining both problems and solutions makes all the difference in public policy.

Outcomes

The Kentucky legislature passed and the governor signed the Kentucky postsecondary reform legislation in May 1997. The act created the Kentucky Community and Technical College System (KCTCS), with its own Board of Regents, separate from the University of Kentucky.

Since passage of the legislation, Kentucky has seen the following results achieved through the work of the KCTCS:

- There was a 58 percent enrollment increase in Kentucky community and technical colleges from fall 1998 to fall 2003. KCTCS now enrolls over 72,000 students in credit courses. Also, the system serves about 180,000 Kentuckians a year through workforce training, continuing education, employee assessments, and adult education.
- There was a 23 percent increase in KCTCS associate degree graduates over the period from 1997-1998 to 2002-2003; total credentials earned (diplomas, certificates, associate degrees) increased to 9,918 in 2003, a 46 percent increase in two years.
- KCTCS includes 62 campuses now open or under construction, all augmented by access through the Kentucky Virtual University.
- KCTCS institutions and regional universities are operating or soon will open regional postsecondary education centers in five communities.
- Over 1,000 new career-related programs are available to Kentucky students.
- The system offers 3,600 workforce-related courses.
- Fifty thousand people have been trained.
- The KCTCS has served 1,900 businesses.
- AA and AAS degrees are attainable online.

The KCTCS has been described in the media as follows:

- "One of the best systems in the country" – *Chronicle of Higher Education*
- "Increasing accessibility to higher education" – *Community College Times*
- "A most unqualified success" – *Lexington Herald-Leader*
- "Coordinated workforce development exists because of KCTCS" – *Louisville Courier-Journal*
- "Almost-instant success" – *National CrossTalk*

Kay McClenney is Director of the Community College Survey of Student Engagement and an adjunct professor in the Community College Leadership Program at The University of Texas at Austin.

4. A Change in Board Composition

David H. Ponitz

Context

Crawford Community College is located in a central city with a population of 30,000, a community that is the commercial center for multiple counties. It is characterized by heavy and light manufacturing and emerging high-technology initiatives. Workers in the manufacturing arena belong to a variety of traditional industrial unions.

The Crawford Community College board of trustees is elected, and several members have served multiple terms. Members work in small business and the professions, and one member is a manager of a manufacturing plant. As a group, they like and respect one another, attend many of the same social functions, and find hybrid decisions to a spectrum of college policy issues. During the past year, the finances of the college have been strained, as at all the other community colleges in the state, and projections suggest there will be additional financial reductions by the state government during the next several years. The college has a long history of offering quality liberal arts programs as well as advanced technical courses to serve both university transfer needs and the special employment requirements of area business and industry.

The board and the president respect one another, and together with the faculty, staff, and community have developed a comprehensive master plan within the year. To address growing unemployment in the community, the Chamber of Commerce and other business groups have asked for additional training in electronics, advanced information technology, and automated controls, which will necessitate purchase of updated numerically controlled computer equipment. The board has responded by shifting budget expenditures to these workforce requests, which will provide 500 new technical jobs over the next several years.

The faculty at the college is older, has a strong union, and is very supportive of traditional liberal arts programs. Collective negotiations are adversarial, and there have been several near strikes. The board has always been cohesive on bargaining issues, insistent that the board be in control, and supportive of the president on grievance issues.

Summary of the Case

Things changed at the last general election. Three incumbents, along with a fourth individual heavily supported by the teachers' union, ran for three seats. A board member of long tenure who gave many hours of quality service to both the college and the community was defeated. Both he and the other board members were stunned by the election results.

The new board member once worked in a middle-management position at the college. He was eased out of employment several years ago and is still unhappy about how he was treated. Continuing board members believe he is bad news for the college. They believe that his election platform emphasized total support of the faculty union and embraced a faculty position that placed more emphasis on traditional liberal arts with fewer opportunities for economic development. In addition, expanded faculty control of the curriculum is also part of his agenda. Board members believe he is obligated to the teachers' union, not very knowledgeable about the needs of business and industry, and a "pain in the neck." One board member describes him as angry, defensive, and ready to destroy much of the good work of the past 10 years. With these concerns in mind, several members of the board now come to the president with a number of questions, and ask for recommendations.

Questions to Consider

1. How do we rebuild a cohesive board membership – or is that an impossible goal now?
2. How will the new board member affect collective negotiations preparation? We are afraid that our stand-together strategy has been destroyed, and that the new board member will blab our discussions to the entire union.
3. Should we cocoon the new board member, as some of our business friends have suggested, or do we try to work with him? How should we proceed?
4. We had planned to elect the now defeated board member as our next chair. Should we elect an old hand or a more junior member to better face the new challenges? What talents do we need?

Thoughts and Analysis

Many newly constituted boards hold retreats to discuss goals and ways they will work together, to provide orientation of new board members, and to set priorities on issues for decision and implementation. Some boards facing issues of this type have discussed mutual-gains bargaining and other new governance forms.

The president may need to educate the board on the mood of the community. Is there a real change happening, or did the incumbent board member lose simply because he thought he didn't have to campaign for the position?

The new chair has a special function to help the board work as a unit, and the president shares that responsibility. Formal discussion may be needed to ensure that members of the board as well as the president understand how they should proceed. That will take time and discussion. Cocooning a board member can produce a variety of challenges – some of them very negative.

Outcomes

To produce the best outcomes in this case, the president's role might be that of mediator between the continuing board, the new board member, and various faculty demands. Development of a process plan of action will be most important, and the newly devised master plan might be a vehicle to keep the college moving in a positive direction.

David H. Ponitz is President Emeritus of Sinclair Community College in Dayton, Ohio.

5. An Attempt at Overlegislation

Charles Spence

Context

The community college about which this case study is written is a large, multicampus college with over 100,000 students in a Southern city. Enrollment was about one-third African American, 10 percent Hispanic, and the rest Caucasian. I was president of this college for 11 years. When I arrived, I found a very traditional institution that had had little experience in the planning arena because of political chaos surrounding the previous president. Because the college had also been plagued by a good deal of racial stress, I decided that we needed to take a number of important steps to ameliorate the situation.

We instituted a very aggressive affirmative action plan in the hiring of new faculty; we established a strong program of developmental skills for underachieving students; and we put into place a purchasing plan to assure that minority-owned small businesses were able to fairly access college contracts and purchases.

After undertaking these initial steps, I hoped that the college's new commitment to diversity would gain a natural momentum of its own and thus require less of the president's time. My dream was that once everyone recognized that diversity worked, I could focus my attention on other, equally important issues. In fact, the opposite occurred, because racial prejudice had become severely institutionalized in the college's culture. Moreover, I sadly and rather naively learned that racial prejudice runs very deep and can surface in surprising ways. I found that there were very few decisions I made that did not take the racial-fairness issue into consideration.

After a good deal of soul searching, I decided to take a different approach and involve the college in setting what I considered to be exciting strategic directions about innovation and managing the relevant changes.

As part of these changes, we created a collegewide administrative process in which we encouraged all individuals who were in similar but about-to-be-deleted positions to apply for the new positions. I had hoped to use this opportunity of new positions to add new blood and achieve a higher level of diversity in the staff. Those goals were achieved.

Next, I created a position to encourage and support instructional innovation and faculty leadership. The position had exciting possibilities and needed a respected change agent from the faculty ranks to assume its leadership. The board endorsed the concept, and we started to search for this new leader.

At this point, a very senior state legislator who represented our district approached me and asked that I give his wife this new position. This legislator's wife was a faculty member who had just been promoted in the collegewide reorganization. She was bright and creative but had little support from the faculty because of her weak interpersonal skills. The faculty simply did not perceive her as an effective team player, although I liked her and enjoyed working with her.

I found myself in an extremely awkward position with her husband because he had great control and influence over our budget, special allocations, and even appointments to our board of trustees through the governor's office. He was also a strong voice for the needs of African Americans in the community. I told him that his wife would have to apply for the job along with others and that I would be happy to consider her. His response to me was blunt: He told me in no uncertain terms that he would "get me" if his wife didn't get the job.

In the end, I decided to hire a faculty member who happened to be a White male and was a respected leader of the faculty senate who had also been named Faculty Member of the Year. He did extraordinary work, which has continued for many years and has even been recognized with the Hesburgh award.

The legislative leader then called in state auditors, who were told to examine every expenditure I had approved for the previous six years. Nightly TV newscasts speculated about the audit and its results. I would estimate the cost of this audit to be in the hundreds of thousands of dollars.

During this time, the governor had to appoint seven of the eight college trustees. This legislator solicited members for these positions based upon their willingness to dismiss me. My contract was to be renewed that year.

At the same time, the legislator also released an internal audit report to the press before the audit was completed. The allegations in the audit were outrageous and ultimately proved untrue. I was literally under siege.

Summary of the Case

The community college was a deeply traditional institution with a poor record of racial integration in its faculty and a lingering history of political chaos surrounding the previous president. The institution was in need of some radical changes in its administration and leadership. When I tried to make long-overdue administrative changes to the institution, I came under attack by a member of the state legislature, who demanded that I hire his wife under what would have amounted to a patronage system. Moreover, my fiscal management of the college came under attack, and the renewal of my contract was held hostage by our board. Meanwhile, the media put my management of the college under a microscope.

Questions to Consider

As president of the college, I faced many difficult questions:

  1. Should I just give the legislator's wife the position?
  2. Should I inform the board of this pressure?

3. Should I go public?
4. Should I try to get the legislator to put his demands in writing?
5. Should I resign?
6. Should I go public and fight the allegations one by one or just issue a denial, asserting that I will be cleared?
7. Should I hire an attorney and claim that I was libeled?
8. Should I leak any of this to the press to tell my side?
9. Should I let the chips fall and let the process continue?

Thoughts and Analysis

1. The college is in serious need of change, since it suffered from a kind of institutionalized racism.
2. In the midst of a reasonable attempt to bring change to the college, the president is challenged by a state legislator to appoint his wife to a college position via a kind of spoils patronage system.
3. The college president is put under additional political pressure by this legislator and the governor's office by an audit.
4. The media is reporting on this chain of events and, by its involvement, fanning the flames of controversy.
5. The president's job is in jeopardy if he does not acquiesce to the legislator's demands.

Outcomes

I kept to the high road. My worst nightmare was that our employees would be hurt by innuendo. At the same time, the board reviewed my contract and wanted to weaken it, but I did not allow that to happen.

I was being accused of racism, which hurt me very deeply. After all, we had won the Kennedy award from ACCT and we were recognized everywhere for our determined commitment to diversity. Ironically, in the midst of being called a racist, I was personally given the state's highest civil rights award.

Another wonderful irony was being given the Prudential company's community leadership award for my work in the community. I gave the $10,000 check to our college foundation.

After six months, the audits by the state were finally made public. As television crews covered the board meeting, the board chair, who had cooperated with the state legislator in demanding that I hire his wife, walked out of the meeting when the report totally cleared me.

The board then had to elect a new chair and split 4-4 for three meetings to debate the chair's behavior. A new chair was finally elected, and the board renewed my contract for three years.

I was exhausted. And I was shocked at how people at the college had avoided me while the audits were going on. I realized how alone a CEO can be.

I agonized about whether to stay at the college and determined that I would stay long enough for things to settle down, so that I could protect our employees. I sought professional counseling, which suggested that I so loved the college that I should stay. I stayed for another four years. Meanwhile, I was continually recruited by other college systems and accepted a challenging new position, where I have been very happy.

The state legislator was not re-elected, and the legislator's wife left the college. The board was still so split by the issues that it took two years to hire a replacement. The search was characterized as full of board dirty tricks.

As I review the outcomes of this experience, I am reminded of the Buddhist philosophy that, while it may seem unlikely at the moment, "your enemies make you stronger." In retrospect, I also believe that I should have contacted the state ethics commission and reported the behavior of the board member and the state legislator.

Finally, despite the pain, the threats, and the terrible toll it took on me, I would again deny a job to someone because of threats. In contrast to my earlier experience, I am now blessed with an honest, ethical board.

Charles Spence is Chancellor of Contra Costa Community College District in Martinez, California.

6. System Within a System: The Evolution of Hawaii's Community Colleges

Joyce S. Tsunoda

Context

Hawaii's population at the beginning of the 21st century was 1.2 million, with about 75 percent of its residents living on Oahu. Geographically, the island state is in the middle of the Pacific Ocean, nearly 3,000 miles from the nearest land mass.

The University of Hawaii (UH) is the state's single system of public higher education, consisting of 10 campuses on four islands. Seven of these are two-year colleges, which became known as the University of Hawaii Community Colleges (UHCCs). The remaining three campuses are baccalaureate-granting institutions, including the original UH-Manoa, a Carnegie I Research University.

The UH System is governed by the Board of Regents (BOR). The 12 members of the BOR are appointed by the governor and confirmed by the state senate. BOR members serve four-year terms, except for a student member, who serves two years.

UH was founded in 1907. The Honolulu-based Manoa campus was a selective university serving less than 10 percent of Hawaii's college-going population. This changed in 1965, when the state legislature passed Act 39, which established the community colleges. This landmark legislation was part of a national movement that peaked in the 1960s to expand postsecondary educational opportunities through establishment of low-tuition, open-door community colleges. Act 39 converted five technical schools run by the Hawaii State Department of Education (K-12) into community colleges, and called for opening a brand-new campus in the rapidly growing Central-West Oahu region. A few years later, another community college would open on the Windward side of Oahu.

The rise of the UHCCs was not without challenges. There was opposition, including from baccalaureate-campus faculty who believed that community colleges granting two-year degrees did not belong within a university system. Meanwhile, the statewide K-12 public school system, which ran the technical schools, was not pleased about losing jurisdiction. To this day, this system still hangs on to the adult education function, duplicating many existing programs of the UHCCs.

Organizationally, the seven community colleges experienced much change over the years. Each college is a separately accredited institution with a basic complement of administrative and academic functions and structures. This includes the college president, whose title was provost. At inception, these provosts reported directly to the president of the UH System, with some systemwide support and coordination provided by a statewide office headed by an administrator. The title and responsibilities of this administrator evolved from director of community college operations to vice president for community colleges and, ultimately, to chancellor for community colleges, with much stronger oversight authority over the seven campuses. The last chancellor for community colleges served for 20 years, from 1983 to 2003, and was the first to come from the ranks of faculty.

By the turn of the century, the UHCCs had become the largest component of the UH System, representing more than 60 percent of total headcount enrollment. Collectively and individually, the UHCCs were acknowledged by students, graduates, and the public for their responsiveness, quality programs, teaching-learning focus, and outreach nationally as well as internationally. Many graduates and program participants became productive members of the community, and those transferring to the four sister campuses were successful in completing their baccalaureates as well as advanced degrees.

Most important, the UHCCs were praised from within the UH System as well as the larger community for their organizational coherence, smoothness of operation, collaboration, innovation and creativity, and a strong sense of identity and mission integrity. When the UHCCs celebrated their 25th anniversary as a system, a Honolulu newspaper editorial called the community colleges "one of the proudest legacies of Hawaii's social reform and growth in the last four decades."

The incumbent chancellor for community colleges contemplated retirement at the end of her 20-year tenure and expected to turn over the helm of the UHCCs to a qualified successor, including possible internal candidates who had been groomed as part of the BOR-expected succession plan. However, changes within the entire UH System, especially with the appointment of a new UH systemwide president, affected the anticipated leadership transition and more.

Summary of the Case

In 2000, the sitting president of the UH System announced plans to retire after seven years. His difficult tenure was marked by Hawaii's economic downturn, resulting in continuing deep budget cuts to the UH System, and was exacerbated by faculty union problems, leading to an unprecedented statewide faculty strike. There were also incessant calls from Manoa faculty members for their own chancellor, a backhanded compliment to the UHCCs and the strong advocacy role of the chancellor for community colleges.

The following year, in 2001, the BOR selected a new systemwide president with a reputation as a change agent. He brought a sense of renewal to the UH System, particularly to the Manoa campus, where faculty demands for its own chancellor were heeded. Immediately after taking office, the new president began efforts to reorganize the entire 10-campus system. He suggested the dissolution of the system-within-a-system arrangement of the UHCCs. He wanted each of the 10 campuses to be headed by a chancellor, with all reporting directly to him. He also proposed a new branding of the UH System and doing away with the word "community" in community colleges because, he said, "community colleges have a stigma attached to" the word, particularly from an international marketing perspective. The new president also suggested that the community colleges, particularly those on the neighbor islands (Kauai, Maui, and the

Big Island), move toward offering baccalaureate degrees in response to what he perceived as desire for four-year campuses there.

Questions to Consider

1. Actions of the new president were a surprise to many. They wondered why the UHCCs needed to be reorganized at all. In other words, why fix something that wasn't broken?

2. The major consequence of restructuring the UHCCs would be the dissolution of the office of the chancellor for community colleges and the shifting of its functions to the individual colleges or to various UH System offices. Would this serve the community colleges well?

3. Centralized support services included development and implementation of consistent personnel policies and processes to guide staff hiring, evaluation, and termination functions, which always remained at each college level; coordination of legislative liaison and lobbying; a unified response to workforce training needs of local businesses and industries to minimize negative competition among the colleges; the conducting of institutional research and provision of transactional support for individual college program reviews and assessments; formulation of statewide vision and strategic planning to guide resource allocation, program monitoring, and performance evaluation; and commonly shared advocacy and public information dissemination. In this regard, how many of these functions could realistically be assumed by each college without additional resources? Where would such additional funding and positions come from? Could the larger UH System provide the support functions with the same spirit of promoting and sustaining the open-door mission of the community colleges?

4. What would happen to the various staff personnel and administrators in the to-be-disbanded chancellor's office? What about their job security? Would each employee have a say in the future? Who would make the decisions about reassignments, and when would such decisions be made?

5. The incumbent chancellor was offered the position of UH Systemwide vice president for international education, a function she had been assuming as added responsibility during the past 10 years. Now she has a chance to carry out that function on a full-time basis. Should she accept and, if so, where will resources, including staffing, come from?

Thoughts and Analysis

The incumbent chancellor had already decided to retire after December 31, 2003. She had three choices: (1) attempt to keep the status quo by opposing the reorganization initiatives of the new president; (2) take steps to pull the community colleges out of the UH System, an option that had been brought up many times during the 35-year existence of the UHCCs; or (3) accept the changes as inevitable.

To oppose the reorganization would mean mounting a campaign to gain support of various constituencies: the Board of Regents, political sectors, local residents, and internal UH and community college representatives, including provosts, faculty, staff, and students. Although the general reputation and perceptions of the UHCCs among the various constituencies were positive, a campaign that turned negative would force individuals and groups to take sides. This divisiveness would negate the decades of work for the UHCCs to gain acceptance as a vital and indispensable part of public higher education in Hawaii. Furthermore, as a member of the UH administration, any such effort of outright opposition would require the chancellor to submit her resignation or retire prematurely. Such action would disadvantage the chancellor personally, and would not be a desired end to a long and cherished career.

The option to spin off the community colleges from the UH System would require legislative action and would need to be initiated by the UH administration, which was unlikely. Moreover, even if extraordinary and independent lobbying efforts by those opposing reorganization of the UHCCs succeeded in placing a separation bill before the state legislature, it would take much time and many rancorous debates and hearings to pass. Indeed, the chance of such passage was not a certainty, given the state's gloomy financial picture.

On a personal note, the chancellor felt that, if she were to start a fight, she would have to be around many years to finish it. But, at the given point in her career and personal life, she could not envision herself having the time to complete the task.

Another major consideration was the future of the provosts and other top administrative staff of the colleges and the chancellor's office. A potential brouhaha instigated by the chancellor would place each in the untenable position of taking sides, with a wrong choice affecting their futures with the university (most were not near retirement age). Additionally, the president had publicly stated that each provost would become a chancellor, considered a promotion, thus giving each the opportunity to assume increased authority and responsibilities.

The last and most important consideration was the question, "What does all of this have to do with students and their learning?" Negative public debates, fights, and position taking would detract from the focus needed to continue serving students, and might even dissuade some from enrolling in institutions that were embroiled in turmoil.

Outcomes

The chancellor decided to take a fourth option: accept the change, remain an active and contributing member of the new UH administration until her retirement date, and work from the inside to propose measures that would

- Maintain the mission and institutional integrity of the community colleges;
- Keep in close communication with internal constituencies to seek input, and keep all informed about developments in the reorganization process;
- Involve affected personnel in decisions about their futures;
- Maintain stability of operation during the transition;
- Take great care to pay attention to details of the transition, including adhering to external requirements such as institutional accreditation; and

- Continue to encourage constituencies to look for the positives in the change, and take advantage of the opportunity to enhance the role of the UHCCs as an increasingly vital component of public higher education in Hawaii.

On December 12, 2002, the BOR approved the new president's reorganization proposal at a special meeting. The reorganization called for the creation of a Council of Chancellors reporting directly to the president, including the chancellors of the community colleges and chancellors of the three baccalaureate campuses. Eliminated was the office of the chancellor for community colleges, reassigning its functions and staff to various UH system-level vice presidential offices. Each staff member was also given the individual option to remain at these system offices or move to a community college campus of choice.

In a letter dated October 30, 2003, the UH vice president for academic affairs relayed the *Report on the Substantive Change Request Related to the System Reorganization* to the executive director of the Accrediting Commission for Community and Junior Colleges (ACCJC). The report detailed how the Council of Chancellors was working to advocate the mission of the community colleges, assured the ACCJC that UH strategic initiatives were supporting the comprehensive mission of the community colleges, and described how the UH System is addressing the need to coordinate efforts of the community college system.

On November 18, 2003, more than 1,000 people filled the ballroom of the Hilton Hawaiian Village to honor the incumbent chancellor for community colleges for her 37 years of service to the UH System. Event proceeds helped launch the UHCC Leadership Development Endowed Fund, which will enable community college faculty, staff, students, and administrators to participate in leadership training, professional development, and other education-related classes and activities.

Joyce S. Tsunoda is Vice President for International Education at the University of Hawaii. On January 1, 2004, she became Emeritus Chancellor for Community Colleges and Distinguished Senior Visiting Scholar, East-West Center.

Part II

Executive Leadership

1. Styles or Hubris? The Balancing Act for Strong Leaders

J. David Armstrong Jr.

Author's note: The following is a composite from actual situations over the last two decades at multiple community colleges. Names have been eliminated, and some of the contextual information has been obscured out of respect to those involved in the situations and because of the legal sensitivity of some of the situations.

Context

Strong leaders with vision are often sought by governing boards to lead community colleges. Boards of trustees or state leaders charged with selecting presidents and chancellors are seeking leaders who have a bias toward action and a record of accomplishment. In more cases than not, the process of selection of a college leader results in a good fit between the college – its culture, the governing board, faculty, students, community – and the new leader. However, there are occasions when the fit is not so good. Moreover, times change, organizational cultures change, communities change, state or local priorities change, and some leaders who have been in office for many years do not change leadership styles to maintain a good fit, even when there may have been an excellent relationship earlier in the tenure of the leader. In these situations, a college or campus leader sometimes decides to take a position or series of positions not aligned with the other chief elements of the organization. In some cases, this is viewed as bold, visionary leadership. In other situations, it is viewed as arrogance, hubris, or self-centered decision making that ignores the role of other important stakeholders in the college.

Summary of the Cases

The President Who Would Be Entrepreneur. The college president of a conservative midsize city had many interests outside of the normal duties of the president. He had long been involved in athletics and had become a referee of football games. This had led him to develop a relationship with many athletic directors, coaches, and others in the athletic departments of colleges in his state. He eventually became coordinator of referees and umpires for the athletic association, wielding a great deal of influence and control over who was assigned to various games. The president benefited from being a referee himself, and from coordinating the games for athletic conferences. Additionally, the president pursued a business opportunity with a fast-growing multitiered marketing company that sold internet services. He used his influence and power and connections in athletics to build a significant and lucrative business. Additionally, college records eventually revealed that college phones and other resources were being used to support the president's business.

The President Who Did Not Share Victories. The college president of a large multicampus urban college had been aggressively promoted to the college's trustees by a national search firm as a brilliant, visionary leader. After a few years, the president began to lose support from board members on major parts of his agenda, but he pushed ahead, using his considerable personal skill and working hard to develop support in the business community. He was often granted, and gladly accepted, credit for accomplishments in news stories and chamber meetings, and sought state and national recognition for his institution's accomplishments under his leadership. Unfortunately for him, his board members did not share the same sense of accomplishment, nor did his faculty or political leaders. Board meetings became increasingly contentious, and split votes on the board eventually brought the president's agenda to a painful crawl. Outside consultants were brought in to provide mediation. One consultant observed a telling symbol of the problems in a newspaper photo where the president was prominent in the foreground with uplifted, victorious, celebratory arms in front of a new building that was being dedicated for the college. Very small in the background, and barely noticeable, were a few members of the governing board of the college, legislators who had provided funding, and city leaders who had helped promote the new facility.

The President Who Outgrew His College. The president of a megacollege with multiple campuses had been one of the first faculty members when the college was founded. He had gradually grown into progressively higher positions as the college grew in size over many decades. In that time, he and the college had come to be known leaders nationally. He became well regarded and respected by his peers, and the college was considered one of the best anywhere. As he and the college grew, the community changed in many ways, both in size and culture, and the governing board wanted changes for the college. The board also wanted quantitative performance from the president and adjustments to respond to the changes in the community, including more diversity among employees and more responsiveness to community needs via new programs. They also believed that the president was not strong enough in controlling costs at the college, which were outpacing revenues. Faculty salaries were escalating while hiring was increasing, and other expenditures were growing to support the many good ideas and projects from the college's aggressive leader. The president, proud of his many years of service and success, was insulted by the board's growing engagement in the direction of the college.

The President Who Would Not Be Intimidated. A relatively young president was selected by a split board vote to lead a college that had a history of disagreement and turmoil between the previous president and the faculty, which was represented by a faculty union. The faculty union believed that with a new president, they finally had an opportunity to advance an agenda of higher salaries and pay that had been at the heart of most of the strife in the past. The president wanted to work with the faculty, having been a faculty member earlier in his career, but he recognized that student enrollment and the college's need to expand programs were rapidly outpacing financial support from the state and local revenues. He offered long-term commitments to address faculty salaries and benefits, but proposed that in the short term, limited resources should be used to hire more faculty and staff, to expand access to more students. The board, community, and students applauded the move. The faculty met and voted no confidence in the still relatively new young president.

Questions to Consider

1. Should a president (or other college leaders) seek employment outside his or her college job?
2. What role should state leaders play as regulators, or outside but interested parties, in issues that cross the boundaries from one college to another?
3. Who really deserves credit and recognition for the successes of a college?
4. Who is responsible for bad fits between a college and its leaders, and what are the resolutions to these situations?
5. Are there situations where the stature of a college leader's success and recognition as a leader provides special protection from a board's desire for new directions, or accountability for items not important to the leader?
6. Should faculty salaries and benefits always be an entitlement that supersedes other needs of a college? How should presidents and faculty resolve these conflicts?
7. Where does a college leader develop support for an agenda when one or more stakeholders are opposed?
8. Who really governs a community college?
9. Are failed presidents always poor leaders, or are they possibly bad fits for the situation?

Thoughts and Analysis

Many great leaders with long lists of accomplishments have been forced out of their jobs because of pride, hubris, or unwillingness to share governance or accomplishments of a college. Other leaders with vision and commitment to community college values have lacked the strength to make tough fiscal decisions to direct limited resources to priorities supporting their good ideas. In truth, many people or groups govern a community college formally, legally, or informally. State and local governments who provide significant funding for colleges obviously have an interest in the governance of a college. Consequently, elected officials of those units of government have to be considered, consulted, and provided some degree of ownership of the governance of the college. More directly, boards of trustees, elected or appointed, are often the principal formal governing bodies that must be more than recognized for their role – they should be nurtured, cultivated, informed, and engaged in the direction and policies and strategy of the college and its leaders. Faculty and students, major stakeholders in the organization's core function of teaching and learning, are critical to the success of a college.

Outcomes

All of these presidents were considered to be successful at one point in their careers. However, the first three situations resulted in forced resignations or retirements. In the final example, the president was strongly supported by the board, community, and political leaders, and the faculty union lost a great deal of credibility for its vote of no confidence in the relatively new leader.

In the end, the importance of developing meaningful relationships with all the principal stakeholders through integrity, inclusion, involvement, sharing of success, and intensive communication, is critical to the ongoing success of a college's governance. Less than that can lead to the perception, if not reality, of a leader losing touch with the board and community, or worse, committing the classic sin of hubris that can lead to the downfall of the best leaders, no matter what the record of success.

J. David Armstrong Jr. is Chancellor, Florida Community Colleges and Workforce Education in Tallahassee, Florida.

2. Growing Our Own Leaders

Michael B. McCall

Context

The Kentucky Postsecondary Education Improvement Act, from 1997 legislation, reformed two-year education in the Commonwealth of Kentucky by joining 13 of the 14 community colleges and all 15 technical schools into one system – the Kentucky Community and Technical College System (KCTCS).

Until then, 14 community colleges were part of the University of Kentucky (UK), the state's flagship land-grant university. The Cabinet for Workforce Development, an agency of the executive branch of state government, operated the 15 technical schools.

Since 1999, KCTCS technical and community colleges have merged and now have single accreditation or are seeking accreditation membership from the Commission on Colleges of the Southern Association of Colleges and Schools (SACS). With consolidation, KCTCS comprises 16 colleges, with 62 campuses open or under construction. KCTCS colleges are strategically located across the commonwealth and serve Kentuckians by offering associate degrees; diploma and certificate programs in occupational fields; pre-baccalaureate education; adult, continuing, and developmental education; customized training for business and industry; and distance learning.

The system enrolls more than 72,000 students in credit programs and touches the lives of over 300,000 people a year through all programs and services. The colleges of KCTCS confer three types of credentials, view postsecondary education as a crucial resource for economic development, and enhance learning opportunities for all Kentuckians through noncredit continuing education. From personal improvement to cultural activities, community development programs at KCTCS institutions meet local needs.

Only six years old, KCTCS is meeting its legislative mandate and exceeding the expectations of its founders. The system has achieved its successes largely because of strong leadership exerted by the 14-member Board of Regents, which includes eight citizen members appointed by the governor and six members elected by KCTCS constituencies: two faculty members, two staff members, and two students.

The Board of Regents is involved in the development of policy and in assessing the results of the implementation of that policy but does not engage in operational matters. In December 1998, the Board of Regents hired the system's founding president. Creating a structure for leadership of the system was a priority. The president's cabinet at the system office and 16 college presidents compose the President's Leadership Team (PLT). With policy guidance or approval from the Board of Regents, the president and the PLT have led KCTCS through a period of rapid and successful change in many areas, such as

- Merging 28 colleges into 16, with single SACS accreditation;
- Increasing credit enrollment 58 percent in five years;

- Developing a Workforce Investment Network System to expand workforce-training initiatives;
- Creating an administrative information technology network that provides systemwide registration, data collection, and reporting;
- Establishing KCTCS as a leading provider of distance learning; and
- Developing a reputation for success that is rapidly becoming known across the nation.

Summary of the Case:

In 1996, before the Kentucky General Assembly approved creation of the Kentucky Community and Technical College System (KCTCS), the commonwealth's community colleges and technical colleges were administered by separate and often competing organizations. For KCTCS, leadership at all levels was essential to bring future stability and growth to the system. A leadership shortage is an issue community colleges across the nation are facing. The increasing numbers of retirees and the decreasing budgets have created a need for colleges to promote from within. Faculty and staff within an institution bring both knowledge and experience that provide excellent sources of leadership.

However, local college leadership development opportunities often do not exist or do not adequately prepare internal candidates for the scope and depth of leadership responsibility. In the case of KCTCS, creating a new organization demanded leaders with knowledge and understanding of the issues and concerns of all the stakeholders. Preparing leaders from within the system became the challenge, not just for positions as college presidents, but also for leadership in all levels of the colleges. It was equally important to prepare leaders in faculty positions as it was to prepare division chairs, deans, counselors, and vice presidents. Some resistance could be an issue, as college presidents were asked to support internal candidates for professional development beyond the scope of the individual college. Some apathy among the faculty and staff was observed, since the changing cultures had created some distrust of administration and fear for job security. The combining of two distinct educational cultures presented the challenge of creating a shared vision and shared goals among current and future leaders.

Questions to Consider

1. Should a leadership development program be designed at the college level or system level?
2. Could a program be designed that would facilitate leadership development at all levels in the college, rather than focusing on primarily college presidents or upper-level administration?
3. Would developing an internal program to grow our own leaders promote leaders with too-narrow viewpoints?
4. Who should lead and take responsibility for the leadership development program?
5. Who should pay for it?
6. Who should be allowed to participate?
7. Faced with increasing budget cuts, how could the system maintain the program?

Thoughts and Analysis

1. If each program addressed the specific leadership requirements determined by the college faculty, staff, and administration, it could respond to the local needs but might not provide the breadth and depth of leadership development necessary for opportunities within the system at other colleges. A systemwide development program could provide for broader viewpoints of leadership styles versus the limited scope of modeling a single college management team, therefore providing an open yet confidential forum of discussion with additional growth opportunities for faculty and staff. It could also provide an opportunity for creating a shared culture.
2. Supporting the philosophy of being a leader at any level, a program needed to be designed so that a faculty member not wishing to move into administration could still benefit from the contents.
3. In order to avoid a narrow definition of leadership and provide a variety of viewpoints, the program was developed to include national, regional, and state leaders.
4. The leader of the program needed to be someone who would take the responsibility to give it the importance and credibility necessary to obtain the acceptance of the college presidents and the participation of the leaders and potential leaders within the colleges.
5. Since the program would promote capacity building within KCTCS, it would be appropriate for the system to fund the project.
6. If leaders at all levels was the goal, then it was important to solicit participation from all levels of the organization, both faculty and staff.
7. With increasing demands on the system and decreasing resources, leadership development was a priority issue. The program could offer alternatives for using resources to be more efficient and effective.

Outcomes

While the goal was to grow our own system leaders, the design and creation of the appropriate program needed to be far broader in scope. The KCTCS president called on an external consultant to offer expertise in design and delivery. In order to develop leaders with exposure to diverse viewpoints and backgrounds, national leaders were invited to serve as presenters. Diversity in topics, speakers, and program offerings would offer a variety of skill sets.

The program was designed to consist of two separate seminar sessions. A fall session focused on listening, learning, lecture, and participative presentations. The spring session focused on individual leadership traits and styles, as well as a group project relevant to the system goals. It was decided that it would be a statewide program, created to provide leadership development theories, concepts, and strategies to a broad audience. It was designed to offer leadership traits and skills to faculty and staff at all levels in the system.

The president of KCTCS led the project, committing his time to the entirety of the program. Applicants were encouraged from all positions within the colleges, with college presidents having the opportunity to give their opinion and support for their participants. Applications were accepted from all colleges via a competitive process designed to determine individual participants' professional goals. The office of the KCTCS president funded all costs associated with the program.

Named the President's Leadership Seminar (PLS), the program is now in its fifth year. It has encouraged leadership, participative decision making, and accountability throughout the system. The faculty and staff (up to 30 per year) go through an application process and are selected based on a variety of factors, including review by previous PLS graduates. Gender, racial diversity, experience, credentials, and faculty-staff ratio are integral components of the selection process.

Presenters are selected from nationally known leaders. The topics and issues are based on national, regional, and local trends. The range of subjects goes from history and philosophy to conflict management and personal leadership styles.

To date, over 110 faculty and staff have participated in the PLS. Applications for participation have grown from 35 the first year to over 80 for the 2004 class. Only four graduates have left the system. Return on investment in the program has included promotions, increased responsibility, leadership at the college and system level, and greater involvement in planning for the future of KCTCS.

The investment in growing our own leaders has proven to be a valuable use of resources. The multiple gains include advocacy created for the new system, the leadership developed at the college level, and the participation of the graduates in the decision-making process at the system level. All of the outcomes have been tremendous results of the initiative, and of great benefit to KCTCS.

Michael B. McCall is President of the Kentucky Community and Technical College System.

3. Leadership for Transformation

Byron N. McClenney

Context

The Community College of Denver (CCD) is a multicampus community college serving the largest urban center in Colorado. It will be used as an example to illustrate principles of organizational change. The perspective comes from the 14-year administration (1986-2000) of its longest-serving chief executive.

The institution launched a systematic process in 1986 to match college efforts with community needs. Environmental scanning in the community and internal studies on student progress and success drove annual planning and budgeting for over a decade as CCD pursued continuous improvement. Early studies demonstrated poor outcomes for students in developmental courses and a major gap in minority student achievement and attainment, compared with majority students. Studies also demonstrated that few recent high school students were entering the community college.

Compounding the task for CCD as a relatively undeveloped community college was the fact that it shared a large campus with Metropolitan State College and the University of Colorado at Denver. Known as the Auraria Higher Education Center, the campus presented distinct challenges in addition to the usual issues related to college development.

Summary of the Case

In a community where only half of the students who enter ninth grade graduate from high school four years later, and where the largest concentration of poor people in Colorado live, a community college set out to make a difference. Only six students in CCD's entering cohort for fall 1986 had graduated from high school the previous May. At a level below the general population of Denver, the people of color represented 27 percent of the enrollment and only 13 percent of the graduates in the previous year. A majority of the first-time enrolled students started with at least one developmental course, and the pattern was for only about one-third of them to be successful.

By FY 2000, total college enrollment had more than doubled, and people of color represented 56 percent of the enrollment, which exceeded percentages in the general population. People of color as a percentage of transfers and graduates moved beyond 50 percent to the point of equity. The college had become the leading point of entry to public higher education for Denver citizens, including hundreds of recent high school graduates.

Questions to Consider

The people of CCD were guided by the following questions:

1. Do we understand the realities and constraints within which we must work?

2. Do we have a way of developing a collective vision of our potential future?
3. Do we have a way to identify institutional priorities for a given year?
4. Do we properly link plans with the allocation of resources?
5. Have we identified our competition and defined our place in the higher education market?
6. Do we have processes in place to properly inform and involve constituent groups in planning and budgeting?
7. Do we have a way to learn from assessment of outcomes and apply the understandings to alter practices and processes?
8. Does our budget implement the important values?

Thoughts and Analysis

The approach taken here is to offer general observations about how to bring about institutional transformation, but also to demonstrate what was actually done during the 14-year period at CCD by dealing with the principal ingredients. The reader may then readily adapt the general discussion to his or her own institution and setting.

Missing in many discussions about leadership, quality, and excellence is the identification of essential ingredients for individual leaders and their organizations. The essential ingredients are the willingness to dream, the will to decide, and the courage to take risks for the benefit of the organization. Establishing a direction for the future, in concert with the people in the college, is crucial if an institution is to avoid drift and decay. A leader who decides to make a difference needs to be constantly involved in defining the difference between what is and what ought to be for the organization.

In the final analysis, leadership has been exerted only when there is movement toward desired outcomes. Any leader seeking to develop excellence must decide to take the risks inherent in assessing the current state of affairs. Shared goals are more likely to emerge when there has been a shared struggle to identify and deal with the significant issues of the organization in the local context. That means internal and external assessment is crucial. The impact on students should always be at the center of the review.

Deciding to focus on issues and reinforcing the expectation that people of good will can come together to solve problems and set standards is an important step. Open discussion, honest debate, and forthright decision making should prevail if leaders hope to establish a positive climate. The leader has an opportunity to set the tone for the institution by demonstrating an ability to sort through the significant issues, select through an interactive process the ones with the greatest significance, and lead discussions geared toward enhancing the organization.

Commitment to a set of key principles can set the stage for continuous improvement in the life of the college. Among the most critical are the following:

- Create a collective vision to drive activity.
- Develop related strategies and priorities to allow pursuit of the vision.
- Commit to use data in planning and decision making.

- Foster collegewide participation.
- Identify best practices and share ideas.
- Develop teamwork across organizational boundaries.
- Encourage open, constructive problem solving.
- Facilitate leadership at all organizational levels.
- Reduce unnecessary and counterproductive bureaucratic constraints.
- Modify policies, structures, and systems to support change.
- Link plans to the allocation of resources.
- Provide professional development, coaching, and training.
- Establish incentives to encourage vision- and mission-related outcomes.
- Develop information systems to communicate across the campus and beyond about institutional performance.
- Celebrate progress and success.
- Evaluate outcomes.

Critical to implementing these principles in organizational life is the creation of an annual cycle of activity through which the college works to tend the essential ingredients. Baseline evaluation of student outcomes, along with environmental scanning, should be used as a foundation for planning future activity. What is learned about student retention, student satisfaction, graduation, transfer, job placement, employer satisfaction, and alumni satisfaction should drive the thinking about next steps. That thinking could lead to alteration of the vision or to adjustment of priorities for the coming year.

For example, assessment of current performance might yield the insight that minority students are not achieving or attaining at the same level as majority students. It might also show that part-time students lag behind full-time students in similar comparisons, or that males lag behind females in the comparisons. Such realities should be forthrightly addressed in planning and resource allocation.

Outcomes

Illustrative milestones and outcomes at the Community College of Denver included the following:

1. Exit competencies were specified for all programs.
2. Assessments were developed for all competencies.
3. Assessments were incorporated into regular program reviews.
4. A Teaching-Learning Center was developed for faculty.
5. Minigrants were awarded to faculty to pursue college priorities.
6. Five Critical Skills-Across-the-Curriculum were adopted.
7. Values for Teaching and Learning were adopted.
8. FY 91 was the first time people of color had higher transfer rates than their peers.
9. FY 95 was the first year students who started in developmental courses were as likely to graduate as those who did not.
10. FY 98 was the first time cohort tracking yielded no significant difference in student success on the basis of race, ethnicity, age, or gender.

Three years after launching the process of cohort tracking (1986-1989), 21.2 percent of the students had graduated, transferred, or were still enrolled. For the entering cohort in 1993, results three years later were dramatically different. The percentage of successful students had reached 47.1 percent, even though the institution serves the most disadvantaged and diverse population in Colorado.

A crucial element throughout the 14 years was the adoption of no more than five Action Priorities for the next year in the life of the institution. Although there were many different priorities during those years, it is significant that the climate for learning, cultural pluralism or diversity, and technology appeared in some form on each list during most of the 14 years.

A relentless focus over a period of years is what will be required to deal with the challenges faced by community colleges in the new century. Closing the gap between people of color and Whites in achievement and attainment should be on the agenda for most colleges, just as it was for CCD. While each college is different, the general principles will apply in the hands of effective leaders. There are no short cuts.

Byron N. McClenney has joined the team of the Community College Leadership Program of The University of Texas at Austin following his retirement from 32 years as a community college chief executive and 42 years as an educator.

4. Daring to Leave a Legacy

Pamela L. Whitelock

Context

Gulf Coast Community College (GCCC) is a single-campus, comprehensive community college located along the some of the world's most beautiful beaches in the panhandle of northwest Florida. The college operates from its bay-front main campus in Panama City, with three additional dedicated centers strategically located across Bay, Gulf, and Franklin Counties. Accredited by the Commission on Colleges of the Southern Association of Colleges and Schools, GCCC is governed by an autonomous District Board of Trustees composed of nine members appointed by the governor. Representatives of the area's Air Force and Navy military bases, the president of GCCC's Student Government Association, and the chair of each of the three GCCC employee councils serve as nonvoting guests of the board. Responsibility for college administration is delegated by the board to the president. Recently, the board negotiated a prompt rehire of its retired president, who, after 34 years of service to the institution (16 as president), was selected to ensure institutional stability during an era of dramatic change, as well as to leverage the institution's enviable political alliance during an era of unprecedented legislative clout. Established in 1957, GCCC was the first college to open its doors after Florida created its community college system, thus early demonstrating the vision, drive, dedication, and leadership that has been its sustaining hallmark and that lays the foundation for this case.

The citizens who insisted on a community college for their future are similar in nature to those supporting Florida's Great Northwest (FGNW), the region's first nonprofit economic development partnership. As FGNW declares, "Northwest Florida has long been known for its extraordinary environment, friendly communities, and unmatched quality of life," a legacy to preserve and nurture. "Today, it's a region on the move, with public and private sector leaders joining together to push for regional infrastructure improvements while aggressively pursuing world-class economic development opportunities that mesh with existing regional needs. FGNW is committed to building awareness of the 16-county region among site selection consultants and key decision-makers around the world." Gulf Coast is an active player in that initiative, established through the leadership of the St. Joe Company, the region's largest landowner, in collaboration with multiple stakeholders.

On the other hand, the vast size, compactness, and quality of the St. Joe Company's land holdings, and its aggressive conversion thereof from pine tree forests for paper mills to real estate development, or "place making," as they intend it, renders it "No Ordinary Joe" among the region's influences. Joe is not alone. Golfer Greg Norman has partnered with other out-of-state companies to establish an exclusive golf club and residential community that caters to the wealthy elite from all over the southeast, many of whom build million-dollar vacation homes at Wild Heron for occasional use. The nature and extent of such growth have met considerable resistance from the old guard. It's both the gorilla-sits-anywhere power struggle and the clash between former and emerging regional demographics.

Convinced that educational opportunities play vital and pivotal roles in building community, the president compels college philosophy and practice to proactively position the institution not only as the community's space for deliberation of critical issues, often regarding the direction of certain growth, but also as a catalyst for and partner in guiding many dimensions of innovative, constructive economic development. Staff is encouraged to look for more and better ways to meaningfully engage the college in community building and is extended a highly desirable combination of support and independence in management. An impressive track record of $5,700,000 in externally funded projects flanks the staff request that is the subject of this case.

At the same time, very conservative institutional fiscal policies historically have protected GCCC against funding shortfalls, sustained enrollment growth, and forestalled repercussions of threats to the area's predominant, seasonal, and vulnerable hospitality and seafood industries. Therefore, new programs – often conceived by creative, energetic lifelong learning personnel – must first be tested over a reasonable period of time, prove themselves, and, typically, be externally funded before successfully competing for greater allotments of precious institutional resources. Always, there is a greater abundance of worthy ideas than resources, and some ideas initially appear almost too far-reaching to consider.

It is in this context that lifelong learning staff suggested to the president that the college not only lead a grassroots campaign, prompted by a citizen's letter to the editor, to save from real-estate development 180 acres of priceless gulf-front and Outstanding-Florida-Waterway-situated property, but also to establish on the property a long-imagined, world-renowned Environmental Education Center, a center that would function as a working laboratory for the best principles in sustainable design and as a learning and discovery center to encourage preservation and stewardship of a diverse ecosystem and promote creativity in the sciences, arts, and humanities.

Summary of the Case

The challenges of institutional change, coupled with those of dramatic service-district and regional change, demand progressive and judicious leadership. Sustaining old institutional friendships while cultivating new ones is paramount and tricky, particularly regarding politics and external fundraising. The staff's ambitious plan includes mobilizing and shepherding a viable community advisory team; state purchase of the targeted $15 million site; expansive collaboration for external fundraising to support planning, design, and construction of a complex estimated at $22 million, as well as ongoing program and facilities maintenance; and curriculum development. The president must weigh the opportunity and plan in light of recent trends that suggest downturn in and competition for philanthropic support and volunteers; some historical community leaders' skepticism, even mistrust, of new personalities bearing gifts; no otherwise available site; no traditional funding anticipated for facilities absent from the institution's master facilities plan; no revenue stream to support additional personnel or operations expenses; insufficient resources to meet all currently identified, priority-ranked institutional needs; no related existing certificate or degree programs; and increasing employee inexperience. (Due to retirements, 50 percent of the college's employee group has five years' or less experience).

Questions to Consider

1. Should the president approve the project? If so, what factors might prompt him to do so, and who else should he involve in the decision-making process?
2. If the president agrees to the project, what institutional considerations would be placed at risk?
3. What intangible payoff might the president presume to be the sustaining driving force behind commitments staff are willing to make?
4. If approved, what parameters might the president need to establish to ensure staff pursuit if the EEC does not deplete institutional resources already earmarked for more pressing purposes?
5. Should the president approve the plan, how might he deal with board members, foundation officers, and influential community leaders who may question feasibility or wisdom of novel strategies or the uncustomary alliances that surely would evolve and seemingly compete with existing initiatives?
6. What accountability and performance indicators might keep the president appropriately informed as to return on institutional investment?

Thoughts and Analysis

1. The project is quite staff specific and likely could take 10 years; the president has a three-year contract, the dean is approaching retirement in two years, and the key coordinator is subject to move – all could be gone before project completion.
2. Sustained artfulness is required to employ benchmarks to gauge progress, without discouraging initiative and enthusiasm, and to nurture staff return on intangible investments.
3. Some key administrators and influential others may be more inclined to be gatekeepers than innovators.
4. The college enjoys enviable positive relations with local media; the project would be high profile and potentially controversial.
5. The college already is under construction with four fully funded new building projects, and anticipates at least two additional ones with the next round of legislative appropriations.

Outcomes

The president and board approved the project. The Nature Conservancy bought the property from the developer and held it for state purchase; the college led a citizens group to persuade the governor's cabinet to position the parcel for state purchase; a 50-year sublease was executed by the college for 35 of the 180 acres; a state park was established on part of the property and an unprecedented partnership forged between two state agencies for land management; thriving new business partners underwrote the cost of project planning, architectural renderings and subject-matter expertise in support of an articulated master development site plan and engineering design work; and two federal-to-state grants have directed $1.5 million for infrastructure work.

A consulting agreement negotiated continued engagement of a key staff member with the dean, despite the staff member's relocation to another state, and continuity of project leadership and program development is assured over time. A strategic plan for external fundraising, tapping of state matching funds, incorporation of EEC plans with long-term instructional aims, and grant seeking has been formulated and is being guided by a campuswide, multidisciplinary instructional team. Area leaders tout the venture as indicative of the president's vision, unswerving institutional commitment, and courageous and expert partnership in the region's growth. The EEC is destined to serve as a catalyst, hub, and international resource for environment-related business and cultural expansion and unparalleled interactive learning experiences to support degree, certificate, and continuing education programs.

Pamela L. Whitelock is Dean of Lifelong Learning at Gulf Coast Community College in Panama City, Florida.

Part III

Administration and Finance

1. Build It and They Will Come

John Anthony

Context

The Collin County Community College District (CCCCD) was established in 1985. Approximately 15 miles north of downtown Dallas, the district boundaries are the same as Collin County's, approximately 900 square miles. At the time of the election to create the district, the county had a population of some 205,000 residents. Almost 60 percent of those residents lived in the southern part, in or near the city of Plano. The county seat of McKinney, near the county's center, had a population of 19,500, and Allen, a bedroom community between McKinney to the north and Plano to the south, had the third largest population, with 19,000 residents.

Collin County was one of the most rapidly growing suburban areas in the United States; increases in population were averaging close to 15,000 annually. Within the county, however, growth was unevenly distributed. The southern portion had grown by over 60,000 people in the six years prior to the college's founding, and while there had been growth throughout the county, Plano was the dominant expansion area. Projections through the year 2000 indicated the probability of over 400,000 residents, with the majority residing in Plano, Allen, McKinney, and Frisco.

The younger population resided primarily in the southern portion of the county – most notably Plano, while the northern and central parts of the county showed a significantly older population with many retirees. Median income for county residences was 45 percent higher than for the state; there was little poverty, with only 5 percent of the families below the poverty standard, and unemployment was less than 4 percent. While there was considerable commuting out of the county for work, the economy was strong and growing, with more and more business and industry moving into the area. The annual assessed tax value of the county was $10.4 billion, an increase of 35 percent from the preceding year. This increase was due almost entirely to new residential and commercial construction occurring in the southern part of the county.

The population was served by one major highway, U.S. 75, running north-south through the middle of the county. Route 380 provided the only adequate east-west artery, running through the center of the county and intersecting with U.S. 75 at McKinney. Plans were under way to construct an extension of the Dallas North Tollway to run north-south in the western part of the county to accommodate the rapid growth projected for that area.

The Collin County Community College District was formed when fewer than 10 percent of registered voters approved its creation. Citizens were asked to vote for three ballot measures and a nine-member board of trustees. The district was approved with 61 percent of total votes cast. A $70 million bond issue for land acquisition and campus construction was approved by 56 percent of the vote, and a maximum tax rate of 8 cents for operations and 12 cents for debt services was approved by 54 percent. Nine trustees representing 7 of the 14 incorporated cities and towns located in the county were selected from a slate of 15 candidates. The majority of the positive votes came from the southern part of the county, with every precinct in the city of Plano approving all ballot measures.

The only other city to give citywide approval for the creation of the district was the rapidly growing city of Frisco. Upon certification of the election results, the newly elected board set out to conduct its first order of business, the hiring of a college president. Within months, the president was hired and immediately charged with the responsibility of acquiring an interim site to start classes in the fall; selecting a permanent campus site or sites; and building strong, positive relationships with all the communities in the county – especially those that did not support the creation of the college district.

Plano wanted one if not two campuses located in its area, and McKinney was pushing for a campus as well. Several sites were considered in McKinney for the interim campus, including the old Job Corps facility, which had ample space but was badly in need of repairs; an empty shopping mall of 160,000 square feet, with ample parking but limited access from U.S. 75; and a new 90,000-square-foot speculative office building near the intersection of U.S. 75 and Route 380, but carrying a hefty price tag. Consideration was also given to constructing a tilt-up facility in Plano for the interim campus – a process that would take about four months but would require major infrastructure upgrades to provide adequate access. It was recognized that a key to gaining countywide support for the college district was the location of the college's interim and permanent campuses.

Summary of the Case

The CCCCD was approved by a small percentage of registered voters casting ballots. An even smaller percentage approved bonding and tax measures to support the district's creation. (It should be noted that 10 years earlier, the voters approved the creation of a college district but failed to approve bonding and tax measures to support its creation and operation.) The majority of votes in favor of the district's creation occurred in the southern part of the county, an area represented by a rapidly growing, young, affluent population, in contrast to the older, more conservative, rural population in the rest of the county.

Demographic data projected continued rapid residential and commercial growth in the southern and western parts of the county and only limited growth north of the county seat. Projections indicated that more than 400,000 individuals would be residing in the county by the year 2000, and that Frisco would be the most rapidly growing city in the county. If the growth rate held to projections, the college's $70,000,000 bond issue and its 8-cent operational task rate would be insufficient to buy land, construct facilities, and operate campuses to handle the growth. The college had to make some immediate decisions regarding the number, the location, and the maximum size of its campuses, recognizing that these decisions would affect the character of the district throughout its history.

Questions to Consider

1. With the district representing an area of less than 900 square miles, should the college consider constructing one major campus in the center of the county that

would put all residents within a 15-mile commute of the facility?

2. With major population and economic growth occurring in the southern part of the county, should the college consider constructing one major campus in this location to meet the needs of its strongest support base? This would require students in more remote areas of the county to travel as much as 25 miles to the campus.

3. How should the college address the needs of the rapidly growing and supportive area in the western part of the county represented by the city of Frisco?

4. Should the college consider constructing three campuses to serve its projected enrollment needs? Additional resources beyond those approved by the voters would be necessary to buy sites and to construct and operate three comprehensive campuses.

5. For its interim campus, should the district build a fast-track tilt-up facility or look for an existing facility that could be remodeled? Where should this interim facility be located?

6. If the college builds more than one comprehensive campus, how does it avoid the duplication of services, program isolation and competition, communications difficulties, and remote supervision commonly associated with multicampus districts?

Thoughts and Analysis

1. The district should establish a strong visual image, one that makes a statement about its direction and mission in the community. The diversity of the district calls for individual campus identities – centers of community within a larger center of diversity.

2. Campuses should be strategically located to serve existing and future concentrations of development and population.

3. From the students' point of view, commuting distances between home and campus should be no greater than 15 miles.

4. Campuses should be close to the confluence of major north-south and east-west arterials.

5. Campuses should be buffered by means of intervening land use or on-site development from residential or industrial property.

6. Campuses should be located to take maximum advantage of joint-use opportunities. The college should locate near community facilities that complement its mission and offer opportunities for shared development and maintenance costs.

7. Based on data from the Dallas and Tarrant County Districts, it seemed reasonable to assume that total head count in credit courses for CCCCD would be approximately 3 percent of the total population of the county. Population projections of 400,000 by the year 2000 would indicate a total enrollment in the district in excess of 12,000 credit students.

8. Interests of both the students and the citizens of Collin County could best be served by a campus of at least moderately large scale.

Outcomes

The college chose to develop three campus locations, strategically located to serve both existing and projected concentrations of development and population. The first campus was planned to serve the major population center of Plano and the southern portion of Collin County. The second campus, not located in a major population center but within the city of McKinney, was planned to provide easy access within a reasonable period of time for all residents in the northern half of the county. The third campus was planned to address future demands that would result from projected growth in the western part of the county near Frisco. The first campus in Plano and the second campus in McKinney were developed as soon as possible. The third campus was to be delayed until population figures justified the need for its construction. It was estimated that eventually, the Frisco campus could well be the largest in the district.

In a bold move, the board sold $70,000,000 in bonds and purchased 115 acres of land and the 90,000-square-foot speculative office building in McKinney for its interim site, and agreed that with proper planning and development, the office building could become the centerpiece for the permanent second campus. It also purchased 115 acres of land in Plano for the first permanent campus and started immediate planning for the construction of an initial 400,000-square-foot facility in that area. Within two years, the board acquired the necessary land for its third campus in Frisco.

Today, CCCCD operates three comprehensive campuses. The interim campus became Central Park Campus in McKinney, specializing in allied health and public service programs and serving an estimated 2,200 credit students. Spring Creek Campus in Plano houses the majority of the college's award-winning fine and performing arts programs; it serves approximately 9,800 credit students. Preston Ridge Campus in Frisco houses the majority of the college's engineering and computer science programs; it serves 2,600 credit students. In addition, the college has an 80,000-square-foot Center for Professional and Economic Development in west Plano, and a 25,000-square-foot facility in Allen built in conjunction with the new Allen High School.

Efforts by the district administration have been successful in getting other parts of the county to buy in to the community college. In 2003, voters approved by a 64 percent vote a bond issue of $57,000,000 for the expansion of the three campuses and the acquisition of land for additional sites in the northern and eastern parts of the county. These additions should help the college more fully accommodate the needs of a growing county population of 450,000 residents and its rapidly expanding student body of 16,000 credit students.

John Anthony is President Emeritus of the Collin County Community College District in Collin County, Texas.

2. Thinking Through a Financial Dilemma

Leonardo de la Garza

Context

The Tarrant County College District (TCCD) is a two-year comprehensive community college providing degree programs toward an Associate in Arts and an Associate in Applied Science. In addition, the college offers certificate of completion programs designed to meet specific needs of the community. In fall 2002, Tarrant County College was ranked the eighth largest community college or university in Texas (fifth largest among community colleges). The fall 2003 credit enrollment totaled 32,657 students. Consisting of four campuses and a district office, the college employs approximately 2,800 people, 1,320 of whom are full- and part-time faculty.

The Tarrant County College District was founded on July 31, 1965, when the voters of Tarrant County approved the sale of $18,144,000 in bonds for construction, elected a seven-member board of trustees, and approved taxes for debt service and operations. These actions resulted in the creation of the Tarrant County Junior College District. The word designation of junior college remained until the board of trustees voted in February 1999 to change the name to Tarrant County College District.

On September 9, 1965, the board named the college's first president, a title later changed to chancellor. Three months later, the board announced acquisition of land for the multicampus district and commissioned architects to begin planning the first two units. Educational specifications for the South Campus were given to the designing architect on February 1, 1966, and first work began on the 158.5-acre site that May. The general contract for building construction was awarded in August 1966. Thirteen buildings on Loop 820 in south Fort Worth were completed by September 1967, in time for the first classes to begin. Work on the Northeast Campus started in the summer of 1967, with the awarding of general contracts for building construction, and initial use of the new physical plant began in September of 1968.

In December 1968, the college was given 193 acres of land in northwest Tarrant County for a third campus. A $20 million bond issue approved by voters in 1971 provided funds for construction of the Northwest Campus and second-phase construction on the other campuses. The Northwest Campus became fully operational in January 1976. In March 1983, the May Owen District Center opened in downtown Fort Worth. This facility currently houses the College District office.

The voters reaffirmed their support of the college in September 1985, approving a $50 million bond package, $43 million for new construction, renovation, and equipment on present campuses, and $7 million for acquisition of future campus sites. In the fall of 1987, TCC purchased a 123-acre site near the intersection of Interstate 20 and Texas 360, for an Arlington campus. A $70 million bond package was approved overwhelmingly by Tarrant County voters in August 1993 for the construction of a fourth campus, for renovations and new classroom facilities on the existing three campuses and the May

Owen Center, and for the purchase of a new mainframe computer system. This bond package allowed for the construction of the Southeast Campus, which opened in fall 1996.

Through the years, three individuals have served as chancellor of the Tarrant County College District. On January 25, 1997, the Board of Trustees named the college's third and current chancellor.

Summary of the Case (circa 1996-1997)

Following the common practice of all Texas public community colleges, the Tarrant County College District historically has funded major purchases of equipment and all capital outlay expenditures for new construction or repairs and renovations to college facilities through the issuance of general-obligation bonds authorized by voters. Through this practice, by 1997, the college has accumulated the highest tax-supported bonded indebtedness of the 50 Texas public community college districts and has depleted the funding made available through the last bond issue.

Furthermore, the college has been facing declining enrollments during the last few years. As a result, increases in tuition and fee income have not been substantial. Increases in state funding, driven by enrollment, have also been affected. The college has accessed its reserves in order to achieve a balanced budget. Thus, the college has been experiencing several years of stagnating revenues and inability to fund the operating budget adequately, with particular negative impact on salaries, equipment, and deferred maintenance.

The current (1996-1997) external environment is not very positive. The economy has undergone a severe decline, and although the state's economy has been recovering, demands for revenue far exceed available funds. Education is one of many state priorities, and given limited resources, current levels of state funding are likely to be increased at a level far less than costs.

From a financial perspective, the college has three major sources of revenue: (1) state appropriations, (2) tuition and fees, and (3) local ad valorem taxes. Of the three sources of revenue for the college, local funds comprised of tuition and fees as well as local tax revenues provide more flexibility in the use of such funds. For example, state appropriations may not be used for construction of facilities or for repairs and renovations for those facilities. On the other hand, tuition and fees may be used for any legal classification of expenditures, and local tax revenues provide some flexibility. Specifically, the local tax revenue is divided into two categories: maintenance and operations funding and funding for debt service on general obligation bonds. The latter are for paying principal and interest on funds used for construction and other capital outlay needs and may only be used for such purposes. The college's current tax rate is one of the lowest among all community colleges within the state. In addition, tuition and fees charged for two 15-hour semesters are below the state community college average. The college is now working to develop a new fiscal-year budget. The chancellor faces the challenge of developing a budget that meets the needs of the college. He acknowledges the pressures that have been placed on college staff during the last few years. Therefore, the identification of new sources of funding has to be a principal focus, given that the last several years have been difficult ones. Furthermore, he recognizes the need for a long-term financial strategy – one that will ensure the college's future financial stability.

As the new chancellor thinks about the college's financial future, he might consider the following options:

1. Recommend to the board of trustees that it seek citizen approval for the issuance of new bond issues for the college. Despite the fact that the college's enrollments have been declining, the citizens of Tarrant County have always been very supportive of the college. The prospects of obtaining voter approval for a bond issue are excellent.

2. Review the current budget and reallocate funds toward capital improvement projects. Some budget categories might be reduced or eliminated, thereby making funds available for capital improvement projects.

3. Place most, if not all, capital improvement projects on hold until funding becomes available. Despite the facts that maintenance has been deferred for the last few years and that the college's service area is expected to continue to grow (given that is located in one of the state's fastest-growth metropolitan areas), the college's facilities may be able to weather an extension in repairs, renovations, and additions.

4. Identify and implement a new financing strategy that provides funds not only for capital improvement projects, but also for ongoing operating budget needs of the college. The new chancellor believes there is a new, viable financing strategy that will provide funding for the college's future growth and expansion, while recognizing the institution's continuing enrollment growth during a period of decreasing state support.

Questions to Consider

1. What are the advantages and disadvantages of each of the options described above?
2. Whom should the chancellor involve in his decision-making process?
3. What forms of communication should the chancellor consider as he moves forward with any of these options?

Thoughts and Analysis

During the last five years, the college district has undertaken a major transformation in regard to a central aspect of its financing strategy. The result, fashioned over 18 months of intense work with the board of trustees, was the chancellor's recommendation of a new pay-as-you-go funding strategy, *i.e.*, paying in cash, to ensure the college's future growth and success. In 1998, the board of trustees approved a new pay-as-you-go approach to funding yearly multimillion-dollar capital outlay construction projects and equipment purchases. The initial phase called for trustees to increase the maintenance and operation tax rate from 5 cents to 10 cents. While some of the revenue derived from this increase was to go to current-year operating expenses, the majority was dedicated to capital outlay. The plan thus provided the college with a steady, predictable source of capital-outlay funding to be expended in accordance with a rolling five-year facilities plan. It also removed the necessity of having to fund capital outlay through voter-approved general obligation bonds, with the attendant interest payments equaling roughly one-third of the total bond amount. In 2002, the board of trustees extended the plan by enacting a 3-cent maintenance tax increase earmarked for the construction of a fifth comprehensive campus. As of FY 2004, the college district will have invested over $117.6 million in capital outlay expenditures – all to be paid in cash.

The methodology used to develop the pay-as-you-go approach was based on a strategy of research, assessment, consultation (chancellor and board), and planning. The first step in this process was to determine the college's actual financial needs. The overall intent was to make sure that the college realistically determined its needs in order to maintain student access and educational quality while simultaneously remaining competitive within the existing market environment. Clearly, there was a need to consider historical information and to generate viable projections of optional paths toward self-sufficiency and excellence for the district. For example, information on past and projected salary increases was obtained from several comparable Texas multicampus, urban-based colleges, as well as those located within the college's service area. Internal estimates were projected for technology-related equipment, general equipment, capital improvement projects, staffing needs, and other operational expenditures. To ensure inclusiveness, faculty and staff were asked to prioritize their needs. Survey information obtained from faculty and staff ultimately served as a guide during the decision-making processes. The possibility that funding might or might not materialize was communicated, given the understanding by the chancellor that he would have to convince the board of trustees to take unprecedented and courageous action toward securing the required resources.

The initial assessment and budget-planning efforts provided the college with solid information to use in its implementation phase. Another important step was conducting budget workshops with the board of trustees. The chancellor provided detailed information and possible funding options that could be adopted by the board. For example, the college's maintenance and operations tax rate was identified as being the lowest in the state, while maintaining the highest bonded indebtedness of Texas' 50 public community college districts. Thus, increasing the maintenance and operations tax rate became a viable option. This and other information provided to the board at these sessions allowed them to feel comfortable in acknowledging and embracing the pay-as-you-go concept, thereby ensuring the college's continued growth and success.

Outcomes

Dissemination of information to the community and the college family was a significant factor during implementation. The chancellor and members of the board met with the local newspaper's editorial board, and the chancellor presented the case for the intended action with community leaders, service organizations, and business and industry. The goal was to provide information on the college's intent and the benefits of implementing this type of strategy. In addition, Tarrant County citizens had the opportunity to express their support or concerns during a public hearing prior to the board's review and approval of the funding approach. Budget presentations were conducted on each campus and at the district office to ensure full understanding of the actions taken by the board and their implications. These budget presentations continue to be made to the college family.

The board of trustees, on the recommendation of the newly appointed chancellor, approved the new pay-as-you-go approach in 1998. It involves the use of maintenance and operations (M&O) mil-levy revenues in lieu of interest and sinking-fund mil-levy revenues. The additional M&O tax revenues will continue to be available and used for many capital outlay projects. As of FY 2004, the district will have invested over $117.6 million in capital outlay expenditures – all to be paid in cash. Most recently, this included a new state-of-the-art fire training facility, now fully operational and with no outstanding debt. Another positive element of this new funding strategy is that the Tarrant County College District will save millions of dollars in interest expense that normally would have been paid through the traditional debt-service method, using general-obligation bonds.

Leonardo de la Garza is Chancellor of the Tarrant County College District in Fort Worth, Texas.

3. Raising Tuition: A Conflicting Argument

Glenn DuBois

Context

The Virginia Community College System (VCCS) is one of the nation's largest college systems. There are 23 community colleges, with 40 major campus locations. With few exceptions, Virginians are within a 20-mile drive to a community college campus. The system serves 225,000 credit students and another 125,000 students in noncredit programs.

Organized in 1966, the Virginia Community College System has one chief executive officer with the title of chancellor. Reporting to the chancellor are 23 college presidents and a senior cabinet of seven administrators. The chancellor reports to a 15-member board of trustees, all appointed by the governor, with each board member serving a term of four years. No board member can serve more than two consecutive terms.

Summary of the Case

In July 2001, the eighth chancellor of the Virginia Community College System took office. He arrived on the first of the month from a New England state where he had held similar CEO responsibilities in the community college system. The new chancellor's approach was to lead initially with his ears, not with his mouth. But within five months of the start date, the Virginia Community College System found itself facing a fiscal crisis, the worst in 30 years in Virginia. Listening sessions were over quickly.

The chancellor and his college leaders were now faced with unprecedented budget cuts in state support – a historic $75 million. The wounds went deep, generating dramatic losses of students, employees, and programs. The stakes couldn't have been higher. The system was massively depleted, like a great ship, its sails ripped, struggling to stay afloat in a storm.

The college system had come to rely on state aid to fund up to the level of need, with tuition increases used as an undesirable last resort. While "community colleges" might have become a household phrase in the last few years, the understanding of community college work and mission, both within the Virginia legislature and throughout the state, was woefully inadequate. At best, we were known as Virginia's best-kept secret. To be vaguely understood was a tremendous disadvantage at a time when the state was facing a $6 billion shortfall. The crisis was real.

The good news is that a crisis will bring people together – really fast. During a crisis, leaders can ask some tough questions about core operations and motivate large institutions to organize and cooperate. A crisis galvanizes and soon separates the crew from the spectators, *i.e.*, points out to the CEO those who can lead and those who cannot. When the seas are calm, anyone can pilot the ship. But when it gets rough, the captain of the ship finds out who can really sail. If managed right, a crisis can strengthen an organization, generate huge stakeholder support, and create new opportunities and markets for community colleges.

Determined college leaders soon emerged. Together, they designed an aggressive advocacy campaign to raise awareness about community colleges in the legislature. Their efforts, in effect, reduced the cut in state aid from a possible $75 million to about $50 million – less than what was proposed, but a substantial and far-reaching reduction nonetheless.

We'd done an admirable job. And yet, it became baldly apparent that the time had come to ask the state board to act on tuition – a step that would stir a fiery debate.

At that time, in 2001, 46 other states had tuition levels higher than Virginia. Even so, our governing board members, like those on so many other community college boards, arrived at their posts already convinced that tuition increases are bad: They hurt students, reduce access, and fly in the face of the community college mission. So how do you make the case to substantially raise tuition? Not without a carefully considered strategy.

The challenge was to convince a reluctant and nervous governing board to substantially increase tuition. Without a substantial tuition increase, the quality of our VCCS programs and the scope of our services throughout the state would inevitably change, with more program closures and cuts in staff. To remain viable, the community college system needed to increase tuition by 30 percent.

Questions to Consider

1. What overall strategy would you design to achieve a tuition increase of approximately 30 percent?
2. How would you use college presidents in your strategy?
3. In what ways would you involve students in your strategy?
4. What kinds of information would you present to the board to raise their awareness and understanding of the issue?
5. How would you deal with the press once it got hold of a whopping tuition increase story?
6. What would you say to legislators?
7. Should you go for 30 percent or just enough to get by?

Thoughts and Analysis

Tuition and enrollment behavior is a complex relationship, difficult to understand or to predict. Price certainly affects behavior. But tuition is less about price and more about affordability. The fundamental questions to ask are centered on the percentage of income its takes to attend college and your tuition rate, compared with your competitors' rates.

Many students, particularly those from low-income families, aren't directly affected by tuition increases. For some students, Title IV funds would cover any tuition increase. Other students have sufficient tuition benefits from employers. In dealing with tuition, it is critical to know the impact on your current students, particularly on those who have little or no financial assistance.

Asking for a significant tuition increase puts a new chancellor on the spot. Credibility and job security are at stake.

Outcomes

The VCCS state board raised tuition by 30 percent, with only one dissenting vote. The tool the chancellor used to persuade the board members was a six-year strategic plan called Dateline 2009, the development of which involved college presidents and students.

Dateline 2009 contains seven major measurable goals for the colleges, but at the same time, it focuses on critical needs of the state. This plan has provided much-needed guidance to the system of colleges, and it has shaped a useful context for board members in exercising their governing responsibility. Board members frequently ask how any recommendation fits into Dateline 2009.

Board members, particularly at the state level, need additional context. They need to see students, visit campuses, and get to know college presidents. For a clearer understanding of the college system, board members must get out of the boardroom and visit students and faculty at college campuses.

A critical piece of the development process was this: Individual college presidents invited board members to visit their campuses. In the setting of the campus itself, they would discuss the impact of any tuition increase. These discussions were between college president and board member, not college president with chancellor and board member. Presidents were asked by the chancellor to make the case and ask the board member for his or her support. The chancellor had his own conversations with every board member.

Student leaders were asked if they could support a tuition increase. Many student government associations sent resolutions of support. Students wrote letters to the chancellor, often claiming that they would rather have a tuition increase, so their college could continue to promote access and opportunity to future students, than cut back.

System office staff prepared detailed presentations on the issue of tuition over the course of several board sessions. Board members were apprised of the number of students who would be covered by federal and state financial aid and employer benefits. Staff also presented college plans assuming no tuition increases and cuts of 7 percent, 11 percent, and 15 percent. Tuition rates were also compared to national levels and competing in-state institutions such as private colleges and public four-year colleges. It was demonstrated that the gap between the community college tuition rate and that of the average public four-year college or university was widening, making the community college more competitive on price.

Finally, various recommendations were presented to the board, including no tuition increase (and what that would look like in program closures and staff reductions) and several different tuition increases and their impact. Finally, our preferred recommendation was Dateline 2009, which contained the largest increase ever enacted, demonstrating how those dollars would keep us moving toward the goals adopted by the board and reflected in Dateline 2009. The increase did not cover all the cuts, but did generate revenue adequate to keep access and opportunity prominently featured in our mission. To date, not one student or parent has ever complained to the chancellor's office about our tuition increase.

We learned some valuable lessons about working with governing boards:

- Have an exciting strategic plan with measurable goals focused on the unmet needs of your service area. Tie all your actions to that plan.
- On significant board items, count your votes before the vote is taken.
- Get board members out of the board room.
- Use other stakeholders, such as students, alumni, and parents, to make your case to the board.
- Do your homework, be prepared, and know when it's time to strike.
- Be straight and responsive when dealing with boards.

Glenn DuBois is Chancellor of the Virginia Community College System in Richmond, Virginia. For more information on Dateline 2009, visit http://www.vccs.edu/magazine.

4. Anatomy of Financial Crises

Rufus Glasper and Debra Thompson

Context

The Maricopa Community College District is among the largest community colleges in the nation, with 10 independently accredited colleges. Enrollment growth has been steady over most of the district's 40-plus-year history, and the 10 colleges collectively now offer credit classes to over 233,000 students and noncredit classes to another 35,000. The district's Fiscal Year 2003-2004 combined operational and capital budget totaled $725 million. The strategic and tactical implementation of the district's goals regarding teaching, learning, and community service, including enrollment growth and management, are facilitated by a resource base that generally has been growing, although not without limitation and not without issues at times.

Summary of the Case

The Maricopa Community College District now enjoys an AAA rating from two of three investor rating agencies. This is the highest measure of credit worthiness possible. The district also holds reserves that total at least 8 percent of General Fund revenues, further evidence of financial strength and stability. However, it was only about a decade ago that a series of financial issues converged, causing significant financial pressure in the district. Cases of financial stringency catching higher education institutions unprepared are becoming all too common. In general, "pre-exigency planning"[1] is the key to preparing for and reacting to a fiscal emergency and, subsequently, minimizing potential impact. It is instructive to explore some of the factors that led to fiscal emergencies, and the planning activities that institutions might undertake to avoid emergencies or to mitigate financial issues, as well as the longer-term positive benefits of sound fiscal practices.

Questions to Consider

Some fundamental questions must be considered to understand the conditions that might result in fiscal emergencies, prevention and mitigation strategies, and practices that can lead to enduring fiscal health.

    1. What is a financial crisis?

The financial condition of every business, institution, government agency, and the nation as a whole are subject to continual response to both external and internal factors. For example, the 1990s were deemed a time of prosperity for the nation and the State of Arizona. Many new businesses were created, and many companies posted record earnings. Employment rates and wage levels increased, inflation was low, and the stock market reached numerous milestones, all of which further amplified the wealth of many. The exceptional economic climate shored up the finances of many governmental institutions as well, including the federal government, the State of Arizona and the Maricopa Community Colleges.

[1] Richard J.Meisinger, Jr., College and University Budgeting (NACUBO, 1994)

In recent years, signs of weakening and economic pressures have abounded. Layoffs and restructuring, stock market declines, and energy crises in some major states have negatively affected business and individuals. When the economy weakens, the loss of taxes generally weakens the finances of government agencies. In Arizona, the governor and legislative leaders forecasted annual revenue shortfalls of approximately $1 billion in recent years. It is not surprising that the state served notice in each of the prior two years that community colleges should prepare for state aid reductions.

For either a private or public entity, managing operations with limited resources is not a financial crisis. Similarly, when actual resources are less than planned, managing within reduced revenue forecast guidelines may not necessarily lead to a financial emergency. However, mismanagement of difficult financial conditions may result in financial crisis. There is no substitute for leadership's diligence and action to ensure that expenditures remain aligned with revenues, and that the institution continues to operate effectively. The financial crisis occurs when the financial condition of an institution deteriorates to the point that the entity is on the verge of, or reaches, insolvency.

2. How is a financial crisis caused?

The immediate cause of a financial crisis is the failure of an organization's leadership to align spending with available or reasonably projected resources. A financial crisis may occur when an institution elevates spending above available resource levels or fails to reduce spending to meet current resource levels.

Like many business entities, both public and private higher education enterprises have succumbed to financial pressures and crises. The following examples illustrate paths, or in some cases, blind alleys taken by several higher education institutions that led to financial problems.

One university long relied on its prestigious medical center to help support enterprisewide costs. As a result of Medicare and Medicaid cuts, however, the medical center's revenues declined, and the institution elected to establish the medical center as a separate entity to financially protect the parent institution. Concurrently, student enrollment was decreasing, resulting in tuition losses. Despite these notable revenue declines, the university continued expanding programs. Annual operating deficits well in excess of $100 million resulted from the combination of these contributing factors.

Another institution, which had operated continuously since 1909, announced in the late 1990s that it was closing because of "financial problems" based, in part, on the inability to compete with for-profit technical institutions.

The Maricopa Community College District has avoided financial crisis per se, but did face financial pressures between Fiscal Years 1991 and 1993 that required the college district to take significant corrective actions. The pressures were caused by both external and internal resource-limiting factors. During this period, the economy in Arizona was very weak, creating several years of declining assessed valuations and limited annual growth in property taxes. At the same time, state aid remained fairly level until Fiscal

Year 1992, when, because of its own fiscal pressures, the state determined midyear that the full appropriation to community colleges would not be made. This created a huge revenue shortfall for all college districts. Internal issues concurrently exerted additional financial pressure. Two colleges had exceeded allotted budgets in the process of recruiting and serving additional students. Further, costs rose significantly as a result of a multiyear salary agreement that was inclusive of successive cost-of-living adjustments of   4 percent, 5 percent, and 6 percent. All told, spending exceeded revenues.

3. What can be done when an institution faces financial pressures or a crisis?

The Maricopa Community Colleges avoided a financial crisis because it was able to draw down $23 million of its $26 million fund balance to pay salaries and bills and cover all other costs. Several expenditure-reduction initiatives were initiated, including a revision to the third year of the three-year salary agreement, a hiring freeze, and temporary and permanent budget reductions. These were short-term solutions; to avoid serious financial problems in the future and to restore and then advance its financial health, the Maricopa Community Colleges implemented a number of new policies and practices.

Thoughts and Analysis

Many financial professionals judge Maricopa Community College District's future by its high standards of financial stewardship and planning practices over the last decade. "Notable is the district's strong long-range financial planning. Although spending pressures associated with new and growing facilities should continue, financial stability assumes that management will continue to exercise the strong fiscal discipline that it cultivated in the early 1990s when lagging state aid for community colleges hurt financial margins."[2]   Since then, the institution has enhanced its financial stability in many ways, including placing an emphasis on shared governance practices, *i.e.*, power, authority, and influence over resource distribution.

Maricopa Community Colleges' resources are dedicated to support its mission to "create and continuously improve affordable, accessible, effective, and safe learning environments for the lifelong educational needs of the diverse communities we serve." To safeguard the financial resources of the institution and to ensure business and operational continuity, a series of governing-board financial policies exists that specifies expectations for financial planning, financial condition, asset protection, executive constraint, and communication and counsel to the governing board. These policies help set parameters for enterprisewide financial and operational practices. Broadly speaking, these are designed to ensure that the enterprise will avoid financial crises.

A financial crisis is not necessarily a terminal condition. Assuming that no alternative revenue sources can be identified, if a financial crisis appears to be imminent, a number of recourses may exist. All require the concerted efforts of leadership in the organization. Expenditure reductions may include hiring freezes or layoffs, compensation reductions or deferred increases, travel prohibitions, service reduction, and program cuts or elimination.

[2] Fitch IBCA, Duff, & Phelps, Maricopa Community College Credit Rating, 2001

A careful assessment of the nature, magnitude, timing, and expected duration of the problem is critical in determining what and how much action must be taken. Also critical is a careful assessment of the types and levels of services and expenditures required to continue to operate at an acceptable level.

The short-term strategies taken by the Maricopa Community Colleges were noted previously. The following synthesizes the longer-term preventive actions taken by Maricopa Community Colleges to build a strong financial condition:

- Discontinuation of multiyear labor agreements
- Adoption of a districtwide strategic planning process to set goals and implement action plans
- Long-term financial planning (annual public presentations and annual updates of 3-year and 15-year financial forecasts)
- Governing-board adoption of a Financial Stability policy (nonadherence denotes a cost recommendation that is equal to financial stability of the institution)
- Implementation of an enterprisewide carry-forward provision of prior-year unexpended college balances as an incentive to spend more wisely
- Emphasis on interest income as a more significant funding source
- Increased participation of faculty and staff on advisory councils for finance, technology, strategic planning, and capital development planning
- Decentralization of spending responsibility granting authority and accountability of total budget allocation
- Lobbying of coalitions and increased briefings with legislative staff and major taxpayers
- Adoption and strengthening of governing-board policies regarding financial planning, condition, asset protection, executive constraints, and counsel to the board
- Formalization of Intervention Strategies when expenditures exceed budget
- Enhancement of Financial Advisory Council (FAC) process and increased Chancellor's Executive Council involvement in budget processes
- Strengthening of role of Audit and Finance Committee
- Adoption of policy that no new buildings and facilities could be opened without budgeted operating costs
- Establishment of operating-cost formulae and approvals by FAC and Capital Development Advisory Council
- Establishment of regular monitoring reports
- Recapture of expenditure limitation (temporary solution, allowing phased-in approach to reduced expenditures)

Many of the strategies implemented to address resource shortfalls were painful, but becoming financially stable and implementing financial management practices has long-term rewards and benefits:

- Greater ability to plan and commit funds to advance operational priorities
- Strong financial condition and stewardship contributing to AAA bond ratings, reducing debt service payments, and relaxing tax requirements
- Strong reserves that guard against temporary shortfalls
- Greater ability to respond to future problems that are certain to occur

While the Maricopa Community College District has constructed many safeguards to mitigate against a financial crisis, every issue potentially affecting institutional finances requires vigilance. New approaches and solutions are consistently sought, because Maricopa has learned that pre-exigency planning is the key to preparing for and reacting to a fiscal emergency and, subsequently, minimizing the potential adverse impacts.

Outcomes

All institutions, including the Maricopa Community Colleges, will experience strong and weak financial periods in response to internal and external financial conditions. As new threats emerge, prompt and appropriate action is continually required to avoid financial pressures from becoming possible crises. The Maricopa Community Colleges swiftly and collectively addressed its financial stress of the 1990s, and has built a much stronger financial condition and environment as a result. The award of two AAA ratings (the highest possible) on the fourth general-obligation bond issue and subsequent refunding issues is testimony to this fact. The effect of a strong financial condition, built by sound financial planning and management, fosters the enterprise's sustained ability to meet its mission: to create and continuously improve affordable, accessible, effective, and safe learning environments for the lifelong educational needs of the diverse communities we serve.

Rufus Glasper is Chancellor and Debra Thompson is Vice Chancellor, Business Services of the Maricopa Community College District in Maricopa County, Arizona.

5. A College's Response to a Community's Dream

David W. Sink, Jr.

Context

Blue Ridge Community College is one of 59 public institutions in the North Carolina Community College System. Ninety percent of the college's operating budget of $15 million comes from the state, 9 percent from county commissioners for buildings and maintenance, and 1 percent from federal and foundation grants. Capital projects are funded through local and statewide bond referendums and private donations. The college's education foundation, with assets of almost $4 million, contributes approximately $250,000 a year to scholarships, faculty development, and program support.

Blue Ridge operates under the leadership of a president and a 15-member board of trustees and serves 2,000 curriculum and 12,000 continuing education students annually. Located in the Blue Ridge Mountains of western North Carolina, the college's service area includes Henderson and Transylvania Counties, with a combined population of 130,000. The college's main campus is located in Flat Rock, three miles south of Hendersonville, the Henderson County seat. Known for its natural beauty and four seasons, Henderson County has been featured in national publications as one of the best places in the United States to retire. The county is experiencing rapid growth and boasts an abundance of educational, cultural, and arts programs provided by a symphony, the Flat Rock Playhouse (North Carolina's state theater), an arts council, five community theater groups, a quilters guild, and local art galleries. Henderson County's community foundation boasts assets of almost $50 million.

In 1987, a new community college president was hired and charged by the trustees to become active in the community. One of the first things he realized was the need for a large auditorium or performing arts center in Henderson County. Since a blue-ribbon study commission was under way, the president quickly proposed in speeches to the Chamber of Commerce, Four Seasons Arts Council, and various civic groups the idea of locating such a building on the college's campus. The college's director of community relations interviewed community leaders representing the arts, business community, and county commissioners to ascertain the feasibility of this proposal. Those interviewed indicated that the community needed an auditorium; it should be built with public and private donations; and locating it at the college would make it more cost effective. Conservative county commissioners were reluctant to allocate public money for capital construction or building maintenance and were not willing to put the project on a referendum ballot.

The president and chairman of the board of trustees had preliminary plans drawn for a site location and went to solicit support from the chairman of the arts council board, a local attorney influential with wealthy donors and members of the North Carolina General Assembly. This leader voiced concerns raised in the community. Some felt that a cultural facility had to be located downtown, in the heart of the city. Others questioned who would govern the facility, schedule events, and control the content of performances if the auditorium was located at the college. Serving alcohol on campus was also an issue, because it was prohibited by state law except under certain situations. The attorney proposed establishing a nonprofit, nongovernmental entity to own and operate the facility, but trustees were unwilling to hand over control of a campus building. Although the college offered several compromises, including establishing an advisory board to the trustees to oversee facility scheduling and to recommend policy changes, no consensus could be reached.

What followed was a multitude of studies, each with new and differing recommendations about size, location, and partners to be involved. In 1990, the community foundation contracted with a regional university to conduct a cultural-center feasibility study. That study recommended the college as the best location, based on affordability, availability of land, college infrastructure, proximity to a major interstate, and adequate parking space. In 1992, a committee using the feasibility study recommendations projected building costs for a 1,200-seat auditorium located on the campus at $7.4 million. Again, grumblings followed from a small group of city advocates about the distance of three miles from the college to downtown.

Within a year, the attorney opposing the college location became a community foundation board member and chaired a committee that retained a fund-raising consulting firm. These consultants, contrary to earlier reports, recommended the facility be located downtown on donated city land. Estimated cost was $6.25 million–$1 million to $1.5 million from the state, $1 million to $1.3 million from private donations, and $3.45 million to $4.25 million from city and county governments. In 1996, the county commissioners appointed still another committee to explore the possibility of a public-private partnership to help fund a multipurpose building downtown. This committee recommended a facility to house a performing arts center, local nonprofit groups, and the county's agricultural extension agency. The addition of agricultural programs was an attempt to garner financial support from the county commissioners. Even with a reported $2.5 million pledged by local donors, a price tag of $14.6 million was unacceptable to county commissioners and civic leaders alike.

In 1997, the college opened a new allied health building, funded by the passage four years earlier of a $5.5 million bond referendum. Plans called for a 500-seat teaching auditorium, but high construction bids forced the college to shell in the auditorium rather than eliminate it. The untimely death of a prominent Henderson County state senator prompted college trustees to name the unfinished auditorium in his memory. The chairman of the board then succeeded in getting state legislators to appropriate $2 million for the auditorium's completion, over the objections of the state community college system office and other presidents who had agreed not to seek special project funding. Coming on the heels of the derailed downtown efforts, the special appropriation attracted the attention of community leaders. A citizen's committee approached the president with the concept of enlarging the teaching auditorium to 1,200 seats. Architects estimated costs for an expanded facility at $5 million, leaving $3 million to be raised by community partners.

Summary of the Case

The college's emphasis on performing arts is growing, with the addition of an Associate of Fine Arts degree, several concert series, an annual arts symposium, and plans for a drama department. Trustees and college foundation directors are not willing to undertake a capital campaign to raise the additional $3 million, but are open to supporting a community-led effort. County commissioners will not provide funds to operate a large auditorium, although they raise no objections to the smaller one. A CEO of a major industry, highly respected in the community and with strong college ties, sees the opportunity as a win-win situation. He offers to chair a task force and contribute $30,000 in seed money to spark the fundraising effort. The economy is soft and there is a possibility of the General Assembly recalling the $2 million special appropriation.

Questions to Consider

1. Should the president delay the completion of the smaller auditorium to give community leaders time to raise the money needed to expand the auditorium? If so, for how long and under what conditions? If not, what reasons will he give?
2. If private money is raised to expand the seating capacity, how much influence should community leaders have over facility governance, management, and scheduling? How will additional maintenance costs be covered? What position will the president take about requests that alcohol be served at arts events and community fundraisers?
3. If the president decides to complete the smaller auditorium, will there be loss of support from the arts and business communities? How might his decision affect emerging programs, donations to the college foundation, and future collaborative partnerships?

Thoughts and Analysis

1. Community service is a vital part of the community college mission.
2. The president at Blue Ridge has a strong commitment to and reputation for championing the arts.
3. The chairman of the board of trustees is fairly confident that the money escrowed at state level is secure, but has some doubts as to how long the college can delay spending the money before being questioned by state legislators.
4. The business CEO is a strong supporter of the college. He has served on its foundation board, initiated a business and industry scholarship program, and helped fund a two-year technical training program for students.
5. No one person or organization speaks for the various arts groups.
6. The auditorium would house state-of-the-art technology and could be used by business, industry, local government, and nonprofits.

Outcomes

The president delayed completion of the auditorium to give the community the opportunity to raise the $3 million. The CEO formed a task force that projected securing

$1.5 million in private donations and $1.5 from federal and foundation grants. Six months into their work, only a few pledges had been received. The financial picture for North Carolina began to weaken, due to the devastation in the eastern part of the state by Hurricane Floyd and legal rulings adversely affecting the state. The president and chairman of the board were concerned about losing the special appropriation. With no donor willing to make a lead gift, the president concluded that the community was not willing to fund the expansion. He decided to complete the smaller auditorium, which was dedicated in 2001.

Within a year, another community group formed to study the feasibility of converting an old downtown mill into a 1,200-seat performing arts center – this time at a price tag of $17 million.

David W. Sink, Jr. is President of Blue Ridge Community College in Henderson County, North Carolina.

6. Weathering the Storm

Tony Zeiss

Context

Central Piedmont Community College (CPCC) is a multicampus, comprehensive institution located in Charlotte, North Carolina. The college serves 70,000 individuals each year through curriculum courses, corporate and continuing education offerings, and literacy and English-as-a-second-language programs. CPCC receives operating revenue from the state and construction and maintenance revenue from Mecklenburg County. The state legislature sets tuition rates, and the college is obligated to give tuition revenue directly to the state. All student fees are also set by the state. The college is allowed to retain this money, although the fee-generated revenue must be expended in specific ways.

The weak economy began seriously affecting this open-door college in 1999. North Carolina's state revenues were declining as a result of a series of multimillion-dollar civil lawsuits that the state lost, and also because of a decline in tobacco revenue. The year 2000 brought the downward-spiraling stock market, followed by the decline of the state's other two primary job-producing industries: textiles and furniture manufacturing.

State and county revenues decreased severely because of this loss of jobs, but the demands for services from the college increased. This debilitating climate developed with surprising rapidity and presented the college with a challenge for survival. The need for a shift in how the college conducted business and earned revenue became apparent. During 2003, CPCC experienced a 25 percent reduction in public funding, exacerbated by a 28 percent increase in enrollments. This situation produced a net budget gap unparalleled in the college's history.

The CEO, his administrative team, and CPCC's board of trustees faced a critical challenge: How could the college remain an open-door institution when it no longer could afford to be so accessible? Faculty and staff worried about their jobs, programs were in jeopardy, and vendors complained about not being paid by the college. During this period, all faculty and staff experienced increased workloads and elevated stress levels. In the meantime, the college opened two new campuses funded by county construction bonds that had been approved during better economic times. These campuses provided the much-needed space for recent enrollment growth, but the state has never properly funded satellite campus operations. So although the college desperately needed the space, it lacked the necessary financial resources to properly operate them. The college's regional accrediting association visited and required the college to employ three additional librarians for the new campuses, and also strongly suggested that more counselors be provided. Of course, CPCC had no money for these new positions, and state restrictions prevent transferring money from one funding category to another. This was just one of many difficult problems faced by the college.

CPCC also faced a cultural challenge: Would the open-door college be closing its doors? This prospect presented a morale problem for the faculty and staff, who loved the accessibility aspect of CPCC's mission. On the other hand, to maintain quality teachers and teaching, the college could no longer provide all the courses needed by its growing and diverse student body. The threat of inadequate resources made it increasingly difficult for the college to stay true to two of its most revered values. In addition, it was perfectly clear that the decline in public resources was going to be long term, probably even permanent. The college was going to have to become more self-sufficient and move from a public-supported to a public-assisted organization. How could the CEO transform the faculty and staff from being totally reliant on public funding to becoming more self-reliant for funding? CPCC was compelled to transform itself into an education enterprise or risk becoming a mediocre organization whose long-tenured values of accessibility and quality would be sacrificed.

Summary of the Case

Funding from the state and county had declined for the past four years, and there was no sign of improvement in the near future, since the state suffered declines in its top three job-producing industries. The college was growing in student enrollments and was in desperate need of new space. Two new campuses were built from county funds appropriated before the decreases in operating budgets. The combined effects of diminished operating budgets and increased enrollments presented a serious dilemma for CPCC. Furthermore, the college faced the challenge of staying true to its values of accessibility and quality teaching when inadequate resources placed these two values in conflict with each other.

Questions to Consider

1. Should the CEO initiate a reduction in force and eliminate all services that do not generate income? If so, what effect would that have on employees, and how would it affect students?
2. Should the CEO search for efficiencies, close a campus or two, reduce course offerings? If so, what effect would this have on the students and the community?
3. Should the CEO prune the programs and courses and hold tight for the economy to improve? If so, how would this affect the students, the college, and the community?
4. Should the CEO search for new revenue streams? If so, how should he go about it?

Thoughts and Analysis

Community colleges are known for their accessibility, responsiveness, and teaching-learning quality. These fundamental values were in jeopardy because of declining revenues and increasing enrollments. How could the college continue its focus on community and student needs when the resources could no longer support the entire mission of the organization? Should the college remain true to one fundamental value while sacrificing others? Since the reduction in public funding was likely to be permanent, what could be done to increase revenues? How could the college transform itself from an entitlement mentality to an entrepreneurial mentality while staying true to its mission and values? How should the college respond to such challenges while employee workloads were already at the limit?

Outcomes

This case is not yet closed, and likely won't be for several years, if ever. However, some major initiatives have been launched that are paying great dividends.

First, the CEO recognized that he had to rally all of the college's supporters and garner all the good will possible to formulate and navigate a strategic course for the institution. He arranged for a board of trustees retreat with his key administrators to reaffirm the mission, vision, and values of the college. They then established specific parameters and set a course of action that included multiple initiatives to increase efficiencies, enhance existing revenue streams, and generate new sources of revenue. Three of the crucial parameters were that

1. No full-time employees would be dismissed, if that was avoidable;
2. No campus would be closed – the savings would be minimal and the public response would be negative; and
3. The quality of teaching and learning would be preserved.

The course of action involved a determination to turn the CPCC into a more self-supporting organization as rapidly as possible. The board of trustees also agreed to establish a new nonprofit entity that would be a fee-for-service corporation serving as the springboard for turning the college into an educational enterprise.

To accomplish this course of action, the CEO began to garner both external and internal support for this new charge. He met with the college's influential foundation directors and convinced them to begin a new $15 million capital campaign to establish endowments for scholarships, equipment, teaching fellowships, and new program start-ups. (This campaign is in its second year and has exceeded the halfway mark.) He established a president's council composed of 30 top CEOs of business and industry and regularly solicited their advice on how to increase revenue from existing and new sources. To capture the collective intellectual capital of the internal personnel, the CEO communicated with all faculty and staff by email to get their ideas for identifying greater efficiencies. The result was extraordinary, and the existing process review team made up of faculty and staff gained new momentum as it looked for greater efficiencies and better ways to make the college more customer focused. The president then established a team of CPCC's most innovative and creative administrators, faculty, and staff to identify new revenue streams. This high-energy group was named the Resource Enhancement and Creative Thinking Team (REACT). This team examines new revenue opportunities and recommends priority initiatives, serving as a strategic positioning body for the college. Once an initiative is approved, a REACT member spearheads its implementation.

In addition to these initiatives, the president and his staff have spent more time raising grant and earmarked funds from the federal government. With $2.2 million from earmarked funds, CPCC recently established the American Academy for Applied Forensics. The president also spent more time at the state capital and persuaded the legislative leadership to sponsor a bill to provide adequate funding to support satellite campuses. The CEO and college foundation staff have renewed their efforts in annual fundraising and planned giving. They sold class sponsorships and offered naming opportunities for laboratories, buildings, and campuses. A $5 million gift from one individual is the largest single gift to date.

The college's new fee-for-service corporation is helping to reshape the culture of the college so that faculty and staff are encouraged to think about opportunities to bring new revenue to CPCC, to their departments, and to themselves. Through the CPCC Services Corporation, faculty and staff are becoming entrepreneurs. Several faculty members are writing textbooks that will be marketed by a national firm. Proceeds will be distributed to the college, the department, and the faculty members. One faculty member produced a series of DVDs helping Spanish speakers learn English. This program has been purchased by several states. The college's research department is conducting research and providing consulting services for a fee to private entities. The CPCC Services Corporation also generates revenue by leasing space to private companies, restaurants, and universities. Through this corporation, the college established its first national conference, titled *Positive Reactions to Negative Budgets*. It was a success!

To reduce overhead, CPCC also outsourced as many administrative functions as was deemed appropriate. The bookstore operation now produces a minimum of $400,000 per year, instead of operating in the red as was the case prior to being outsourced. Security, housekeeping, parking services, and lawn maintenance have also been outsourced.

The college is pulling itself out of its financial depression and is becoming a much stronger organization because it chose to face adversity with optimism and a positive course of action.

Tony Zeiss is President and CEO of Central Piedmont Community College in Charlotte, North Carolina.

Part IV

Instructional Programs and Services

1. Assessing Student Learning: What's the Big Deal?

Marsha S. Bordner

Context

The dean of arts and sciences at a small community college in Ohio has the opportunity to become the chief academic officer after the current vice president for academic and student affairs takes a presidency in another state. The dean has served seven years as a full-time faculty member and eight years as a dean before the time of her transition to chief academic officer. She knows the campus well.

Her biggest concern in taking the position of vice president is the lack of the campus's progress in the assessment of student learning.

The North Central Association (NCA) had mandated the submission of plans to assess student learning early in the 1990s. Her college's plan was approved early on and was not as descriptive as it might have been. Several years have passed.

In the time since the original mandating of the submission of plans, the NCA has provided no models on how to assess student achievement, leaving the choice with the individual colleges. Many colleges, including this one, are uncertain of a direction to pursue. This contributes to the lack of progress.

Complicating this lack of progress is the site visit the accrediting association will be making to campus in only three years as part of its 10-year comprehensive review.

The vice president clearly realizes that the overall responsibility for learning in academic programs falls squarely at her feet. In fact, she fears that her overall job performance will be measured against her ability to move this initiative forward.

Summary of the Case

The vice president needs to initiate an assessment of student learning process quickly, and *quickly* in an academic culture is frequently a tall order. The North Central Association team visiting in three years will most certainly expect that progress toward the implementation of a plan of student learning will be evident. The vice president also needs to get faculty buy-in and will need their assistance to effect meaningful, systemic change in the way learning is measured.

Questions to Consider

1. Learning is the most fundamental premise upon which higher education, or any education, is based. What is the great difficulty about assessing learning?
2. How should the vice president get started? Should she mandate that learning will be assessed? Some faculty have encouraged her to try to force the faculty to get to work quickly.

3. Is there truth to the faculty's contention that this, too, shall pass? The faculty believe that this is one more of the latest trends that higher education is pursuing. Their resistance is palpable. They have seen other trends come and go.
4. The NCA mandated, appropriately, that there be faculty buy-in. What is the best way to get faculty buy-in?
5. Is there truth to the faculty's contention that they are already too busy? Why can't they just teach, which is what they were hired to do?
6. Does one size fit all? Can all programs and academic disciplines be assessed in the same way in a community college?
7. Is assessment in two-year colleges comparable to that in the four-year environment?
8. How can a two-year college assess general education across the curriculum?
9. How is assessment different from the more traditional program review?
10. Why aren't grades sufficient in the assessment of student learning?

Thoughts and Analysis

Accountability first became important in the business world and then in the health care arena, but was a new concept in education in the early 1990s. There were few good models to draw upon. The ultimate outcome, well-educated humans, is a vastly different outcome from the tangible products that can be generated in a business environment. The concept of assessing learning was very foreign to most faculty members, who frequently teach the way they were taught.

Mandating anything with faculty violates traditional concepts of academic freedom and governance. It seemed more appropriate to encourage assessment because it is the right thing to do. After all, faculty might just improve student learning, an appealing concept to any committed educator.

As pleasant as it might be to hope that assessment will pass, the overall thrust from accrediting associations, the general public, and parents concerned about the cost of education suggests otherwise.

Any systemic change in academic culture requires faculty buy-in. Faculty need to do more than pay lip service if assessment is to be meaningful.

Faculty are generally very busy; however, it behooves everyone in higher education to realize that the life of a faculty member is far less contemplative than it used to be. At one point, it was enough for faculty to know their discipline and to be mildly entertaining in the classroom. There has been a fundamental shift in the profession itself.

Academic disciplines approach assessment in different ways. In the liberal arts, faculty are frequently unfamiliar with assessment techniques. Faculty in business are often equally unfamiliar with assessment, although in the computer field, certifications and other processes help provide viable assessment data. The health technologies tend to be the strongest in assessing student learning, since assessing the state of patients is a natural part of the profession. In engineering technologies, the response to assessment is mixed. In fields dependent on the fulfillment of competencies, assessment of student learning is natural. In areas more theoretical, assessment becomes more difficult.

Assessment in a two-year college is markedly different from that in a four-year college or university. Many community college students are part-timers, many take classes at multiple campuses, and most will not actually complete degrees on a two-year campus. The approach to assessment is far more fragmented on a two-year campus.

Assessing general education across the curriculum, especially with direct measures of learning, is very difficult. The mission of the technical programs and the transfer programs are often at odds in terms of general education outcomes across the curriculum.

The difference between assessment and program review was very confusing to educators at first. After some time, it became clear that program review assessed the program itself, including the curriculum, the faculty, the equipment, and so on. Assessment of student learning focused exclusively on what students should be able to know, do, and value throughout the program as well as at the end.

The traditional method of assessing student learning in the classroom has been grades. However, as all educators know, grades tend to be subjective. They often depend on the teaching style and rigor of the faculty member involved. Assessment of student learning had to include more varied and direct measures of learning than simple awarding of grades.

Outcomes

The new vice president instituted a program of enticement and coercion. She felt that any attempt to out-and-out mandate the faculty to assess student learning would result in certain failure. Hence, she frequently mentioned that the North Central Association visit would be coming in the near future and that faculty would be expected to demonstrate what learning had occurred in their classrooms. She believed that this pressure was as close to coercion as she could get.

She formed an assessment committee and provided release for a coordinator. Occasionally, stipends were given for extra pilot projects as an additional enticement.

After a trial run with two different coordinators, she finally found the right person for the job. This individual reorganized the committee and recruited faculty of high stature to be a part of the group. This provided valuable momentum.

The NCA visit resulted in a focused engagement. The college had five years to demonstrate progress on the assessment of student learning. This focus visit resulted in a progress report to be completed within three years on the demonstration of direct measures of assessing learning in general education.

In addition to the pressure from North Central, the vice president was able to get the health faculty on campus to share models with other faculty on how to assess learning.

The vice president also instituted an orientation program for all new faculty that included assessment as a fundamental component of their jobs.

Nonetheless, with all of the enticement and coercion, it took nearly a full decade to effect a systemic change in the academic culture of the college; however, at the end of this time, the vice president felt that significant progress had been made and faculty buy-in had been secured.

Marsha S. Bordner is President of Terra Community College in Fremont, Ohio.

2. Faculty Load Fairness?

Peter D. Boyse

Context

Delta College is a public community college located in the Midwest. Its fall semester headcount enrollment is 10,500 credit students, with another 35,000 trained through its Corporate Services division each year. The college also has a public television and public radio station. The students come mostly from the three counties served by the college and from several other adjacent counties that are not served by a community college. The students generally reflect the demographic makeup of the surrounding area.

The board of trustees is composed of nine members, with three coming from each of the three counties served by the college. The trustees are publicly elected and represent a cross section of the population served by the college.

Reporting to the president of the college are the vice president of instruction, the vice president of student services, the vice president of business and finance, the executive director of institutional advancement, the executive director of administrative services, the executive director of communication technology, and the executive director of corporate services.

The college senate is an important part of Delta College's shared governance structure and is composed of representatives of the faculty and the administration and professional staff. The senate is advisory to the Delta College board of trustees. The Delta College faculty and administrative staff are not unionized. Hence, the college senate is not connected to a union. As there are more faculty than administrative and professional staff, the faculty maintain a majority of the senate seats. A senate president is elected each year by a vote of all the members of the senate assembly. The current senate president's teaching load would be significantly affected by a change in the above referenced policy.

The Delta College faculty is generally very caring and nurturing when it comes to students. They exhibit loyalty to each other and to the college. Delta College uses a relatively large number of full-time faculty to teach its courses – 65 to 70 percent during the fall and winter semesters. Faculty are paid well in relation to other community colleges in the state, and their pay also compares favorably to community colleges in other states. Class sizes are smaller than most of the class sizes at Delta's peer colleges in the state, and faculty load is 30 hours per academic year.

The Delta College faculty has seen a great deal of turnover due to retirements during the past 10 years. There are still a number of the old guard who were hired during the 1960s and 1970s, but about half have been hired since 1990, and they view the world differently than their senior colleagues. In recent years, there seems to be more of an expectation that if faculty members are asked to do something outside of the assigned teaching load, then they expect extra compensation for their effort.

Summary of the Case

As teaching methods have changed and faculty are using more and more technology, the lines between lecture and lab have become blurred. There is a dwindling number of strictly lecture classes. Most classes involve discussion and student interaction. In addition, some classes that were once classified as lab are now classified as lecture. Needless to say, there are inequities in the system.

When calculating faculty load, Delta College has used the more traditional formula of compensating laboratory sections at 0.8 rather than 1.0 for lecture sections. Thus, if one faculty member teaches 15 hours of lecture per semester (a full load), another faculty member who teaches 5 hours of laboratory per semester would be required to also teach 11 hours of lecture to make up a full load ($5 \times 0.8 = 4 + 11 = 15$). Recently the college senate, which is composed of both faculty and administration, voted to ask the board of trustees to change the policy regarding the lab/lecture ratio from 0.8 to 1.0 to 1.0 to 1.0, regardless of whether these classes are in a lecture or lab environment. However, this change in policy will cost the college over $1 million per year, and the college is facing a severe budget deficit thanks to cutbacks in state appropriations.

It should be noted that Delta College spends a larger portion of its budget for instructional costs than most of its peer colleges in the state. It also has one of the higher community college tuitions in the state. Therefore, the president does not want to take resources from other parts of the budget or to add an extra charge to students to fund this policy change. This would mean that any increase in costs for this policy change would have to come from within the current instructional budget, and that would mean reprioritizing this section of the budget.

Questions to Consider

The president needs to work with the faculty leadership and the Faculty Load Equity Committee to address the funding and equity issue if this change is to be implemented. Following are issues that need resolution:

1. During the last 20 years, a large number of courses that were part laboratory and part lecture were changed to an all-lecture designation, which had the effect of changing the laboratory load factor from 0.8 to 1.0. This was done without any financial planning and, because these were subtle changes over many years, the president and finance office were unaware of these changes as they were taking place. Should all of the classes that have made this change in the past 20 years be re-examined and changes made in the faculty load designation if appropriate?
2. Class size is another issue. Although many faculty state that each contact hour requires the same amount of time and effort, there are variations in class size that indicate otherwise. If faculty want all contact hours compensated at the same rate, should all class sizes be the same?
3. Should there be different faculty-load values placed on a contact hour, depending on a given set of criteria? What criteria should be used to determine the value of a contact hour?
4. What suggestions would you have for how any increased costs due to this policy change should be funded?

Thoughts and Analysis

As mentioned, there are two different cost calculations for funding this change in laboratory load factor. The faculty version assumes that all of the additional hours that faculty will need to teach as a result of a change in the laboratory load factor from 0.8 to 1.0 will be taught by faculty at the supplemental rate (overload pay). This cost is about $600,000. The administrative version assumes that all of the additional hours that faculty will teach as a result of this change will most likely be taught with the same proportion of full-time faculty, part-time faculty, supplemental, and so forth, as currently exists within the faculty pay structure of the college. This cost is about $1.3 million.

A decision needs to be made as to which of these calculations is most accurate, and appropriate policies and procedures put in place to assure that the level of compensation does not change as time passes. Current faculty may agree to teach the "extra load" created by this change at the supplemental rate, but future faculty may not want to do this, thus increasing college instructional costs.

There are faculty who feel that the way to fund this change is to charge students by the contact hour rather than the credit hour. However, students would not receive any added value for this change in faculty load factor, and they already pay one of the highest community college tuitions in the state.

Outcomes

While acknowledging there are some inequities, the president and other staff and some faculty do not agree that every class that is taught requires the same amount of time and energy. The president has asked the faculty to take a look at an entirely new method of determining compensation and evaluate course compensation on a new set of criteria. The lecture-lab compensation discussion has been going on for many years – since the mid-1970s – and no good solution has been reached. Another important point is that most working conditions, including faculty load, are recommended by the senate to the board of trustees for approval and are not subject to salary negotiations.

The difference in the cost estimates depends on whether the college hires new full-time faculty to teach the additional hours or uses adjuncts and faculty overload pay. Of course, there are a number of variations and combinations between those options.

During the fall semester, the college senate approved a change in this policy, requiring all faculty to be compensated the same regardless of what they teach. The senate then made a recommendation to the board of trustees for approval of this change. However, the college administration did not recommend board approval until a method for funding this proposed change could be developed. Therefore, the board passed a motion asking that the administration and faculty work together to develop a recommendation on faculty teaching load that addresses both equity and funding.

Peter D. Boyse is President of Delta College in University City, Michigan.

3. Creating a Faculty Workload Policy

Diane M. Calhoun-French

Context

Jefferson Community College is a multicampus comprehensive community college with campuses in downtown and suburban Louisville and Carrollton, Kentucky. It also offers classes at a newly constructed campus in Shelbyville, Kentucky; at United Parcel Service's Worldport Air Hub; at three state correctional facilities; and at numerous other off-campus sites. Its sister institution is Jefferson Technical College, a multicampus institution with campuses in downtown Louisville and Shelbyville, programs in five state correctional institutions, and an aviation-maintenance partnership at Shawnee High School in Louisville. Together, these institutions comprise the Jefferson Community and Technical College District of the Kentucky Community and Technical College System. Already collaborating on many services and programs through a Memorandum of Agreement, Jefferson Community College and Jefferson Technical College are preparing to pursue accreditation through the Commission on Colleges/Southern Association of Colleges and Schools (SACS) as a single institution. The district currently serves more than 13,000 credit students and offers the Associate in Arts and the Associate in Science degrees, primarily designed for students seeking a baccalaureate degree; adult basic and developmental education; and certificates, diplomas, and Associate in Applied Science degrees in more than 25 areas of study.

Faculty Workload Issues, Jefferson Community College. In 2001, Jefferson Community College faced a perfect storm that led to serious re-evaluations of many of its policies and processes. Among the conditions that prevailed were a reaffirmation of accreditation visit in April 2001 that produced numerous serious recommendations requiring written and committee follow-up; a fiscal crisis that necessitated a revamping of budgeting and financial management practices; and changes in leadership in a number of crucial administrative positions.

Among the recommendations that emerged from visiting committee interviews with faculty and a review of institutional policies was one that cited lack of evidence that "procedures [existed] for the equitable and reasonable assignments of faculty responsibility." While academic administrators on both campuses could cite usual practice, written policy was limited to the general statement that the normal teaching load was 15 credit hours per semester. In addition, the institution's fiscal challenges made examining released or reassigned time for faculty as well as class sizes (both of which have a substantial impact on a large adjunct faculty budget) an immediate priority. Finally, the appointment of new leadership resulted in a greater role in decision making for the division chairs, who, as faculty members partially reassigned to administrative duties for three-year terms, function as the primary managers of the college's academic units.

Faculty Workload Issues, Jefferson Technical College. With its roots in vocational-technical education and its relatively recent change from clock-hour to credit-hour scheduling, Jefferson Technical College's possible consolidation with Jefferson

Community College will compound the challenge of creating a unified workload policy perceived to be equitable by faculty often working from different pedagogical models. This will be further compounded by the technical college's tradition of operating with single-teacher programs, where one faculty member will teach the entire curriculum, necessitating often being directly engaged with students in lecture or laboratory as many as 30 to 35 hours a week. On the other hand, historically, this model results in many small classes, often with as few as four or five students at a time, thus making the equation of workload with traditional three-credit-hour courses with upwards of 25 students, the norm at the community college, difficult. In addition, providing adjunct instructors who can assume duties to reduce the contact hourload of the faculty in single-teacher programs would require significant new expenditures of dollars never before required for the technical college. Finally, in contrast to community college division chairs, who are teaching faculty members only temporarily and partially rotating into administrative positions, technical college division chairs are permanent, full-time, nonteaching administrators. This makes their participation in determining faculty workloads qualitatively different in that they are not determining policies to which they themselves will ultimately be subject.

Summary of the Case

Jefferson Community College and Jefferson Technical College, then, continue to face the multifaceted challenge of creating a written faculty workload document, consistent across the district, sensitive both to immediate fiscal exigencies and the ongoing need for efficient use of human resources, and broadly supported by faculty from what may soon be one institution with disparate traditions. While issues of faculty participation in student advising, service (internal and external), and professional development are inextricably intertwined with the question of credit- and contact-hour teaching load and numbers of students in classes, the immediate issues this workload policy needs to address are instructional expectations for faculty and course enrollment limits.

Questions to Consider

1. By what process(es) and by what individuals or groups should this issue be addressed?
2. How should differences in the nature of the courses taught (*e.g.*, content versus skills-based, developmental versus college-level, lecture versus laboratory) be accommodated by the policy?
3. How should the use of nontraditional or experimental teaching methodologies and technologies (*e.g.*, team teaching, interdisciplinary courses, online or web-enhanced classes) be addressed by the policy?
4. Where program or division administration is done by faculty, how should this administrative service be factored in? How can the variety in size of staff, faculty, and student population in the program be acknowledged and accounted for by the policy?
5. How can the policy accommodate the additional workload on administrators in programs that have special requirements (*e.g.*, accreditation, internships)?
6. To what extent should the financial exigencies of the moment or ongoing fiscal

realities influence the policy development or be explicitly referred to in it?

7. In what ways can or should flexibility be built into the policy? If exceptions are to be possible, at what level should they be approved? What kind of documentary record, if any, should exist?

8. To what extent should class enrollment limits be determined by the pedagogical preferences of the individuals teaching them? Should they be standardized?

Thoughts and Analysis

- Given the fact that concerns about faculty teaching loads were surfaced by the faculty to the accrediting team, it is critical that the faculty be primary drivers in the proposed policy, that representation on a faculty committee addressing the issue should be broad, and that this committee should seek input districtwide.

- Prior to making recommendations, the committee should review data on teaching loads, course enrollments, and released-time decisions. A process should be instituted by which these data are regularly gathered, analyzed, and appropriately disseminated. When determining equivalency of effort required for instruction in institutions historically different, the committee will need to take special care to understand the cultures being brought together and to base its decisions on a thorough review of information from each one.

- Any policy should be re-examined and redistributed annually, and adherence to it should be monitored, since division and program leadership changes, especially at the community college.

- The policy should accommodate the differing requirements of courses and disciplines but also recognize that the sheer number of students with whom faculty deal each semester also affects workload. While writing classes, for example, require frequent and close grading of texts, these classes traditionally have lower enrollments; classes with larger numbers may require less of such grading but interaction with many more students. While experientially-based courses such as laboratories might require more hours, there might be significantly fewer students to work at any given time and less grading and preparation required.

- When equating teaching and administrative loads to determine released-time equivalents, the policy must take into account the size of programs; the number of full-time and adjunct faculty; the location of programs; and special requirements such as accreditation, certification, selective admissions, and clinicals.

- There must be room for exceptions to the policy, but it must be clear by whom these exceptions will be made, what kind of documentation will exist to justify them, and how these exceptions will be communicated to all stakeholders.

- The policy should acknowledge the additional time that may be required when using experimental or nontraditional methods. However, the opportunity to use these should be made available to all faculty.

- There may be increased workloads or class limits approved and accepted by the faculty during times of financial crisis, but any policy should make clear the temporary nature of such measures. Academic administrators, up to and including the academic deans and provost, should share increased teaching burdens during such times.

- All those involved in developing and administering such a policy should recognize that it will never resolve inequities in faculty workloads. The nature of the teaching-learning experience is such that preparation, incubation, presentation, facilitation, and grading time will always vary widely – not only by disciplines and settings, which a policy can attempt to address, but by individuals, whom no policy can.

Outcomes

Jefferson Community College. When this issue arose during Jefferson Community College's accreditation visit in 2001, the college took immediate action in preparation for responding to a SACS recommendation. A Faculty Workload Committee was appointed, composed of faculty from across the institution representing a variety of disciplines and campuses. This committee did its work in two stages: (1) determining, codifying, and publishing current accepted practice in a newly-developed college faculty handbook, which was approved by the faculty and the College Leadership Team in fall 2001; and (2) during the 2001-2002 academic year, critically examining current practice; identifying inconsistencies and gaps; clarifying policies subject to multiple interpretation; and expanding the scope of the existing document to include the issue of class limits, which often varied widely across campuses.

In May of 2002, using the findings and recommendations of the Faculty Workload Committee, the acting provost, acting deans of academic affairs, and division chairs presented this expanded workload policy for adoption by the College Leadership Team. After ratification, the policy was distributed to faculty immediately, as well as published in the revised fall 2002 faculty handbook. The policy addresses

- exceptions to the normal teaching load of 15 credit hours (*e.g.*, for faculty teaching English composition);
- released time for division chairs and academic program coordinators (department heads) dependent on several variables (size of division, number of adjunct faculty or sections taught by adjunct faculty, and whether the program had accreditation requirements or involved internships or clinicals);
- released time for faculty coordinating or working in student support labs;
- adjustments to workload based on team teaching and the creation or implementation of new online or telecourses; and
- course enrollment limits for traditionally lecture-based courses, laboratory or practicum courses, developmental and ESL classes, technology-based courses (where equipment may determine enrollment limits); writing and public-speaking courses), telecourses, web-based courses, and interdisciplinary studies courses

All exceptions to the policy must be supported by a written justification and approved by the provost. Continued refinement of the policy to take into account such issues as teaching at multiple locations is also necessary.

Jefferson Technical College. As Jefferson Technical College and Jefferson Community College move toward accreditation as a single institution, joint workgroups are being established to address consolidation issues. At least three of these will consider items related to workload: the Structure of Academic Divisions workgroup, the Personnel Issues workgroup, and the Building a Shared Vision workgroup. The contact-hour-based curricula, the difficulties created for single teacher programs, and nonfaculty status of division leadership have already emerged as topics to be addressed.

Whether immediately or in the long term, should consolidation occur, both the traditional practices at the technical college and the now documented policies and processes at the community college will need to be examined, reshaped, and communicated with a process similar to that described above to ensure flexibility, accountability, and – most important – faculty ownership.

Diane M. Calhoun-French is the Provost and Vice President for Academic and Student Affairs for the Jefferson Community and Technical College District, with campuses in Louisville, Carrollton, and Shelbyville, Kentucky.

4. Partnerships in Technical Programs

Susan A. May

Context

Fox Valley Technical College is a multicampus technical college serving a 2,400-square-mile, five-county district in northeast Wisconsin with its main campus in Appleton. Fox Valley has a long history of offering high-quality technical programming including Associate of Applied Science degrees, technical diplomas, and certificates. In recent years, over 50,000 people have enrolled at the college annually. More than half of these students are served through training contracts with their employers.

Several of Fox Valley's specialized training areas have found a niche in national and, in some cases, international markets. One of these niche areas is in flexographic printing, a printing process commonly used for printing a variety of flexible packaging or materials including plastic film, wallpaper, gift wrap, labels, and corrugated packaging and displays. The flexographic printing industry has a strong presence in northeast Wisconsin, but is also found in various locations throughout the country, as well as worldwide.

Keeping technical labs equipped with not only up-to-date, but leading technology poses a significant challenge to community and technical colleges. It is even more challenging when industrial presses are a critical component in an instructional program's equipment requirements. This type of programming cannot realistically be taken into the workplace because few printers will stop production on their multimillion-dollar pieces of equipment for educational purposes, even for the training of their own employees.

When Fox Valley, through a local and state partnership, built a dedicated facility for business and industry training in the mid-1980s, a section of the building was used to establish the Flexographic Education and Research Center. At that time, the national Flexographic Technical Association donated a substantial piece of equipment: a used wide-web press that served the college well for a number of years. Fox Valley funded additional lab equipment and several narrow-web presses over the years. The flexographic printing industry, both locally and nationally, has been immensely supportive of this program with donations of ink, paper, film, substrates, anilox rolls, and ancillary equipment.

Summary of the Case

Fox Valley's Flexographic Education and Research Center built strong degree and diploma programs from the mid-1980s to the late 1990s. The center also developed a very strong contract-training and technical-assistance arm by offering national seminars and hands-on workshops and by assisting companies with research and development. Companies were given the opportunity to schedule press time on the college's equipment and to receive technical assistance to run trials and applications on new products. By the late 1990s, it became clear that the college's equipment had to be dramatically updated to new technology if this center was going to meet the needs of industry and thrive in the future. Two needs converged at almost the same time. A new

$2 million wide-web flexo press was needed within a few years, and there was great interest on the part of local industry and the faculty to expand into corrugated printing and die cutting, which meant another $2 million-plus of equipment investment. The cost of these two pieces of equipment represented more than the combined total capital equipment budget available to all 70 degree and diploma programs of the college at that time.

Questions to Consider

1. How do college administrators balance the needs, interests, and enthusiasm of this industry and dedicated faculty with the reality of the budget resources available?
2. What partnership opportunities should be considered when embarking on this level of programmatic investment?
3. What level of risk should the board of trustees enter into with the anticipation of corporate support for a major project?
4. What can the college administration and board expect from faculty and staff in terms of return on investment in a discipline such as this?
5. How much should a department or center's track record of success factor into decision making for strategic investments?

Thoughts and Analysis

1. If the occupational programs of a community or technical college are to be relevant and highly regarded by the industries served, the college's faculty and administrators must find creative ways to keep those programs technologically sound.
2. Some occupational programs simply require a greater capital investment than others. If a college is going to be in a given business, it is important that the programming receive maximum support for success.
3. It is most effective to engage industry directly in addressing issues of equipment and technology. No longer can colleges expect handouts or outright donations; they are rare. Win-win partnerships have to be initiated, nurtured, and maintained.
4. National or international associations or foundations may be more likely and capable of working on behalf of their member companies in partnership with a college versus partnerships with individual companies that may have more limited resources and less influence within a given industry.
5. If faculty have achieved results as successful entrepreneurs for the college, enhancing its service to the industry and elevating the college's reputation and stature within a major industry, they deserve the full support and encouragement of administration. These kinds of individuals make it worth taking a risk, and they are most likely to succeed in showing a great return on whatever investment is made.

Outcomes

In the late 1990s, voters in the Fox Valley Technical College district endorsed a $25.6 million capital referendum that addressed the facilities needs of 40 of its programs. While this referendum did not include equipment specific to flexographic printing, it did include $1.5 million toward a deeply discounted offset press for the lithographic printing programs. At that time, the college did not have immediate plans to replace its wide-web flexo press; however, expanding into corrugated printing and die cutting was of interest, and there was initial support expressed by a major local employer.

On speculation of potential events, the administration decided to build a 5,000-square-foot addition onto the Flexographic Education and Research Center as a future corrugated press bay as part of the capital referendum. At the same time, college personnel began to work more closely with the corrugated industry and the International Corrugated Packaging Foundation (ICPF) headquartered in Alexandria, Virginia. When the executive director and board members of ICPF visited Fox Valley, in addition to showing them what we had accomplished on behalf of the flexographic printing industry in related areas, we were able to show them a 5,000-square-foot space (essentially a sand pit at that time) that had been made available to house a corrugated press. Imagine the reaction.

This was definitely a build-it-and-they-will-come proposition. ICPF went to work to get a $2 million corrugated press and die cutter donated to Fox Valley by press manufacturer Workhorse Industries in Jacksonville Beach, Florida. In this process, the college administration and faculty collaborated with ICPF officials to create a partnership agreement whereby both the college and the International Corrugated Packaging Foundation brought benefits to each other and, most important, to the industry that both were interested in serving. The J. Richard Troll Technical Lab (named after a prominent national leader in the corrugated industry) and its premier centerpiece, the Workhorse corrugated press and rotary die cutter, was dedicated in May 2000.

The wide-web press replacement challenge was addressed much differently. In working closely with Fox Valley's program advisory committee, we determined that the technology needed to attract and serve the needs of the industry in the years to come was an Avanti gearless wide-web central-impression press. This press is manufactured less than 30 miles from the campus by Paper Converting Machine Company (PCMC) in Green Bay, Wisconsin. The college was able to attain a half-million-dollar discount from PCMC, a significant contribution toward this $2 million acquisition. Fox Valley embarked on a national fundraising campaign with the flexo industry to equip this national training center. In the end, the press was purchased through a combination of resources: manufacturer discount, local and national corporate donations, and the college's capital equipment budget over two years. The Avanti Press dedication occurred in the fall of 2002.

Today, the college's Flexographic Education and Research Center is highly regarded and well used by the industry. National seminars are held regularly. Several faculty positions are dedicated strictly to contract training and technical assistance for employers, both at the center and onsite in companies in the U.S. and Canada. This type of educational center is made possible only with the right combination of resources: faculty with a great service and support attitude and strong technical ability, curriculum that is relevant and important to the industry, equipment that reflects the future of the industry, supportive industry leaders and advisors, and college administrators and trustees who are creative and willing to take risks in making strategic investments on behalf of the institution.

Susan A. May is Vice President and Chief Academic Officer of Fox Valley Technical College in Appleton, Wisconsin.

5. Making the Case for the Baccalaureate Degree

Eduardo J. Padrón

Context

In the fall of 2002, Miami Dade College (MDC) began the process of petitioning the State of Florida for authorization to offer the baccalaureate degree in education. The possibility of such a proposal had its roots in a 1999 report of Florida's Postsecondary Education Planning Commission (PEPC) that documented the low number of baccalaureate degrees per capita in the state. Spurred by an expanding shortage of teachers and nurses and a burgeoning high-tech economy, legislative interest in expanding the production of baccalaureate degrees took shape.

Summary of the Case

Ensuing legislation invited the expansion of partnerships between community colleges and four-year institutions within and outside the state. At that time, several of the state's community colleges were host to these arrangements, allowing a student to complete a four-year degree from a partnering institution at the local community college campus. While community college leaders applauded the general direction, a clutter of complex provisions in the legislation dampened the enthusiasm to propose new community college baccalaureate programs.

The need remained, however, felt acutely in the county served by St. Petersburg Community College (SPCC). With neither a university partner in tow for the recognized need in education nor the local presence of a state university, students at SPCC found themselves place bound with regard to attaining a four-year degree. With the aid of a state senator who authored simplified and specific legislation on its behalf, SPCC made a successful case for offering four-year degrees in education.

Though SPCC proved a valuable ally in preparing MDC's four-year proposal, dramatic changes in the structure of the state's educational bureaucracy served to alter the application process. No longer could a single legislator author and champion legislation for his or her home district. A multistep process that included a preliminary review board and a new K-20 State Board of Education ensured that multiple viewpoints and influences would come to bear on the prospective four-year institution.

The entire proposal process lasted close to two years. The significant steps in the process included the following:

- *Proposal Development.* This involved research and development of the academic and budgetary aspects, including consultation with other schools and a very thorough effort to gather expressions of support locally and throughout the state.
- *Presentation to the Council for Education Policy Research and Improvement (CEPRI).* CEPRI replaced PEPC in the state's new education strata. Beyond its predecessor's research function, this nine-member citizen board was charged by the legislature to

develop a long-range plan for K-20 education. Its responsibilities included the evaluation of statewide issues of concern, including the college's proposal to offer four-year degrees.

• *Proposal to the State Board of Education.* Under Governor Bush's K-20 reorganization, the state board oversees K-12 and all two- and four-year state institutions. The eight-member board is comprised of educators, business people, and community leaders from across the state and had the final word on our proposal.

We began our journey knowing full well that both the CEPRI and state boards included individuals who harbored doubts about the viability of our proposal. For both political and economic reasons, joint-use arrangements that employed existing facilities, similar to the partnerships already in place, were attractive to some of the members. CEPRI's assignment was two-fold: (1) Determine if the need for the program was genuine. Our proposal sought authorization for four-year degrees in education, focusing specifically on elementary education, secondary science and math, and exceptional student education. The college needed to demonstrate that its program would be a necessary component, beyond the efforts of the private and public universities in the region, in meeting the demand for teachers. (2) Having established need, the college then had to persuade CEPRI's board that it could effectively meet the challenge. The latter alluded to a subtle bias that a community college baccalaureate degree would be less rigorous than one offered by a four-year institution. It was essential to dispel that notion via the proposal and numerous presentations throughout the process.

The college's proposal team consisted of a campus president who served as the project manager, the director of the college's School of Education, our director of governmental relations, our chief financial analyst, and one of our academic deans. Surveying the faculty, including the faculty union leadership, and soliciting feedback from specific individuals across the college established an important network of feedback. To be sure, however, the team's dedication was irreplaceable. The members' willingness to leave no stone unturned proved critical, not only in developing the proposal but also in communicating with principal players throughout the education and state bureaucracy.

Having spent countless hours in Tallahassee during my tenure, I lent strategic and political perspective, continually identifying the challenges we faced and the effectiveness of our approach. I also stressed the vital importance of demonstrating support from our South Florida community, and meetings with local leaders, including colleagues from the local universities, served to maintain an open dialogue. It was crucial to keep abreast of the impact of our efforts on a variety of people and concerns. That point cannot be stressed enough, and the team was diligent in relating to a range of people in education and state policymaking. We called upon friends throughout the state to support the college's proposal and engage those who would ultimately decide the proposal's fate. Our proposal included 20 letters of support from legislators and community and business leaders. Throughout, we sought to gauge the impact of an MDC baccalaureate, cognizant of specific viewpoints and objections from the various players and institutions.

Questions to Consider

Primary among our concerns, of course, were the CEPRI and sate boards. During each juncture in the process, members of our team met individually with each, developing relationships that would serve us well as we made our formal presentations. As we learned their personal viewpoints, we were diligent in delivering a quick response to their concerns. In fact, many of their contributions were thoughtful and helped to strengthen our proposal.

For both the public and private universities in South Florida, MDC's size and potential raised obvious concerns of competition for students. In the extreme, the expectation loomed well beyond the proposal in education. In the immediate, there was concern over the loss of joint-use programs, which we assuaged by recommitting to maintain our existing programs.

While the four-year schools insisted that their capacity was sufficient to meet the demand for teachers, the statistics argued otherwise. Within the initial two pages of MDC's proposal, the supply-demand gap was articulated while noting the first strategic imperative of the Florida Board of Education: "to increase the supply of highly qualified K-12 teachers." The report cited the need for approximately 6,500 new teachers annually for several years to come in Miami-Dade County and neighboring Broward County. Punctuating the need for a new source, only 1,600 teacher candidates emerged from the seven colleges and universities in South Florida in the 1998-1999 graduation. Less than half of the new teachers hired in Miami-Dade County Public Schools were educated at local institutions.

Additional concerns required our attention as well. Legislators worried that MDC would abandon its mission of affordable access and ready response to workforce needs. At the same time, lawmakers applauded the possibility of a lower-cost baccalaureate in education. Community college leaders wondered if MDC was seeking an elite status and, more important, if already limited resources from the general fund for community colleges would be diminished yet again to pay for the baccalaureate program.

Thoughts and Analysis

To effectively counter the collected concerns, our proposal had to be impeccable and thorough, accompanied by a budget that genuinely supported the academic intent of the program. As the newcomer from the world of open access, we needed to demonstrate the distinct value that MDC's approach would bring. In responding to the contention that joint use was the most efficient route, we stressed that an MDC bachelor's degree delivered a product beyond the economy of brick and mortar. In fact, the community college environment provided nurturing not found at most larger university sites. MDC baccalaureate students would benefit from small class size, schedule flexibility for working students, targeted support initiatives, and, most important, the best teachers from an institution that encouraged teaching excellence.

Our proposal also emphasized the exceptional access the college offered to an uncommon pool of future teachers. Many of MDC's students cannot avail themselves of the more expensive baccalaureate options in the state. They constitute the new reality in higher education: employed, older, more mature, seeking career elevation, and, very often, from the ranks of low-income minority families who haven't had the chance to become teachers. In Miami-Dade County, such a population is large and underserved. Confirming our forecast, 81 percent of our inaugural class was minority, and almost half were over the age of 30.

The curriculum proposed reaffirmed the standards of all state-approved teacher education programs as well as the most highly respected accreditation agencies. But the proposal again offered distinctive quality. Combating the typical problem of high teacher attrition in the early years, the program offered hands-on exposure to the classroom from day one. Service learning, collaborative learning, learning communities, and web-enhanced courses also contributed to a rich curriculum.

Providing a budget that truly supported our aims and was justified academically also proved a decisive point in our favor. Promising specific standards and not providing the practical means to achieve them would have painted a careless picture. The proposal made two significant points about teacher responsibility relating to technology: (1) Teachers are the vessels for future scientists and mathematicians; and (2) teachers are change agents, and their facility with technology would enable them to make of it a viable resource for academic pursuits. An MDC bachelor's in education would prepare teachers to lead their programs into the future as knowledgeable acquisition coordinators and consultants for labs and other classroom technology. From this understanding, we budgeted for additional electronic classrooms and refurbished state-of-the-art science labs, among other technological requirements.

Outcomes

In the end, CEPRI did pass on the proposal to the State Board of Education, albeit without an endorsement. While they acknowledged the quality of the proposal, the CEPRI board reasoned that more research on university partnerships should be pursued.

CEPRI's decision is instructive. We had done our homework and did defuse the major objections effectively. There were simply differing opinions and allegiances that would not be moved enough to engender a recommendation. We accomplished what was possible at CEPRI by foreseeing the objections and providing well-reasoned, data-driven responses.

In March 2002, MDC's proposal was presented to the State Board of Education for the first time. Discussions continued with members as the proposal was reviewed, and by the final presentation in May, our supporters on the board were in the majority. While the board did rule against the elementary education proposal on grounds of insufficient need, there was unanimous assent to our proposals for secondary math and science and exceptional education. The programs were authorized to begin in the fall 2003.

This was a very gratifying achievement for the college. Confronted by deep-rooted historical traditions and a diversity of objections, we made a compelling case and were heard. We were able to affect a profound new opportunity in Florida higher education.

MDC's inaugural class of 129 students did indeed begin their baccalaureate degree studies in the fall of 2003. The class was predominantly female (99 students) and minority (107 students). Seventy-two had earned an associate's degree from MDC and, as indicated earlier, almost half were over 30 years of age. The class chose majors in exceptional student education, biology, chemistry, physics, earth science, and mathematics. Once again, a community college had dug deeper, unearthed potential, and given its students and community new opportunity.

Eduardo J. Padrón is President of Miami Dade College in Miami, Florida.

6. A Message of Change

Barbara Sloan

Context

Tallahassee Community College (TCC) is a single-campus, comprehensive community college located in the capital city of Florida. The college also serves two other counties, including a rural county with one of the lowest income and education levels in the state among a predominantly Black population. Because of the proximity of two state universities, the college attracts numerous out-of-district students, over 60 percent of the 24,000 annual enrollments. As a result, 47 percent of the student population is under 22 years of age, 48 percent attend full time, and 80 percent are interested in the university transfer degree. The college also has one of the highest percentages of Black student populations in the state system, at 30 percent.

TCC faculty were among the first in the state to develop online courses; they developed other alternatives such as telecourses and self-paced courses. They teach in alternative semesters of 8, 12, and 20 weeks. A year ago, at the time of the CEO turnover, they were assessing the general education package, focusing on outcomes rather than courses. And they were redesigning their advising responsibilities to shift from emphasizing scheduling courses to academic and career planning.

The college has had a relatively stable 38-year history, experiencing steady but manageable growth, excellent relationships with the universities and the community, a reputation for providing quality education, and a low turnover of faculty and staff.

When the TCC Board of Trustees began its search for a new president, the interim president was the favorite of the faculty and much of the community. The interim president had come up through the TCC ranks and had successfully resolved a number of difficult issues involving faculty salary concerns and shared governance processes. However, the board was interested in looking nationally for candidates as well as at some candidates whose political experiences were stronger than their educational leadership experiences. In the end, the board hired neither the interim president nor the political favorite. Instead, it hired a highly respected, experienced community college president, but not before some strained meetings and decisions that left the faculty, among others, feeling somewhat distressed by the process and the treatment of their candidate, and even a bit suspicious of the new president who emerged.

When faculty returned to campus in fall, the new CEO had been on the job for three months and had begun to put into place the people and processes needed to implement his vision. At the fall convocation, he spoke to faculty about his goals. He had realigned resources and created a vice-presidential position and division in economic and workforce development. He also shared college data that indicated areas of academic weakness; he brought in a national speaker who challenged faculty to become a part of national trends supporting the learning college; and he questioned some of their teaching methods and processes. By the time they left the auditorium, many faculty were angry and suspicious. They felt threatened by the shift to workforce, and they were determined to resist changes they felt challenged their credibility. The president, however, had begun his journey to move the institution in new directions. For the next several months, the president planned to spend much of his time in the community, working to heal the lingering wounds, to develop relationships with community leaders interested in the new emphasis on economic development and workforce training, and to lay the groundwork for the college's upcoming capital campaign.

Summary of the Case

A mature, relatively stable and successful community college is undergoing a change in leadership. While most agreed the board's choice was outstanding, some missteps in the process left both the college and some in the larger community suspicious and angry. The new CEO began in high gear as an agent of change on campus, but also recognized that he needed to address the concerns of the community. College faculty and staff resisted the message and the messenger, believing their years of success, their excellent local reputation, and their experience earned them a message of support rather than challenge. How can the president's vision be advanced in this climate?

Questions to Consider

1. Should the president modify his plan to spend time in the community in favor of building relationships within the institution?
2. Given the tension and suspicion created by the president's presentation of his vision, should the chief instructional officer begin to implement change immediately or slow down the process?
3. If movement toward change begins immediately, what should be done to prevent further conflict between the faculty and the president?
4. How should the differing perceptions of the president and the faculty regarding the current success of the institution be handled?
5. How should the president handle the faculty's fears that the shift to focus on workforce will decrease funding and support of the college's traditional programs and mission?
6. What should be done about the strong opposition among some faculty to the language of the learning college?

Thoughts and Analysis

1. Without personal knowledge of the president, rumors and suspicion in the community were likely to grow. In addition, the college was about to start a capital campaign. Making himself known in the community seems critical to the president's mission.
2. The president made his goals clear; there probably isn't an option to slow down from his point of view. But beyond that, faculty reactions provide the opportunity for dialogue and for exploration of the president's ideas as well as their values. Issues should be addressed immediately.
3. Lack of conflict cannot be guaranteed. Opportunities can be provided for the

president to interact with the faculty so that a dialogue can begin. However, the chief academic officer has the primary responsibility for advancing the shift in the teaching-learning paradigm.

4. Data about the institution should be readily available to everyone. Faculty need to examine the evidence themselves.
5. The president is focused on developing relationships in the community and on positioning the college as a resource for economic and workforce development in the community. It is unlikely that the president will be able to devote as much time and energy to addressing faculty concerns as they may like.
6. Concepts are more important than terminology. While the president's vision clearly embraces a paradigm shift from the instructional to the learning paradigm, there may be ways to approach the concepts without insisting on language the faculty resists.

Outcomes

Follow-up on the president's message began immediately. On the day of the convocation, faculty were divided into small groups and were given details of the data presented by the president, as well as some questions to discuss and opportunities to suggest solutions. The chief academic officer selected faculty team leaders who had already been involved in the college's current student success initiative. Many areas of agreement were quickly found, and several actionable ideas emerged.

Data was made available to everyone on campus. The strategic planning committee looked at growth projections and community economic needs as well as at student demographics and success patterns. The strategic plan developed to incorporate the student success goals and the values of focusing on student learning, although without totally embracing the language of the learning college.

More data was gathered. The college administered a student perception survey and found 20 areas of strength and 5 areas of challenge. Feedback provided faculty with opportunities to reinforce their claims of excellence; it also helped them focus on areas that needed serious attention. Analysis of data was followed by faculty teams researching the literature and looking for best practices in areas where TCC needed to improve.

Financial resources were aligned with the values presented in the president's vision. Rather than seeing resources diverted to other purposes, faculty found that professional development funds and funding for teaching excellence were available to those willing to engage in research and experimentation. Reassigned time was given to faculty on the student success teams; money was provided to travel to conferences and to colleges with excellent programs. The entire budget was made available to everyone on campus, so that anyone interested could examine the allocation of funds to various areas of the college.

The president did spend much of his time in the community in the first year, and that reaped great benefits in terms of support and confidence in the college. Although some felt the president was not visible often enough on campus, faculty and staff were given the opportunity to interact with the president through a series of scheduled forums.

A year later, the president's message addressed areas of progress and strength as well as need for change. The college is a long way from being transformed, but it is far from standing still. While there is still plenty of skepticism and some resistance, the journey is well under way, and faculty are providing both leadership and support.

Barbara Sloan is Vice President for Academic Affairs at Tallahassee Community College.

7. Ensuring Full-Time Quality With Part-Time Faculty

Linda Thor

Context

Rio Salado in Tempe, Arizona is a nontraditional college without walls that is one of the 10 Maricopa Community Colleges. When it was established 25 years ago, the college was charged with meeting the needs of unserved and underserved student populations, particularly working adults with families who desire to pursue their degrees but experience severe time constraints if they attend traditional classroom instruction. Through the years, Rio Salado has met their needs by effectively using distance learning formats, particularly e-learning courses, and through collaborative partnerships with businesses and government agencies whereby students take their classes onsite at their places of employment.

The emphasis at Rio Salado has always been on cost effectiveness, particularly in an era of declining public resources. Despite having no bricks-and-mortar campus, Rio Salado is approaching annual headcount of 40,000 credit students. To serve such a large student population would normally require hiring an enormous amount of full-time faculty at considerable expense. However, Rio Salado has chosen a nontraditional approach whereby more than 95 percent of its faculty members serve in an adjunct capacity. Rio Salado places value on the fact that these instructors are working professionals in their disciplines and therefore bring a hands-on approach to classroom teaching. Since the introduction of Rio's e-learning formats in 1996, there has been a significant increase in the number of adjuncts, which currently number nearly 800 each semester. At the same time, the college employs only 28 permanent residential (full-time) faculty, including 19 faculty chairs that serve as curriculum specialists and discipline leaders.

Although most of the college's students reside in Maricopa County, Rio Salado is not limited by geographic boundaries as pertains to its distance learning formats. The college has enrolled students in nearly every one of the 50 states, as well as on six continents. Adjunct faculty members can likewise reside anywhere, but most are residents of Maricopa County.

Summary of the Case

Rio Salado adjunct faculty members work for a college that has been an active pioneer in distance learning and e-learning. With more than 20,000 online students annually, the college now stands as one of the nation's largest premier colleges specializing in web-based learning. Also, during the 1990s, Rio Salado began to forge collaborative alliances with local corporations and government agencies for in-person course delivery at places of employment.

The lack of a physical campus and the unusual dependence on a high number of adjunct faculty members would seem to raise issues of faculty cohesiveness, recruitment, support, training, and overall quality control that demand nontraditional solutions.

Through the years, the college has faced many such challenges – for example, how to develop a reliable system for recruitment of thousands of qualified adjuncts. Above all, the college needed to identify strategies that would enable it to ensure full-time quality with part-time faculty.

Questions to Consider

1. What should be the basic philosophy of the institution toward adjuncts, and how can the college exemplify an atmosphere of inclusiveness?
2. How can this college achieve buy-in for its policies and practices from adjuncts?
3. How can the college develop a system whereby it can identify and maintain a sizable pool of highly qualified applicants from which to recruit adjuncts?
4. What types of support services do adjuncts require, and what is the best means to provide them?
5. How should the college provide consistent, effective, and ongoing training to adjunct faculty members?
6. How can such a college monitor and ensure quality control issues in teaching and learning?

Thoughts and Analysis

1. Many myths and assumptions exist in academia regarding adjunct faculty members. One is that they lack the same stature as full-time faculty. Another is that they should be able to function without the same level of support full-time faculty have. The college desires to shatter these myths internally and externally.
2. Hiring so many adjuncts in a timely manner is challenging, because the small number of full-time faculty who would normally assume this role at a traditional campus are unable to take the lead in such a massive recruitment process.
3. Major challenges include the need to develop a formal system for providing support services plus professional development for faculty who have no campus to visit.
4. The college is located in a major metropolitan market that is home to several other institutions of higher education, including Arizona State University and the University of Phoenix (world headquarters), plus several smaller colleges. Furthermore, nine additional Maricopa Community Colleges are located within the geographic area. This would seem to be both a positive factor (access to a larger population of qualified applicants) and negative one (significant competition exists).
5. The college takes seriously its responsibility to maintain a faculty pool that is multicultural and promotes diversity.

Outcomes

Rio Salado believes it has found the solution to the dilemma of achieving full-time quality through part-time faculty with strategies that are based on a philosophy of organizational responsiveness to specific identified needs. In fact, organizational responsiveness has been incorporated into the college's mission statement as a means through which Rio Salado transforms the teaching and learning experience. When applied to the teaching experience, Rio has focused on building quality through four strategies:

- A systems approach to teamwork
- An innovative approach to recruitment
- Sophisticated support services
- An atmosphere of inclusiveness

Systems Approach. The college's emphasis on organizational responsiveness begins with a goal to provide flexibility and convenience for all instructors as well as students. To achieve this, the college uses a systems approach, based on principles found in learning organizations, that places less emphasis on formal departments that operate in isolation and more emphasis on teams working closely together to provide support services to both faculty and students. Teaching and learning are at the center of the systems approach, with all support services integrated to provide exceptional support. Several components of the systems approach are further described under "Sophisticated Support Services."

Recruitment. Before the college could fully undertake the task of deciding how to train and support an ever-growing number of adjuncts, Rio Salado first had to develop a specific and innovative model for recruitment. It found the solution in Faculty Services, which represents a radical departure from the traditional means used to recruit plus maintain a pool of available adjuncts that numbers in the thousands. Faculty Services centralizes the hiring process for professors and also assumes responsibility for anticipating staffing needs, screening applicants by phone or in person, maintaining the databases for the faculty pool, coordinating new adjunct faculty orientations, placing textbook orders, and disseminating course materials. Under this streamlined process, potential instructors apply once rather than filling out multiple applications for more than one discipline or assignment. In effect, Rio Salado's Faculty Services division has become the Human Resources function, working closely with each discipline's full-time faculty chair in the final selection process, yet freeing them from the time-intensive responsibility of spending countless hours courting new faculty. Faculty Services also ensures that the college maintains consistent recruitment standards that reflect the college's sensitivity to diversity issues.

As its e-learning programs grew in the middle and late 1990s, Faculty Services recognized that it needed to do more than maintain a substantial faculty pool; it had to adopt a proactive stance toward recruitment by anticipating needs well in advance. For example, when microbiology's e-learning curriculum was approved as part of an online nursing program, adjunct faculty members were already in place who were not only experts in the discipline, but could also transition smoothly into the web-based aspects of teaching.

Sophisticated Support Services. Both full-time and adjunct faculty members receive the same exceptional support services that ultimately free them from routine tasks so they may focus exclusively on instruction. Examples of primary support services that are components of Rio Salado's systems approach are an instructional helpdesk, a technology helpdesk, course support, tutoring, testing, and courier services.

The instructional support helpdesk members serve as faculty chair communication links for adjuncts, and answer questions for both adjuncts and students. They facilitate communication between instructors and students, provide information for first-time e-learning instructors and students, and troubleshoot miscellaneous needs. They also conduct new faculty orientations, online training, and specialized program training.

A different kind of support is found in the technology helpdesk, which assists faculty members as well as students in overcoming any technological barriers that may arise during their online experience. Typical assistance would include opening files, downloading materials, and troubleshooting email problems. Access is provided seven days a week.

The course support team distributes introductory materials to distance learning faculty and students. Course support provides faculty with basic office supplies and facilitates the delivery of mailed or faxed assignments from students to faculty.

Rio Salado also assists instructors with time-management issues by providing student tutoring, including call-a-tutor, online tutoring, block tutoring, and in-person one-on-one tutoring.

A testing division has formalized the process for midterms and finals, which are taken at testing centers or, in the case of out-of-county students, are proctored.

Finally, adjuncts do not need to worry about physically commuting to the college to pick up homework or supplies, because a team of couriers who work directly for the college makes deliveries to them during normal work hours.

Inclusiveness. Rio Salado adheres to the philosophy that an atmosphere of inclusiveness is healthy and that adjunct faculty will perceive they are valued by the organization if they can benefit from the same caliber of professional development as full-time faculty.

In order to encourage such an atmosphere, Rio Salado has developed specific strategies that encourage professional development in teaching and also provide guidance in each instructor's discipline. Every adjunct works under the direction of a faculty chair in a specific discipline. Thus, each adjunct benefits from the expertise of a knowledgeable professor with a holistic approach to understanding where the individual discipline fits into the college's mission and vision.

Continuous learning takes several forms. Twice a year, All-Faculty Learning Experiences are conducted onsite at the college. During these sessions, adjuncts can engage in discipline dialogues and workshops, plus benefit from speakers of a national reputation who are well versed in educational issues and trends. Adjuncts also participate in in-person semester instructional workshops on topics such as electronic library resources, plagiarism, and multicultural communication. Online workshops and seminars have recently been introduced.

Adjuncts also benefit from shared knowledge that comes from faculty continuous improvement teams such as the Development Team, which studies the latest advances in technology and e-learning on a weekly basis. As the college shifts to a new course-management system for its e-learning programs of the future, adjuncts will benefit from additional intensive training available to full-time instructors.

Orientations and training cover mutual expectations: the college's expectations of faculty in their roles as adjuncts and the students' expectations for prompt grading of assignments, plus what Rio Salado adjuncts can expect in the form of support and training from the college.

After more than a decade of practicing organizational responsiveness in teaching and learning, Rio Salado's adjunct faculty turnover rate is less than 5 percent annually. The process of preparing for the college's 10-year reaccreditation and site visit by the North Central Association provided occasion for the college to survey its adjunct faculty on its collective level of satisfaction with the college. Survey results were compiled and placed in the college's Self Study Report. From this survey, the college learned, 95 percent of adjuncts report that their work helps Rio Salado accomplish its mission. The vast majority reported that they felt respected on the job, that they had access to the resources they needed to do their jobs well, and that they felt valued for the quality of work they perform.

Linda Thor is President of Rio Salado Community College in Tempe, Arizona.

8. Instructional Programming on a Shoestring

B. Kaye Walter

Context

Kansas City Kansas Community College (KCKCC) is a comprehensive community college located in Kansas City, Kansas. An urban community within the Greater Kansas City metropolitan area, Kansas City, Kansas has a population of 157,900 that is very diverse both ethnically and economically. The ethnic breakdown of the community is 48.2 percent White, 28.3 percent African American, 16 percent Hispanic, 1.6 percent Asian, .7 percent American Indian, and 5.2 percent Other. Economically, the community has an unemployment rate of 11 percent, which is the highest unemployment rate in the state. The community also has some of the highest local taxes in the state, while 27.5 percent of its families are living in poverty.

The student population of KCKCC closely mirrors the community population. The ethnic breakdown of the student population is 65 percent White, 25 percent African American, 5 percent Hispanic, 2 percent Asian, 1 percent American Indian, and 2 percent Other. In excess of 60 percent of the students attending KCKCC receive federal financial aid. Sixty-seven percent of students at KCKCC attend part time and are employed. The average age of students is 29 years.

KCKCC is coordinated by the Kansas Board of Regents and governed by a six-member elected board of trustees. The president of the college is responsible for administering the day-to-day operations of the college. The president has divided the college into three areas of responsibility – academic services, executive services, student and administrative services – and, with input from the vice presidents supervising these areas, sets direction for the college.

The chief academic officer supervises the academic services area and is in constant conversation with the deans and directors in her area regarding the use of technology on campus and its importance in instruction. These academic leaders have concluded that the college must expand its technology infrastructure, develop online courses to provide instructional options for students, establish a major web presence, and increase the technology staff of the college to meet the growing needs of its student population. The group recognizes a number of challenges they must face to move the college forward:

- Budgets are frozen and will most likely decrease in the coming year.
- Many faculty feel threatened by online courses and fear they will lose students or be replaced by faculty in a box.
- Establishing online classes will necessitate training for faculty.
- The academic services area must sell its proposal to the executive council (three vice presidents and president). At least one of the other vice presidents does not support large technology expansions or the addition of online courses for the campus.
- The academic services area must sell its proposal to the president and board of trustees. The elected board must deal with state budget cuts, excessively high local

taxes, and a community that does not understand the importance of technology for future economic development and growth.

Summary of the Case

The world is changing. In order for graduates of KCKCC to compete locally and globally for employment opportunities, they must have both a working knowledge of technology and the ability to use technology in their place of employment. This means that the campus must expand its technology infrastructure and technology staff so that students may be afforded the opportunity to prepare to use technology in the workplace. To better serve its adult, working student population, the campus must develop online delivery services that will allow students to access courseware anytime, anywhere. This will require additional staff and hours of professional development for both faculty and staff. KCKCC is located in a depressed urban area. The college must discover a way to expand its technology presence and instructional services without expanding its overall budget. Faculty, staff, administration, and the board of trustees must be convinced that the plan developed by the academic services area to expand technology is both appropriate for students and affordable for the community.

Questions to Consider

1. What options does academic services have for increasing staff without increasing the budget significantly?
2. What options does academic services have for increasing the technology budget without increasing the overall budget?
3. How will the deans and directors get faculty on board?
4. How should academic services approach the executive council?
5. How should academic services prepare to sell its proposal to the board of trustees?

Thoughts and Analysis

1. Community colleges must prepare their students to work in an increasingly technological world.
2. Academic services must consider all funding options available to it.
3. Academic services must be creative and look at nontraditional staffing options.
4. Faculty must be recruited to help design the online proposal and actively direct and engage the college in the development of online courses.
5. Academic services must market the proposal to faculty so that it is nonthreatening.
6. The college's service provides significant challenges because of the lack of resources available to the community.
7. Academic services area must devise a strategy for selling the idea to the president and board of trustees.

Outcomes

After agreeing that the college needed to expand its technology infrastructure, develop online courses to provide instructional options for students, establish a major web presence, and increase its technology staff to meet the growing needs of its student population, the academic deans' and directors' council developed a strategy for moving forward.

The first order of business was to recruit faculty who were interested in helping to lead the effort. To the surprise of the council, seasoned faculty emerged who were not only interested in the effort but dedicated to moving it forward.

Since funding was scarce and no new funds were available to hire additional staff, the group brainstormed about new ways of staffing its effort. To accomplish what they were proposing, at least five new positions would need to be created. These positions included two computer technicians, a director of information systems, a webmaster, and an online project director. It was decided that two student interns could function in the roles of computer technicians until the full-time staff positions could be added. It was recommended that the webmaster's and the online project director's positions be filled with full-time faculty who would be given complete release time from their teaching responsibilities. Adjunct faculty could fill their positions until additional positions could be secured. Two outstanding faculty emerged to fill these positions. They were given full release time with a guarantee that they could return to their teaching positions if at any time they felt they no longer wanted to function as the webmaster and online project director. One retirement occurred, which gave the group a position that could be converted to the director of information systems.

The staffing plan was presented to the executive council and the board of trustees. Both supported the effort and gave their approval for the plan to move forward. They felt the plan showed creativity and was within budget constraints.

The new webmaster began working with faculty from across the campus to expand the college's website and create a dynamic presence that would attract students. The new online project director enrolled in an online certification class at a well-known university. After completing the class, the online director established an online design team of faculty members from across campus. Criteria were established for the creation of KCKCC online courses. An online course for faculty was developed and taught by the online project director. All faculty interested in developing and offering courses online were required to successfully complete the online training course.

Within a five-year period, KCKCC has established a dynamic web presence. KCKCC now offers over 200 online courses, which generate approximately 25 percent of the total credit hours each semester. Both the original faculty webmaster and the online project director remain in their positions. They are stars, and the college is very grateful for the work they have done and continue to do. After two years, the board agreed to add two additional faculty positions so that new faculty could be hired to fill the teaching positions vacated by the webmaster and online project director. Two full-time technician positions were secured for the two student interns after the first year. Both technicians still remain important members of the information-systems team.

This year, in an effort to continue the development of our technology effort, the library joined instructional technology and information systems. The three departments became the KCKCC Information Services Division, led by an instructional dean. We believe this to be a very important step in converting our library to a high-tech information supplier. We are also hoping to complete our last phase this year in the conversion of our college into a wireless-enabled campus.

We learned a valuable lesson from this experience: Never let the lack of funds or staff keep you from meeting your students' needs. Everything you need might be right in front of your eyes. Learn to look at what you have in a new and exciting way.

B. Kaye Walter is Vice President of Academic Services at Kansas City Kansas Community College.

Part V

Student Life

1. The Diversity Protest

George R. Boggs

Context

Palomar College is a single-campus, comprehensive community college located in northern San Diego County, California. The college operates from a main campus in San Marcos and several smaller education centers throughout a 2,500-square-mile service area. The college district is governed by a five-member elected board of trustees with delegated responsibility for administering the college given to a superintendent/president (CEO). Although the board elections are nonpartisan, the members reflect the very conservative Republican views of the electorate. The president of the Associated Student Government sits at the board table and, as this story begins, does not have a vote.

The CEO is in his eighth year of leadership of the college and, for the last few years, has given direct attention to improving both the quality and diversity of the faculty and staff. Student enrollment has grown during the eight-year tenure of the CEO by 39 percent to 21,500. At the same time, the communities served by the college have become more ethnically diverse. Twenty-six percent of the population served by the college is minority, with Hispanic population growing significantly. The college has done a good job of providing proportional access to the population: Twenty-nine percent of the students are from minority groups.

On the other hand, employees of the college do not reflect the ethnic makeup of the communities served. During the tenure of the CEO, the percentage of full-time faculty from minority groups had increased from 9 percent to 12 percent; that of administrators had increased from 12 percent to 21 percent; and that of classified support staff had increased from 17 percent to 21 percent. The CEO was just concluding a difficult struggle with faculty to change the employment policies and procedures, requiring sufficient numbers of qualified candidates and sufficient gender and ethnic representation in the applicant, interview, and finalist pools. Under the proposed policy, the CEO would interview the top three or more unranked candidates for each faculty and administrative position and, after meeting with the search committee, would recommend his selection to the board for employment. At any time the administration felt that the pools did not have sufficient diversity or sufficient numbers of qualified candidates, the search would either be extended or canceled. The CEO could waive these requirements in highly unusual circumstances (*e.g.*, lack of male applicants for nursing faculty positions after evidence of unsuccessful attempts).

The policy and procedure changes that the CEO had sought had, after several months and not without opposition, made it through the college internal governance and were scheduled to appear for information at the next meeting of the board of trustees. However, before the board meeting, the CEO received a letter from the State Chancellor's Office stating that Palomar College had not met a state-mandated goal that 30 percent of new employees in a three-year period should be members of ethnic minority groups. The chancellor notified the CEO that he would be dispatching a Technical Assistance Team to Palomar College, as well as to other colleges in similar circumstances, to review employment policies and practices and to make recommendations to the CEO and the board. Although the CEO saw the review of the Technical Assistance Team to be positive in helping the college to focus on improving policies and practices, conservative local newspapers ran stories that portrayed the visit as punitive.

When the CEO introduced the board agenda item to change the employment policies, board members were influenced by the negative newspaper stories about the scheduled visit of the Technical Assistance Team. The board chair commented that he resented interference by the state. Another trustee, who was a retired faculty member, said that she did not like the emphasis on diversity in the proposed policy, and that Palomar should hire quality, not diversity. Their comments were reported in three local newspapers the following day.

The comments from the board members inflamed the minority communities. At the following board meeting, the president of the North County NAACP joined minority faculty members and students in condemning the comments from the two trustees as being insensitive and potentially racist. Despite words of caution from the CEO, the board chair angrily gaveled down a student who called the board racist. The following day, minority students, led by MEChA, the African-American Student Alliance, and the Native American Student Alliance, paraded through the campus with mock coffins for the board chair and the trustee who made the comment about hiring quality rather than diversity. With the encouragement of minority faculty members and community members, the students decided to turn their demonstration into a campout in front of the campus and pitched makeshift tents. The two coffins were predominantly displayed near the tents along Mission Road near the campus entrance.

Local newspapers ran front-page stories on the protest. The CEO received notes from a few faculty members urging him not to cave in to pressure from liberal minorities. A nonminority male student came to the CEO's office saying that he was thinking about organizing a counter protest of White students. The protesters received notes handed to them from passing automobiles, many in support of their efforts. However, one note threatened that they would be shot if they continued their protest. The national head of the White Aryan Resistance, a separatist organization, lives in the college district.

Summary of the Case

The community served by the college is changing demographically, becoming more ethnically diverse. However, the community and its leadership remain very conservative. The CEO has been successful in leading the college through several financial and political challenges during his eight-year tenure. His efforts to bring greater quality and diversity to the faculty and staff have not necessarily been welcomed by faculty and trustees. Trustee comments about proposed policy changes and an impending state Technical Assistance Team visit ignited a student protest and presented the CEO with the need to protect freedom of speech, protect the safety of the student protesters, and keep the situation from escalating further. Three local newspapers are competing for readership. One of the newspapers has assigned the story to a young, aggressive investigative reporter who has interviewed community leaders, students, board members, and the CEO. She is following the story closely. The trustees to whom the CEO reports are under attack by the protesters.

Questions to Consider

1. Should the CEO allow the protesting students to continue their camp-out protest? If so, under what conditions?
2. If the CEO allows the protest to continue, what should he do to ensure the safety and security of the students and the campus?
3. How should the CEO respond to the student who suggested a counter protest?
4. Should the CEO delegate dealing with the student protesters to his Vice President for Student Affairs or to one of his minority administrators?
5. How should the CEO deal with his board members?
6. How should the CEO deal with the press?
7. What, if anything, should the CEO report to the State Chancellor's Office?

Thoughts and Analysis

1. College campuses are historically centers for freedom of speech. If the CEO were to consider a forced end to the demonstrations, he would be acting against his own values and would need legal advice.
2. Classes end at 10:00 p.m. on the San Marcos campus of Palomar College. The campus generally closes at 11:00 p.m., all facilities, including restrooms, are locked, and Campus Security leaves for the evening.
3. With the strong emotions involved on both sides of the diversity issue, and with the head of the national White Aryan Resistance living in the college district, there is a very real threat of violence.
4. Since the protesters are calling for the removal of the board chair and another trustee, the CEO's job security may be at stake.
5. The student protesters have no single authority to represent them, and the Hispanic and African-American students do not always agree, making it difficult to negotiate an agreement to end the protest. The Native American students pulled back from the demonstration.

Outcomes

The CEO decided to allow the minority students to continue their protest. He arranged to keep restrooms near the campsites open throughout the evenings, had water delivered to the students, and assigned 24-hour security to protect the students and the campus. He successfully discouraged the nonminority students from mounting a counter protest by pledging to work on behalf of all students and to seek a peaceful resolution to the protests. The CEO kept law enforcement officials, the trustees, the State Chancellor's Office, and the press informed of developments on a regular basis. He wrote an opinion editorial for the largest of the local newspapers, outlining the college's efforts to improve both the quality and diversity of its faculty and staff. The CEO decided to negotiate with the student protesters directly and at the campsite rather than delegating the responsibility or requiring the students to come to his office. During the 11-day protest, the students and the CEO developed a respectful and trusting relationship.

After the student protesters told the CEO of the threat of a shooting, he ordered the protesters to move their tents to the interior of the campus. The protesters refused to obey the order, saying that they were prepared to sacrifice for the rights of minority students. The CEO told the protestors that he was responsible for their safety and would contact the sheriff's department and have the students arrested if they did not obey. The students responded that the CEO could do what he had to do, and they would do what they had to do. The CEO called the sheriff, and deputies arrived in about a half hour along with the investigative newspaper reporter. The deputy said that he had to hear the students disobey the CEO's order before he would arrest them. The CEO called the students together and again asked them to move their tents to the interior of the campus where they would not be susceptible to a drive-by shooting. The students changed their minds and agreed to do so, ending the standoff and a certain front-page newspaper story.

In the course of the protest, the students presented a list of demands for changes that they felt would improve the climate for diversity at the college. The CEO worked with students, community members, faculty, and trustees to achieve a mutually acceptable resolution to the issues that were raised. Discussions with the protesters were conducted in a respectful and nonconfrontational atmosphere. In all of the meetings with the protesters, the CEO affirmed the right to free speech and the college's commitment to increase the diversity of the faculty. Throughout the negotiations, the CEO was focused on ensuring freedom of speech, open discussion of the issues, academic freedom, open communications to all concerned, and the safety and security of the students and the campus.

The protest ended with an agreement on a plan for increasing diversity awareness that included the formation of a task force to address diversity issues, the recommendation for cultural awareness courses for employees and board members, recommendation for an advisory vote for the student trustee, and continuing dialogue between students and administrators. The state Technical Assistance Team's major recommendation to improve the hiring rate of minorities was to give less weight to previous teaching experience when evaluating resumes. The CEO's recommended new employment policies were approved unanimously by the board of trustees. The CEO was named as an Honorary Elder the following year by the Western Region of the National Council on Black American Affairs.

George R. Boggs is the President and CEO of the American Association of Community Colleges and the Superintendent/President Emeritus of Palomar College in California.

2. Collaboration Leads to New Student Success

Vernon O. Crawley, Mary Kay Kickels, Patricia Bauhs, and Delores Brooks

Context

The second largest Illinois community college, Moraine Valley Community College is located in the southwest suburbs of Chicago. Situated on 294 acres of partially forested, scenic land in a university-like setting, Moraine Valley serves residents and businesses in 26 suburban communities.

Moraine Valley offers more than 100 associate degree and certificate programs, continuing education opportunities, fine and performing arts activities, and special events and services. More than 45,000 students annually enroll in credit and noncredit courses, including approximately 300 international students representing over 45 countries. The college hosts over 100,000 people a year who attend world-class entertainment and performances staged in the contemporary Fine and Performing Arts Center and in other campus venues.

One of the fastest-growing community colleges in the country, Moraine Valley is a member of the North Central Association and is accredited by the Higher Learning Commission. A charter member of the League for Innovation in the Community College, Moraine Valley is one of 12 community colleges nationally named a Vanguard Learning College.

The student population is 59 percent female, 41 percent male, with 28 the median age. Approximately 65 percent of the students attend classes during the day, with 39 percent enrolled as full-time students and 85 percent working and attending college. Multicultural students comprise 23 percent of the enrollment, with 77 percent White, 8 percent Black, 9 percent Hispanic, and 2 percent Asian. Average class size is 23 students. Moraine Valley employs 182 full-time faculty and approximately 900 part-time instructors.

Moraine Valley commits fully to living the following pledge: *We promise to provide a student-centered environment and to focus all college staff and resources on student learning, student development, and student success.* However, living the pledge challenges some of the very systems upon which the institution, like many others, is founded.

Summary of the Case

Recognizing that students' experiences during their first semester in college are critical to their academic adjustment and social integration, and are a major determining factor in whether they succeed or fail in their college years, Moraine Valley decided to take deliberate steps in helping students to integrate successfully to college life. The first step in this effort was the establishment of a cross-functional task group co-chaired by a counselor and a faculty member reporting to a senior administrator.

The task group began by researching best practices, reviewing high school and college student data, assessing the effects of the college's counseling and advising programs and services, and analyzing other information prior to recommending action. The survey of the situation confirmed that Moraine Valley students were faced with many academic and personal challenges that inhibited their academic achievement and their successful transfer to four-year colleges or universities.

- Students were not using the academic-advising and course-planning resources of the college to the greatest extent possible.
- Moraine Valley students who transferred to some four-year institutions experienced lower success rates at the end of their first year of transfer than comparable community college transfer students.
- It was evident there was a need to develop a program to help new students make a more successful transition to the college environment by helping them develop basic academic skills and learn about themselves in relation to the demands of higher education.
- It was determined that a required course would provide the most effective approach to helping students succeed.

Questions to Consider

The college's task force recommended to the college president and vice president of academic affairs that action focus on the development of a collaborative, intensive, and comprehensive first-year experience that would address the following:

1. What student behaviors are most critically related to success in learning?
2. How does the college promote and support these behaviors?
3. How can our college effectively assess, benchmark, monitor, and improve student success during the first-year college experience?
4. What fundamental institutional practices have we found to be linked to student success, student retention, and positive learning outcomes?
5. How would a new, required one-credit-hour course for degree-seeking full-time students affect the certificates and degrees that already were approved at the maximum credit-hour limit?

Thoughts and Analysis

The faculty and administrators at the college and the union leadership on campus recognized that a student's first semester is a critical period for intervention. Academic and student development departments collaborated in developing a comprehensive First-Year Experience program that combines mandatory placement testing, new student orientation, and enrollment in a one-credit-hour student success course. Each component of the program, with appropriate supportive services, is required for all new, first-time, full-time students during their first semester at the college.

The course, College-101: Changes, Challenges, Choices (COL-101), became a mandatory graduation requirement for all entering first-time, full-time students effective the spring 2000 semester. In addition, the college incorporated into the First Year Experience Program that all new full-time students complete placement testing in reading, writing, and mathematics to ensure that students begin classes at a level where they can achieve success.

Major challenges were affecting the institutional systems at the college as well:

- The sheer number of entering students each fall required that nearly 100 sections of the new course be offered each term.
- Scheduling nearly 100 sections of a one-credit-hour class would stress the already near-capacity campus classrooms.
- Identifying faculty interested in teaching 100 sections would be a challenge.
- Most faculty, full-time and adjunct, were untrained in addressing the student needs that were anticipated in this kind of course.
- Many full-time faculty were already teaching at maximum load.
- The union faculty contract governing pay practices would raise issues of inequity for other qualified staff and adjuncts who would teach the new course.
- Finally, the course needed a home in the organizational and management structure at the college. Who owned the course? Who would be responsible?

Recommended action included a complete review of all challenges to successful implementation and included these actions:

- Identifying a campus leader who would be responsible for course development, scheduling, faculty development, and assignment
- Initiating the course scheduling process
- Developing and introducing a mandatory professional development program for faculty teaching the COL-101 course
- Resolving faculty contract matters, including adjustment of maximum load, salary issues, and equity for all assigned faculty

The college class schedule was closely examined to assure that the one-credit-hour class could be offered at times convenient to students' schedules, while assuring that the college continued to maximize the use of classroom space both on the main campus and at extension centers. Issues such as full-time student load and daytime, evening, and weekend scheduling were addressed in Year One.

In keeping with the principles of a true learning college, teaching faculty collaborated with counselors to develop a five-hour course that would be mandatory for all full-time, adjunct faculty, and professional staff who would be teaching the class. Minimum teaching criteria included an earned master's degree. It was determined that if full-time faculty and qualified staff were to teach this course, respective of their content-area specialization, the students would benefit greatly from taking the course from dedicated faculty. However, the faculty contract did not provide adequate guidance in integrating the one-credit-hour course into the full-time faculty load. In addition, the issue of fair compensation for staff was discussed.

Compensation issues creating challenging dialogue caused some delay in the implementation of the program. Yet in principle, all agreed on the value of the new course, and all were committed to assuring its success at Moraine Valley. Much to the credit of those on either side of the bargaining table, decisions were made and compromise was reached based on a single deciding question: What is best for the students?

Discussions about requiring this course continued over a period of two years; at the same time, administrators and faculty planned for the full implementation of the First Year Experience program. The underlying assumption was that if this were good for students, the college and its representative groups would find a way to assure that the program would be fully implemented. Indeed, the college community collaborated successfully on this major initiative.

Outcomes

The First-Year Experience course was introduced at Moraine Valley Community College as a special service for students to assist them in engaging with the college. The goals for the course and the end competencies include decision-making and goal-setting skills, critical thinking, moral and ethical choices, living in a diverse world, communications skills, career and college-major exploration, time management, study skills, and using information and technology responsibly.

Over the four years that the course has been offered, the Office of Institutional Research has tracked the progress of all students enrolled in COL-101, comparing their success with other groups. Outcomes include the following:

1. The First-Year Experience at Moraine Valley Community College has resulted in positive academic and life-skills development for freshman students.
2. The successful students who took the course earned credit hours, average GPA, and across-term retention rates significantly higher than those same indicators for the "did not take" and the "unsuccessful" students.
3. Over a four-year period, 354 sections of COL-101 have been offered, with over 6,000 students enrolled.
4. Student feedback on the course has been interesting and upbeat. Some comments derived from evaluations include the following:
    - "No one told me how worthwhile the course was."
    - "It provided me an opportunity to become more confident in my studies."
    - "Fun and very helpful. I expected the class to be a lot harder."
    - "Enjoyed the writing techniques workshop; it helped to rebuild my writing skills."
    - "I will admit it: When I first heard about the class at orientation, I was against it. But overall, this is a good class to take. It helps you discover the right way you should be studying and taking notes."

The administrators and faculty involved in the difficult discussions that changed the systems to accommodate this new course take pride in their role in introducing this initiative and in supporting students in their academic goals. Each knows that this success lies in the details of challenge and compromise, details that led to a clear choice and a singular voice for students and their success. Differences were set aside; the decision was made to dedicate all energies toward student success. In the process, the learning college principles served to guide and direct the actions that we took in this regard.

The First-Year Experience program has received national recognition for the success it has created for Moraine Valley students. Honors include the Exemplary Practice Award from the National Association of Student Personnel Administrators; the 2003 Best Practice Award from the National Council on Student Development; the 2003 Terry O'Banion Shared Journey Award from the National Council on Student Development; and the 2003 Illinois Community College Board Excellence in Learning-Centered Instruction Award.

The leadership and responsibility for The First-Year Experience program is a collegewide priority and function of many departments, academic disciplines, and individuals, including the college president, the senior vice president for academic affairs, the vice president for student development, the assistant dean of new student retention, the Orientation Committee, the First-Year Experience Task Force, and the Moraine Valley faculty.

Vernon O. Crawley is President of Moraine Valley Community College in Palos Hills, Illinois. Mary Kay Kickels is Senior Vice President for Academic Affairs; Patricia Bauhs is Vice President for Institutional Advancement and Execuive Assistant to the President; and Delores Brooks is Director of Marketing and Publications Services at Moraine Valley.

3. Intercollegiate Athletics as an Institutional Priority

Scott Elliott

Context

Meridian Community College (MCC) is one of 15 institutions comprising the Mississippi Community College system. MCC is located in east central Mississippi, approximately 18 miles west of the Alabama state line on Interstates 20 and 59. Enrollment is approximately 4,000 credit students, with many others involved in continuing education, workforce training, and adult education programs. Average age of students is about 28, and most are recipients of some form of financial aid.

Summary of the Case

A new administration came into being at Meridian in the fall of 1998. Shortly thereafter, economic conditions in the state began to decline sharply, resulting in substantial cuts in state appropriations to the community college system. In Meridian's case, the college lost some $2 million over a three-year span – a devastating sum for a small, rural college. Therefore, it was not only a time of establishing priorities for a new administration, but of doing so in a highly challenging fiscal environment.

Meridian had allocated a healthy portion of its operating budget for some years to develop intercollegiate athletic programs capable of regularly competing for National Junior College Athletic Association (NJCAA) championships. This effort involved increased investment in scholarships, athletic facilities, travel, and so forth. It also involved Meridian's seceding from the Mississippi Association of Community and Junior College's state athletic association. Competing as an independent enabled Meridian to schedule opponents from across the nation with rich junior college athletic traditions, and no longer be subject to recruiting and scholarship restrictions imposed by the state association. Meridian indeed developed fiercely competitive athletic teams, winning NJCAA national championships in soccer, track, and softball. Yet the investment required to continue to compete at such a level increased almost annually, and relatively few local student athletes, whose families supported the college through their tax contributions, were recruited to participate on the college's teams. Moreover, out-of-state student athletes are not counted by Mississippi for purposes of state formula appropriations. Therefore, recruiting numbers of out-of-state athletes exacerbated the college's fiscal challenges.

Primarily, state budget cuts compelled an analysis of Meridian's investment in athletic programs. However, the new administration was also concerned philosophically about the congruency of the college's athletic programs with the school's mission. The administration felt strongly that the operative word in the college's title was community, and that the emphasis on competing for national championships did not promote strong participation among community student athletes.

Questions to Consider

1. What effect did having nationally prominent athletic teams have on such issues as private investment in the college or marketability from an overall student recruitment standpoint?
2. In a fiscally challenged environment, could the college continue to support the intercollegiate athletic function at a high level when resources for other programs, arguably more central to the college's mission, were dwindling?
3. Was the college's philosophy on intercollegiate athletics in keeping with its mission as a community college?
4. What would be the effects of changing the college's philosophy on intercollegiate athletics within the campus community and on the community at large?

Thoughts and Analysis

The correlation between intercollegiate athletics and the overall health of the college needed to be assessed. In a major college environment, in which tens of thousands of fans attend football games and some alumni invest heartily in the institution on the basis of athletic performance, that correlation is fairly obvious. It is harder to discern on the junior college level. In an effort to make such an assessment at Meridian, the administration took into consideration such elements as (1) attendance at sporting events, (2) gate receipts, (3) student enrollment trends, (4) student surveys, and (5) any qualitative information that might have connected private giving to the MCC Foundation to intercollegiate athletics. Moreover, a fiscal evaluation was conducted as to how much the college might save if it returned its athletic program to a local and state focus, versus a national emphasis. Expenditures on scholarships and travel, as examples, were considered.

The analysis was conducted by a committee comprised of representatives of the administration and athletic department. The college's business manager assisted in providing fiscal data. Also, the faculty senate was consulted and apprised of the process and results. The study revealed that the college's overall student enrollment had grown marginally during the era when it focused on nationally competitive teams. However, enrollment growth during that era seemed to arguably correlate as much, if not more than athletics, with the advent of a new Tuition Guarantee program, providing financial assistance to area high school graduates. Also, gate receipts during the era recovered only a minuscule percentage of the total cost of operating the programs. Attendance at some sporting events, notably basketball games, did not appear to have a strong nexus with team performance. The lack of strong attendance at basketball games was attributed, at least by some followers, to a dearth of local or in-state student athletes on the men's and women's teams' rosters in tandem with the absence of opponents on the schedule who had once been considered Meridian's traditional rivals. Qualitatively, informal discussions with some key private investors in the community revealed little correlation between those donors' interest in the college and its athletic programs. On campus, those specifically associated with the athletic program were expectantly anxious about any prospective changes in budget and philosophy. Those not specifically associated with the program, based on conferences with faculty senate members and others in the college community, were more concerned about support for those elements of the college operation they considered to be more central to the institutional mission.

Outcomes

After an exhaustive two-year analysis, the Meridian Community College Board of Trustees elected to rejoin the Mississippi athletic conference in the summer of 2001. In coming into compliance with conference rules, Meridian significantly reduced its investment in athletic scholarships and travel, lodging, and meal expenditures, among other direct and indirect costs related to sports programming. The savings realized from changes in the athletic program ultimately helped the college to cope with continued state budget cuts and avoid even more alarming reductions in support to academic and occupational education programs. Absent such savings, the college may well have been faced with a reduction in force in nonathletic areas.

Meridian won regional championships in tennis, golf, and baseball in its first year back in the state conference, thus qualifying for the NJCAA national tournament in each sport. There was very little discernable depreciation in attendance at athletic events. On the contrary, attendance at basketball games increased markedly, with most games drawing capacity crowds. That increase in attendance was attributed by some to more local and in-state players being on the Meridian roster and the renewal of competition against traditional rivals. Rejoining the state association also resulted in about 45 percent of Meridian's student athletes being recruited from within the district, rather than from out of state and out of country. This in itself elevated the college's state reimbursement for students, and supported the "community" element of the college's name. Although three of its teams by the spring of 2004 were nationally ranked by the National Junior College Athletic Association, Meridian's administrative philosophy in athletics focused more on providing local and in-state athletes with opportunities than on competing for national titles. Student surveys indicated that the caliber of the college's athletic teams had little influence on students' selection of Meridian as their school of choice. Private giving to the college's foundation during this time remained strong, and all-time student enrollment records were eclipsed. This led the administration to conclude that the correlation between having nationally prominent junior college athletic teams and such issues as enrollment and private giving was difficult to discern. Moreover, in 2003, Meridian won for the first time Mississippi's Halbrook Award for having the highest junior college student-athlete graduation rate in the state (94 percent).

As to how the decision affected campus and community morale, the administration received very little negative feedback in terms of letters, emails, telephone calls, or media commentary. More prominent was the positive response from constituents who expressed their approval of the college's re-establishing its commitment to the recruitment of local and in-state student athletes. Many also opined that watching Meridian compete against other area institutions, which had once been MCC's traditional rivals, had heightened their interest.

Scott Elliott is President of Meridian Community College in Meridian, Mississippi.

4. Inclusion Rewarded

Dug Jones

Context

Santa Fe Community College (SFCC) is a comprehensive public community college with a fall 2003 enrollment of over 15,000 credit students (about 9,000 FTEs) and another 20,000 students taking noncredit courses. The college is located in the shadow of the University of Florida in rural north central Florida. SFCC sends approximately 2,000 students to the University of Florida each year and places over 90 percent of vocational program graduates in the employment field of their choice.

The college was established in 1965, and has grown to an institution with one large campus and four smaller educational centers. A fifth educational center will come on line within the next year. An eight-member board of trustees appointed by the governor of Florida provides governance for the college.

The majority of students (54.7 percent) are from within the college's two-county district. There are, however, nearly 400 students from other states and over 500 students from other countries. The average age for SFCC students is 24.4 years, and the significant majority (65.8 percent) seek Associate of Arts degrees. More SFCC students attend full time (55.7 percent) than part time. These demographics distinguish our student body as younger and maybe more traditional than most of our sister institutions within the Florida community college system.

Despite the availability of an excellent student activity center and committed college resources (staffing and funding), the levels of organized student involvement in campus and community activities fell well below potential. Students frequently reported either a lack of awareness, a lack of time, or a lack of interest in campus activities and student organizations. College committees and decision-making bodies often lacked a strong, committed student presence. The students who were involved were often overextended, and therefore less effective as leaders. The Student Activities Center was underused to the point that space was reallocated for other institutional initiatives.

The origin of these problems could be attributed to a number of factors. The Student Activities program lost credibility in 1998 as a result of embezzlement by (and the subsequent arrest of) the program's long-term administrator. This disruption and the ultimate departmental reorganization negatively affected staffing and program continuity. Other challenges included the need to overcome the in loco parentis leanings of some staff members and the challenge of dispelling the myth that community college students won't get involved. In some cases, overrestrictive policies and cumbersome procedures made it so difficult for students to use their student center and the associated resources that they just gave up. Another significant impediment was the legitimate perception of students that they didn't really have a strong voice in important decisions like the annual allocation of $1.6 million of activity and service fees revenue.

Summary of the Case

The college community has the goal of increasing student involvement in campus and community activities including shared governance at the college. The college administration has shown strong commitment in the form of building a new student center and allocating adequate resources to support this growth. There is a continuing need to overcome some old paradigms and organizational obstacles to help make this happen. There is also a need to redirect and refocus activities within the Student Life area to revitalize and allow this change to occur.

Questions to Consider

1. How do we make students aware of opportunities for involvement?
2. How do we overcome the myth that students won't find time for campus life?
3. How do we grow a vibrant student government?
4. Should students control activity and service fees revenue?
5. How can we attract students to the student center?
6. What services can we provide to help students succeed?
7. How do we make involvement in the governance process attractive to students?

Thoughts and Analysis

1. Students who get involved in campus life succeed better than those who simply take classes and go back home or to work.
2. The college benefits from greater student involvement in the decision-making and direction-setting processes.
3. Creative approaches to marketing are required to attract the attention of today's students.
4. Students will get involved in governance activities when their roles and influence are legitimate.
5. Removing the obstacles to student involvement is a student affairs role.
6. Students are attracted to a dynamic environment.

Outcomes

The roles for staff at the Center for Student Leadership and Activities fall into three primary categories: attracting students, supporting students, and rewarding students. Initiatives within each of these categories have been developed, and purposeful progress has been made.

To attract students to events, activities, services, and leadership opportunities, the center took on a more creative, dynamic approach to reaching students. Better tools were needed for better marketing. The center acquired the software and hardware needed to create and print full-color, full-size posters in house. A part-time student graphic design position was created and funded. Within weeks attractive posters promoting student organizations, student government, and student activities were appearing on moveable 24" by 36" A-frames throughout campus. Smaller yet attractive color flyers also promoted the services and activities available through the Student Center.

The campus policy on posted information was rewritten to segregate the public bulletin boards from those reserved for college business. Large cylindrical kiosks were purchased and installed at many exterior campus locations to ensure that public-access-type information had an appropriate forum. Maps to these public boards were created and provided to individuals wishing to post commercial, political, and other noncollege information. The college-use-only boards were reserved for use by on-campus entities and clearly marked as such. This change helped SG and student organizations, as well as academic departments and support services, avoid competing with the numerous sales flyers and nightclub advertisements that cover our public boards. College staff is diligent in enforcing the posted information policy on the college-use boards.

A dynamic Student Life website was created and kept current by a student websmith. The site has links to each of the Student Life program areas as well as current information on campus and community activities and deadlines of interest to students. The site includes, as well, information and online forms for most center services and resources. Additionally, students use the site as a forum to find roommates, find rides, sell items, and discuss instructors and classes.

Another marketing effort of interest was the creation of an interactive display case at the entry to the student center. The large, storefront-style area has a motion detector that triggers a 30-second voice loop whenever a person passes. The lighted display area and corresponding voice loop provide student organizations and other campus entities a creative way to draw attention to their events and activities. The goal is to have a new display focus each week.

The initiatives to support student involvement have included focused efforts to ensure that student leaders have access to the resources needed to succeed. Student government and student organization offices are all equipped with computers and private telephone lines. Access to student organization offices and the center's services has been extended until 9 p.m. on weeknights. Student government officers may now access their offices anytime night or day. The Student Senate Chambers has been marked with prominent signage that sends the clear message to all that student government has an active and important role at this college.

Student involvement at SFCC is also supported by the fact that our student leaders have legitimate authority to make decisions and allocate college revenues. Our Student Leadership and Activities Budget Committee transitioned from a group with some student membership to one where 9 of the 13 members are students. This group allocated $1.6 million this year. At the student government level, the $200,000 in funding for student organizations, the student programming board, and student government operations was allocated entirely by a committee of seven students.

Students at SFCC have also been supported within the past few years by the creation of a Student Health Care Center (SHCC) and Student Legal Services (SLS) programs on campus. The SHCC is open 40 hours per week and is staffed by a registered nurse, a health educator, and a nurse practitioner. Students can get most of their medical needs addressed at very low cost or no cost at all. The SLS program provides students access to free legal advice and support 24 hours each week. Programs like these help students address real-life issues conveniently and economically so that they may more easily focus on their educational goals. These programs also serve to attract students to the center and other center-based programs like student government.

Students at SFCC are rewarded for involvement in ways beyond intrinsic satisfaction and résumé lines. The center coordinates an annual Student Awards Night, where each campus entity including student organizations, athletic teams, and academic units are encouraged to identify and recognize students. Additionally, the center initiated and manages the Hall of Fame program, where the top 1 percent of SFCC students are selected and recognized. Hundreds of students are nominated each year by center staff for district, state, and national awards and recognition. Funding to attend conferences and workshops is also provided, as a form of recognition, to students who have distinguished themselves as student leaders.

Activity levels and student involvement have risen dramatically at SFCC. In 2003, the SFCC student government was selected by *Florida Leader Magazine* as Community College Student Government of the Year for the State of Florida.

Dug Jones is the Director for Student Life at Santa Fe Community College in Gainesville, Florida.

5. Introducing Residence Halls to a Community College

Susan Salvador

Context

Monroe Community College (MCC) was founded in 1962 with a mission to provide "a high-quality learning environment to a diverse community." The college is "committed to access, teaching excellence, comprehensiveness, lifelong learning, partnership building, and economic development."

MCC is well supported and valued by the Greater Rochester, New York (Monroe County) community it serves. Its faculty is respected and offers rich perspectives to the 36,000 students educated annually across four campuses, four extension sites, and online. The college is a unit of the State University of New York (SUNY) system, the largest college in upstate New York, and ranks consistently among the top 1 percent of community colleges nationwide, based on the number of graduates. A 10-person board of trustees – including a student-elected representative – governs the college. Classroom, co-curricular, and athletic opportunities abound for students.

Over the years, students and parents increasingly voiced expectations and demonstrated needs for a residence life program. Community colleges like MCC are primarily designed to educate and support local residents, so residence halls are not always part of a college's evolution. With the continued growth and success of MCC's high-demand and highly specialized academic programs (*e.g.*, Automotive Technology, Dental Hygiene, Engineering and Radiologic Technology), and its intercollegiate athletic teams, the idea of offering residence halls became more attractive. The inquiries of local students further convinced MCC leadership that residence halls should be part of the college's future.

The college has enjoyed five consecutive years of enrollment growth, including a 3.6 percent increase most recently. The majority of students are between the ages of 18 and 24, with 25 percent over the age of 30. The college's president is especially passionate and focused on enhancing the student life experience at the college.

It took over a decade for the political and economic climate to become ideal for building residence halls at Monroe Community College.

Summary of the Case

Increasing numbers of students and parents want MCC to offer a residence life experience to complement its academic and co-curricular programs. Neighboring counties do not offer some of the innovative academic and competitive athletic programs that attract students to MCC, so the number of out-of-county students applying to MCC continues to rise. International students desire to live on campus for added convenience and security. Even local students' college choice sometimes hinges on the availability of on-campus housing and the commuting distance. Residence halls would make MCC more attractive to students and competitive with other colleges.

Under New York state law, community colleges may not use operating or capital dollars to finance the building of residence halls. An alternative organization is required. Further, Monroe County owns the property on which the college's campus is located and where the residence halls are envisioned. Some county legislators question whether the plan for residence halls is within the college's mission and is financially viable. Some legislators do not believe that community colleges were intended to provide residence-hall services, and that money would be better spent expanding classroom space. Legislative approval is required in order to lease and develop the six acres of land identified for the residence halls.

Since the campus is located in the Town of Brighton and uses town services, MCC's president proactively engaged the town supervisor and public safety committee in discussing police, fire, and ambulance services for the residence-hall complex. This effort helped to alleviate town concerns.

Questions to Consider

1. Are residence halls consistent with your institution's mission?
2. Do state regulations allow the college to build, own, and manage residence halls?
3. What political issues exist?
4. Does the college president have trustee support for building residence halls?
5. Do you have the staff to plan and then manage the facility?
6. How will local four-year residential campuses react?
7. How will the project be introduced to the community? What will the response be to the commonly asked question, "Is [college name] becoming a four-year institution?"
8. Considering the cost of construction and operation, is the project financially viable?
9. How will you assess the market and the demand for residence halls? Who will conduct market research and help determine target audiences?
10. What rental price will the market bear?
11. What additional security services need to be in place?

Thoughts and Analysis

Factors that influenced the success of the project included the following:

1. Ownership and management of the residence halls were aligned under the MCC Association, Inc., a pre-existing, not-for-profit organization that also owns and manages the MCC Child Care Center, campus bookstores, and other auxiliary services at the college. The MCC Association staff has a defined reporting relationship to the vice president of student services, who also serves as chairperson to the MCC Association, Inc. board of directors.
2. Tax-exempt bonds were used to fund the project. The project was underwritten for a 30-year amortization period.
3. A committee of engineers, planners, student-life staff, administrative services, an outside consultant, and the college's general counsel was assembled to develop a request for proposal. Legal review was a critical element for project success.
4. Targeted audiences included international students, student athletes, out-of-

county residents, and local students.

5. Promotional strategies included a customized brochure, web page, media attention, open houses, tours for prospective students, direct mail, and on-campus communications.

6. Solutions for ensuring secured access and physical safety satisfied students and parents.

Outcomes

The residence-hall project at Monroe Community College received unanimous approval from the college's board of trustees. Two county legislators opposed funding for the project, believing that residence-life services were not within the mission of community colleges, especially at a college where 90 percent of its students live within the county. Community opinion included praise for MCC's decision, stating the housing plans were "progressive" and "wise" in response to increased demand. Local colleges were passive on the topic, as were private apartment complex owners.

College leaders affirmed their position that residence halls fit within the college's mission through community meetings, media interviews, and newspaper editorials. Issues raised by town and county representatives regarding security risks and insurance liabilities were resolved through cooperative efforts to minimize impact on public safety services. Issues of potential security risks and insurance liabilities as well as sewer-system capacity were also addressed and communication protocols were established.

A feasibility study was conducted. The study included written and web-based surveys (30 questions) administered to 6,000 students. Newly registered students were surveyed during orientation programs, via direct mail, and within focus groups. Findings concluded that filling up to 900 beds was achievable.

Ground was broken for the residence halls in May 2002. Three individual buildings (143,000 square feet) with 33 or 34 suites each were built, offering 410 units (beds). Over 630 applications were received from full-time students. The cost of a single room was $2,300 per semester; $2,000 for a double. (Rental charges were calculated based on occupancy for nine months of the year.)

The residence-hall complex was dedicated the Alice Holloway Young Commons in July 2003. The complex is named after the college's board chair emerita, a well-respected retired educator in the Rochester community. Each individual building took its name from MCC history: Alexander Hall, commemorating the college's first campus at 410 Alexander Street in Rochester; Tribune Hall, reflecting the college's mascot; and Pioneer Hall, honoring the early college and community leaders responsible for founding the college in 1961.

The project cost $16.5 million to complete. Suites are furnished and kitchens are complete with microwave oven, stove, refrigerator, dishwasher, and garbage disposal. Rooms were wired for computer and network connectivity and feature two bathrooms, common living space, and air conditioning. The halls are coed, with single-sex suites.

No alcohol or smoking is permitted on the premises. Students gain access to the main entrance to each residence hall by using a key card. Key locks provide security on suite doors and individual bedroom doors. A new residence-hall parking lot was constructed with 205 parking spaces adjacent to the halls (one space for every two students).

On move-in day, August 30, students and their families were welcomed by a host of faculty, staff, and student volunteers. Representatives from dining services, local telephone, cable television, student organizations, and student support services were on hand to assist students and initiate services.

The decision to build residence halls on campus is the first step of a multifaceted process. Students and their families are going to expect more than just buildings and beds from a residence-life program. Establishing a successful program also requires defining a residence-life philosophy and exploring how living and learning will be supported by faculty and staff on campus – a case study to complement this one. From the application process to staffing, community-building activities to room assignments, suitemate conflicts to judicial decisions, the time needed to launch and execute a residence-life program on a community college campus should not be underestimated. Budgets tend to expand easily and need to be well managed. If residence halls are part of your college's future, be prepared for visits from other community college representatives who will be eager to learn from your experience.

Susan Salvador is Vice President of Student Services at Monroe Community College in Rochester, New York.

6. Student and Staff Relational Trust

Bettie Tully and Wright Lassiter, Jr.

Context

El Centro College is the original flagship campus of the seven-college Dallas County Community College District. It is located in the heart of downtown Dallas, with all of the attendant urban stresses such as noise, pollution, traffic, parking, and safety concerns. It is still living up to its reputation as a premier urban educational center. The main campus building is housed in a nine-story former department store, making it a vertical campus serviced by an aging elevator system and with obvious space limitations.

El Centro offers the traditional comprehensive array of academic transfer courses and is constantly applauded for its exemplary nationally accredited health occupations, interior design, apparel design, and paralegal programs. It is equally well known for developmental education and extraordinary support services for underprepared students.

The college president arrived several years ago, a time when the student population was in the end stages of being what most educators would have described as a typical community college student body. There were very few student concerns raised that could not be settled by civil conversation, negotiation, or administrative fiat. College officials and faculty were accustomed to being acknowledged as authority figures and treated with deference.

Four years after the current president's arrival, the open door is beginning to swing shut for a variety of reasons, causing confusion and consternation among students and staff. El Centro students are very rapidly becoming a more diverse group in terms of gender, ethnicity, age, economic level, physical challenges, lifestyle, and level of preparation for college success. Like many urban colleges, El Centro has a high percentage of students who are the first in their families to attend college and who therefore tend to be unfamiliar with the traditions and protocols of academia. It is obvious that these and other catalysts are resulting in marked increases in student activism and other less appropriate ways of responding to their feelings of uneasiness.

In ordinary times, the combination of students from intense competitive programs with very stringent requirements and underprepared students engaged in the tedious and frustrating business of trying to catch up with their peers in college-level courses tends to breed an unusual number of student complaints and grievances, as well as an increased number of disruptive student incidents leading to disciplinary actions. Add to this the inherently stressful urban environment juxtaposed with a budget shortfall, and a domino effect begins to escalate tensions among faculty, administrators, and students.

The president recognizes that the time has come to seek more effective ways of dealing with all college complaints and concerns, hopefully changing the campus environment into a no-fault, problem-solving community rather than continue on the path toward becoming a bureaucratic system characterized by acrimony and retribution. As experienced senior leaders, the president and his vice presidents recognize the potential for the college moving into a downward spiral of low morale and productivity that these administrators had witnessed at other institutions. They want a fresh approach that can be implemented immediately and that would be based on the principles of free expression, confidentiality, and successful outcomes for all involved parties.

All of the administrators believe that issues can best be resolved by those closest to the problem if the institution provides the tools and the opportunity for this to happen. The president knows that El Centro has a Counseling-Human Development Professor who possesses the credentials, skills, experience, and credibility to develop and perform this function. They decide to assign this Professor to the newly designated role of college ombudsperson, inviting her to function as a counselor at large to students, faculty, staff, and administrators. To provide a neutral context, she would report directly to the president, and he would guarantee the confidentiality of her work. Her focus would be on assisting with problem solving, interpersonal conflicts, miscommunications, and any and all relational trust issues, including assistance with negotiating the bureaucracy. She would have license to access any work group and cross all organizational lines in order to informally address problems.

Because of the urgency of the situation, the new position was created and the assignment was made and announced to the college community without the usual and expectedly prolonged processing throughout the organization. It was presented as a distinctive student-faculty-administrator support service aimed at improving relational trust, student retention, and student success.

Predictably, serious objections were raised by various college and district groups:

- Some counseling faculty resented the elevation of one of their peers to such an influential reporting position.
- Some full-time instructional faculty scoffed at the idea that such a position would be viable or helpful.
- Some college administrators were very skeptical about allowing such complete channel-free access to any one person, no matter what the role.
- The president's district colleagues could not believe that he was emphasizing a counseling-faculty role at a time when they were all beginning to de-emphasize and phase out these positions as a cost-saving measure.
- Student leaders predicted that this was an administrative ploy to keep outspoken students at bay; others wondered aloud how one mature white woman could represent the needs of a diverse student body;
- Several staff members said that it was embarrassing to admit that we needed extraordinary measures to deal with these issues.

The president was faced with the dilemma of provoking overt disapproval for arbitrarily deciding to address a serious problem with an unconventional action or risking the consequences of not responding in a timely manner to what could possibly lead to a devastating campuswide decline in climate and morale.

Summary of the Case

The president has detected a sense of unrest among the students, caused by a combination of converging educational trends and social movements. He also recognizes the related anxiety of faculty who are intimidated by the prospects of change and of dealing with overly assertive students. There are signs that some members of the college community are even uncomfortable with the broader community perception that the college has become a minority institution. These issues are being played out most conspicuously on campus by an increased number of complaints, grievances, and interpersonal conflicts.

The Student Code of Conduct and the Professional Ethics Code for staff prescribe procedures for addressing these problems, but have become much less effective in the present environment of tension and change. The president calls on his past experience and present imagination and makes an arbitrary decision to design an informal problem-solving system, create a new college ombudsman position, and appoint a current professor to serve in that position, risking disapproval from campus constituents and loss of credibility if the experiment fails.

Questions to Consider

1. Should the president retreat from efforts to help the college embrace diversity, in the fullest sense of the term?
2. Should the president use a more traditional approach of resolving student and staff issues by causing the student or staff person to pursue concerns through the established grievance channels?
3. How should the president respond to the personal criticism from faculty, student services staff, and other administrators?
4. Should the president propose the ombudsman idea through the more comfortable but time-consuming campus decision-making process?
5. Is the ombudsman service a viable concept for this community college? What alternative approaches would accomplish the same goal?

Thoughts and Analysis

The president decided to proceed with the ombudsman office plan, and appointed the person already on staff to serve in that capacity. Her office was moved to an accessible, easy-to-find neutral area with an inconspicuous entryway, to ensure complete privacy. It is large enough to allow small group meetings of four or five students or faculty who might be involved in the same issue.

Contrary to early signals, and following a low-key introductory period, the service was grudgingly accepted by almost all of the college community. After the second year, an evaluation was conducted, and the results were overwhelmingly positive. The ombudsman program has since been received enthusiastically and with gratitude by everyone concerned. Records indicate that the number of formal disciplinary hearings and grievances have diminished significantly. It is now college policy that all student and staff complaints will be brought first to the ombudsman office. That office has also been designated as the first contact for sexual or other harassment complaints.

A panel of back-up ombudsmen has been established to address expressed preferences related to gender, ethnicity, disability, or age. The panel also provides coverage during times when the ombudsperson might be away from campus.

Administrative time and energy are conserved by having a conflict resolution facilitator available to deal immediately with issues and problems. This immediate response also minimizes the time available for problems to escalate. Campus climate is much improved because of the clear, straightforward, no-fault systems approach to conflict resolution, and the bottom-line intent of helping students and staff solve their own problems has been realized, enabling them to continue their quest for success at El Centro.

Outcomes

The president is now viewed by his colleagues as an innovator and expert in working with controversial and sensitive student and staff problems. In fact, with the El Centro president's permission, most of the other district presidents have since borrowed the services of his college ombudsperson to facilitate problem solving at their own campuses. The most recent tangible outcome was that the El Centro ombudsman service received a commendation from the Southern Association of Colleges and Secondary Schools during an accreditation review.

Bettie Tully is Ombudsperson, Human Development Coordinator, and Counseling Faculty at El Centro College in Dallas. Wright Lassiter, Jr. is President of El Centro.

7. Establishing a Learning Continuum

Karen A. Wells

Context

Lorain County Community College (LCCC) is a single-campus, comprehensive community college located in northeast Ohio in a county that has lost thousands of manufacturing jobs in the past 10 years, more than a thousand of them between 2000 and 2001. The college is the only public institution of higher education in a county that has historically produced the greatest number of associate degrees of any county in the state and the fewest number of bachelor's degrees. The CEO is in his 18th year of leadership of the college. During his tenure as CEO, he has established a distinctive role for the college by strategically engaging the community to raise the educational attainment of Lorain County's citizens from secondary school through graduate school. Dramatic progress has been made since 1995, when the college successfully passed a levy that produced the university partnership that brings eight universities to the LCCC campus to offer more than 30 bachelor's and master's degree programs. LCCC is Ohio's fastest growing college and is guided by its mission: Lorain County Community College, a vital and dynamic leader, serves a culturally diverse community by promoting education, economic, cultural, and community development. The college encourages lifelong learning through accessible and affordable academic, career-oriented, and continuing education.

The community engagement process that was used to shape the university partnership has become a cornerstone of one of LCCC's core values: responsibility to and stewardship of the community. This represents the college's commitment to value the essential support and involvement of the community and to act responsibly in using the resources provided by the community. In its earliest phase, the engagement process brought the education, business and industrial, nonprofit, and faith-based communities together in large groups to demonstrate the need to help people achieve the bachelor's degree. These large group sessions focused primarily on what the college had accomplished in the past, what it was doing at that time, and how a university partnership would bring university instructional services to the LCCC campus. In these large group sessions, participants were asked to identify the programmatic needs of the county relative to market demand. The result was a university partnership that today enrolls over 2,000 students in bachelor's and master's degree programs. Of equal significance, the process resulted in strong connections with the external community.

Subsequently, in 1996, the community engagement process was refined and modeled after the Harwood Institute's civic engagement process. An important outcome of the focus on community engagement was the establishment of a Public Services Institute (PSI) on the college campus. Among its varied responsibilities, PSI organizes, facilitates, analyzes, and disseminates the outcomes of college community engagement activities. The college CEO, using the services of PSI, used the community engagement process to develop a strategic plan-on-a-page, Vision 21. The process that resulted in Vision 21 included 80 listening and learning sessions in which small focus groups of citizens from targeted sectors in the community as well as college employees were asked three questions: What changes are occurring in your field? What should the college do to respond to those changes? And can you offer a building-block idea to the college for the 21st century? The college collected 830 building-block ideas from the 1,100 people who participated in the focus groups. A Vision 21 Council made up of 35 external and 35 internal members worked over seven months to filter through the building-block ideas. They identified six strategic priorities, refined the mission and vision of the college, and identified the core values of the college. Subsequently, 36 initiatives were developed and prioritized to achieve the six strategic priorities, and strategic planning on a page was accomplished.

Summary of the Case

The community served by the college has changed dramatically since 1963, when the college was founded. The county is in the rust belt and has lost major industrial plants and thousands of jobs. This has eroded the tax base for the public schools, and by the 2002-2003 academic year, the two urban school districts in Lorain County were declared to be in emergency status and on academic watch, respectively. Consequently, when state and national foundations targeted Ohio for small high school and early college initiatives, the CEO of the college recognized the opportunity to use the community engagement process to significantly affect secondary education as it had already impacted graduate education in the county. The CEO anticipated that using the community engagement process to impact secondary education as well as graduate education would place the college in the center of a seamless educational continuum. He engaged PSI to organize and facilitate community engagement sessions intended to ensure that internal and external constituents would support small high school and early college initiatives and that external funding would be forthcoming.

Questions to Consider

1. Should the CEO approach the school districts and offer the services of the college to conduct a community engagement process focused on transforming their high schools?
2. Assuming there is interest in engaging the community for this purpose, who should be invited to the community engagement sessions?
3. What questions should be answered by the participants in the focus group sessions?
4. How should the CEO and the superintendents engage their board members with each other and in the process?
5. How should the CEO and the superintendents involve potential funding organizations in the process?
6. How should the information collected during the focus group sessions be reported, to whom, and for what purpose?

Thoughts and Analysis

1. Working with multiple school districts, institutions of higher education, and boards of trustees means accommodating multiple union contracts, policies, and procedures, as well as cultures.

2. Transforming high schools requires flexibility on the part of the Department of Education, the Board of Regents or similar governing body, and four-year colleges and universities.
3. Funding formulas must be revised to ensure that per-pupil funding is sufficient and that the transformational changes are cost effective.
4. Curricula across educational sectors must be aligned, while at the same time, state standards for high school graduation cannot be compromised because of high-stakes testing.
5. Small high schools and early colleges necessitate enhanced student services and require that everyone assume responsibility for student learning.
6. The underlying assumption is that all students can learn and achieve at least the associate's degree.
7. The community engagement process prepares all of the stakeholders to meet the challenges transformational activities always present.

Outcomes

Because the community engagement process has become a cornerstone of LCCC's commitment to community responsibility and stewardship, when the college CEO approached the superintendents of the school districts and offered to work with them to seek foundation funding for transformation of their high schools, both superintendents replied in the affirmative. In fact, both school districts identified the college as their "center of strength" in their subsequent applications for funding.

Throughout the process of developing a response to the proposals of the external funding agencies, five community engagement sessions were held to determine what the community values relative to education beyond high school; to present the concepts of small high schools and early college high schools and to gauge the reactions from community members beyond the leadership level; to identify concerns and perceived barriers to the initiatives for Lorain County; to use community language, provide feedback to the community about their reactions, and help the community to learn and advance its thinking relative to high school transformation. The Community Engagement Plan targeted internal stakeholders (faculty, staff, and administration of the high schools and college; teachers unions; students; and family members) and external stakeholders (employers, government representatives, organized labor, faith-based organizations, law enforcement agencies, and nonprofit organizations) and included small group listening and learning breakout sessions of 8 to 15 people.

As a result of the extensive community engagement process, most stakeholders support the implementation of small high schools in Lorain County's urban school districts as well as an early college high school that will open its doors on the LCCC campus fall semester, 2004. In addition, both initiatives have been funded by state and national foundations.

When the early college high school opens this fall, it will be possible for high school students in the early college high school to earn their high school diploma and their associate degree simultaneously and enter one of the University Partnership's bachelor's degree programs as juniors in college. Lorain County Community College has established a learning continuum on its campus from secondary school through the bachelor's degree and beyond, and the community understands, values, and supports the role the college has played in developing this learning continuum.

Karen A. Wells is Vice President for Learner Services and Chief Academic Officer at Lorain County Community College in Elyria, Ohio.

Part VI

Legal Issues, Politics, and Policy

1. A Web Untangled

Alfredo G. de los Santos Jr.

Context

Immediately after earning my Ph.D. from the Community College Leadership Program (CCLP) at The University of Texas at Austin in May 1965, I accepted the only job offered to me. Folks were not hiring Chicano doctorates in the community colleges in Texas in those days. I went to work as one of the original staff members at what is now Florida Keys Community College in Key West, Florida, as head librarian. The college, founded earlier in 1965, was originally called Monroe Community College because Key West is in Monroe County, and community colleges in Florida had the county as their service area in those days.

The president of the community college technically reported to the county superintendent of public instruction, who in turn reported to the elected county board of education. In effect, the community college was part of the county system of education.

As head librarian of a brand new community college, I got to do what very few people have the chance to do: build and create a library from scratch. I did that for some 11 months until the president promoted me to the position of dean, reporting directly to him. I was responsible for adult vocational and technical education, responsible for building and creating new programs in these areas.

Because the institution was brand new and quite small (as I remember, some 1,000 students were enrolled), all of us had to do a number of things not included in our job descriptions. The president found out that I could write fairly well, and he asked me to take the lead in developing proposals for external funds.

I was responsible for coordinating the planning and writing the proposals for funds from two major sources: the Higher Education Facilities Act (HEFA) of 1963, and the Vocational Education Act (VEA), both of which provided millions of dollars to build up the higher education infrastructure to serve the baby boomers.

The HEFA proposal requested funds for a building to house the transfer-academic programs, library, administrative offices, and so forth; the VEA proposal requested funds to construct a building for the career-occupational programs. The 1960s was the decade when we were building an average of one community college a week in this country. Many of the buildings at these new community colleges – and at institutions of higher education already in existence – were funded through these two acts.

Summary of the Case

In 1966-1967, my responsibility in preparation of the proposals included working with the arts and sciences faculty, the occupational faculty, members of advisory committees to the occupational programs, the executive group, the budget-fiscal officer, and so forth.

I also worked with the facilities planning office of the county school system. In addition, I had to work with the program directors in two state offices in Tallahassee, the state capital.

Given the governance structure then, the county board of education had to approve proposals prior to submission. In spring 1967, we were ready to present the two proposals to the board. In preparation for the presentation, I had briefed the community college faculty and staff, going over the details of space needs, general space layout, and budget.

Both programs required a minimum matching sum from the local governing board. I had gone over the budget very carefully, working with the faculty in each department or occupational program, the chief budget-fiscal officer, and the executive group – especially the president. Everyone involved knew that the local governing board has to provide between $50,000 and $55,000 as matching funds.

A number of the faculty – both academic and occupational – were present at the public meeting of the governing board the evening the two proposals were on the agenda. After the president made a short presentation on the two proposals, one of the members of the board, known to be rather conservative and not too friendly to the community college, asked a series of questions. Some of the questions were: "Mr. President, will this board have to contribute local funds? If so, how much? Where will these funds come from?"

The president, who was sitting at the table with the governing board, responded that no local funds were required, that no matching funds were necessary.

Needless to say, I was very surprised. He had known all along that both programs required some matching funds, however minimal. Two hours prior to the meeting, both the chief budget-fiscal officer and I had gone over the budget with him.

The faculty with whom I was sitting in the audience, who knew exactly what the matching funds would be, looked at me with questioning faces. One of them leaned over and asked, "Did you hear that? Are you going to say anything?"

A lot of thoughts raced through my mind. My president had just lied to the governing board at a public meeting. All my colleagues knew and understood that. They expected me to say something. I was just out of graduate school, and I had no experience dealing with situations like this. I was also away from my home state of Texas and my extended family. I had a wife and two young boys to care for and support. What should I do? I could be fired! Should I just sit there? Who would be blamed a year or so later when the local governing board had to come up with the matching funds? Would I be the goat? Would the president tell the board then that he had made a mistake and accept responsibility, or would he blame me?

I decided that the best thing for me to do was to tell the truth. I stood up in the audience and asked the chair of the board for permission to speak. I told them that I hated to contradict my boss in public, but that the local governing board had to contribute some small amount of matching funds, that we could not be very precise about the amount, but that our best estimates ranged from $50,000 to $55,000.

Questions to Consider

This story, which is a true one, raises a number of questions – personal, political, and ethical:

1. What was the responsibility of the president in this instance? Should he have told the truth to the governing board? Why did he lie?
2. What was my responsibility? Should I have remained quiet? What would have happened if I had not said anything and a year later, the governing board was asked to provide the $50,000 to 55,000 matching fund?
3. What political issues would that have generated? How would the board members react when all of a sudden they found out that they had no choice but to find the funds? What would have been the consequences for the community college, the president, and me?

Thoughts and Analysis

At some time or another, most community college leaders will find themselves in a situation where someone has not told the truth. The ethical dilemma is what to do about it. One can opt not to say anything, in effect committing a sin of omission. It is safe to do nothing.

What happens to a person's reputation when people know that, while one did not lie, one stood idly by while someone else did lie? What are the personal consequences? What happens to someone internally who condones such a thing? Is it possible for such a person to be a real leader? Can one lead with little or no personal integrity?

I decided that I would rather risk losing my job than remain quiet. I decided then and there that I would not break one of the basic values taught to me by my parents and extended family. I don't believe I could have looked my colleagues in the face if I had not spoken up. I don't believe that I could have looked at my own face in the mirror, either.

Outcomes

After some discussion that fateful evening, the governing board approved the submission of the two proposals. The next day I hand carried them to the capital, just in time to beat the deadline. Because of an airline strike, I had to drive from the southernmost tip of Florida to Tallahassee, in the Florida panhandle.

When I returned to my office a day or two later, I found a letter marked "confidential" on top of my desk. It was a letter from the president, telling me that I was wrong in what I had done, that I had humiliated him at the public meeting of the governing board, that he had lost confidence in me, and that I was fired. He would not meet with me.

Later that spring, I accepted a position at Northampton County Area Community College in Bethlehem, Pennsylvania. I was the seventh or eighth employee at this brand-new institution, which I helped to found. We arrived in Bethlehem in late April 1967.

Before we left Key West for Bethlehem, the county superintendent of public instruction fired the community college president. I never saw him after that.

The two proposals were approved by the state agencies and the two buildings were built at Florida Keys Community College. In 1968, now serving as dean of instruction at Northampton, I hired one of the faculty members with whom I had worked at Florida Keys Community College, one who was in the audience that evening when the president lied to the board. When this old colleague and new hire drove up the driveway of our home in Bethlehem, I went out to greet him and his family. The first thing he told me, even before he said hello, was, "It was $52,750."

It took a moment to dawn on me: He was referring to those matching funds at Florida Keys Community College.

Alfredo G. de los Santos Jr. is Research Professor, Arizona State University, Main, and Senior League Fellow at the League for Innovation in the Community College, Phoenix, Arizona.

2. When Politics and Education Converge

Robert A. Gordon

Context

Humber College of Applied Arts and Technology opened in 1967 as one of a system of 22 non-degree-granting postsecondary institutions created to supply Ontario's middle-level infrastructure for the postwar industrial and knowledge-based economy. These colleges were not designed to offer university transfer programs as a formal part of their mandate, but rather to become a viable alternative for non-university-bound students. As such, the colleges concentrated on developing programs, many of a three-year duration, that would allow graduates to obtain meaningful career employment. Recently, the combination of pressure from professional bodies and the demands of businesses on the baccalaureate degree as the minimum credential has begun to alter the playing field for institutions and governments alike.

Summary of the Case

This situation has been most typified in the critical field of nursing. The issue was bound to have direct impact at Humber. A large institution located in diverse, cosmopolitan Toronto, the college had always been heavily involved in nursing, both in graduating students for entry to practice as registered nurses (RNs), and in providing many postdiploma fast-track offerings in specialty areas to upgrade the depth and sophistication of practicing nurses. As part of the college's School of Health Sciences, Humber's nursing program was the largest in Ontario and enjoyed a strong reputation based on high standards and a quality curriculum, delivered by committed, competent, and caring faculty.

Concurrently, health care reform had emerged as a major policy and political issue in Ontario. Nursing was one of the major flash points, having reached crisis proportion. This situation was caused by a variety of factors relating to the squeeze on health care budgets and concomitant escalating workloads of staff, along with early retirement, burnout, noncompetitive wages, insufficient full-time and too many part-time jobs, too few new graduates in the market, and poaching by large American hospitals in states such as Texas, Florida, and North Carolina. For the provincial government, ultimately the only body that could act to address these problems, the relentless pressure from professional associations such as the College of Nurses to legislate the upgrading of their status by requiring the baccalaureate degree as the minimal qualification for entry to practice only raised the stakes. Finally, in early 2000, the provincial government announced that it was going to make the degree qualification mandatory by 2005. Those already practicing under the RN designation, but without a degree, would be grandfathered. The government would also act to ensure that a larger number of new graduates would be available.

Many actors in the field warned that the education and training of nurses presented a political minefield to the government. Nonetheless, the government, through the

Ministry of Training, Colleges, and Universities, decided to proceed with its decision. Some universities immediately argued that degree granting was solely their prerogative and that they should simply increase their nursing enrollments. This scenario suggested that the colleges could increase enrollment in the nursing assistant programs they already offered, to make up nursing enrollment shortfalls in the traditional diploma programs. However, this disregarded the fact that 75 percent of RN education in Ontario was being carried out in the colleges, and that few of the many excellent faculty teaching in the three-year nursing programs were likely to be engaged by the universities, even as their enrollment went up and the colleges' enrollment went down. Conversely, some colleges argued that the solution lay in giving them degree-granting approval for nursing. Not only was this position naïve insofar as few colleges were realistically in a position to offer the degree, but it did not take into account the reaction of the College of Nurses, which, having long battled to gain baccalaureate status for its members, insisted that these degrees must be delivered by established universities. Although the government was in the process of granting some colleges the right to offer a limited number of applied degrees in other fields, the government made it clear that nursing was not going to be one of these.

With such disparate viewpoints emanating from stakeholder groups, the government recognized its difficult position. It soon became clear that some accommodation that would create a working relationship between colleges and universities was essential. Unfortunately, the reality for the colleges, which were eager to and assumed they could cooperate as equals, was that the universities collectively perceived that they had the upper hand and were indeed the senior partners.

The government understood that problems relating to institutional territoriality of degree-granting rights, layoffs at colleges, finding appropriately qualified faculty, increasing lab space, and absorbing higher operating costs at universities all suggested that the only logical solution had to involve colleges and universities acting together. But the government also believed, optimistically, that (a) a major infusion of dollars for operating capital and upgrading of faculty credentials, and (b) a statement that it desired colleges and universities to collaborate harmoniously would be sufficient to produce a smooth and effective transition. In the months following the government's announcement to this effect, it became clear that this harmony would not be easily achieved.

Foreseeing the only viable solution to the nursing crisis, Humber, George Brown College, and Centennial College had entered into discussions almost four years earlier with Ryerson Polytechnic University to develop an integrated, collaborative nursing program in order to be ready when the government moved on this issue. During that time, the agenda focused primarily on academic programming. Despite constant urging by Humber staff, few agreements were reached on matters of policy, operations, or implementation, although Ryerson regularly advised that these would not be problematic. Ominously, one week following the April 12, 2000 announcement, progress ground to a halt. Ryerson's administration advised that they had not resolved a grievance from its faculty, but felt they would be able to do so. By September, not only had they not resolved the grievance, but they now were encountering difficulty in obtaining approval for the entire integrated program (*i.e.*, three years college, one year university), and suggested that the best they could do was an articulated two-plus-two model. They also admitted for the first time that the University Standards Committee and Academic Council would take issue with the qualifications of college faculty and with the fact that the arrangement did not meet the University's 50-percent residency requirement for students, and asserted that these factors would in all probability dilute Ryerson's quality. A huge discrepancy was also revealed in what monies from government funding sources would be required by the universities, which, if taken from a fixed formula, would leave a woefully insufficient amount for the colleges. Because Humber had been assured repeatedly that all matters could be resolved equitably, this new information, in Humber's view, reflected concern about Ryerson's strategic planning abilities and, possibly, bargaining in bad faith.

While Ryerson continued to ask for more time to resolve their issues, Humber realized that Ryerson would not be able to maneuver these matters successfully through its internal governing bodies. Additional evidence began to emerge that supported the perception that university faculty associations across Ontario were being advised to discourage integrated nursing programs. Also, once the government had announced the ground rules, all colleges offering nursing must seek and conclude agreements with publicly funded universities in Ontario in order to qualify for funding; the universities knew then that they could control the process. It became apparent that all colleges were operating from weakness. It also left a bitter taste of betrayal with colleges that had worked diligently on this file for years. Humber was forced to conclude that (a) many of the positions on issues agreed to in principle for four years would no longer be part of the deal, and (b) if it did settle on Ryerson's terms, it would be selling out its own program and faculty. Notwithstanding the facts that students for September 2001 entry into baccalaureate nursing were already being recruited throughout Ontario, and that securing government approval for a new partnership represented major hurdles to overcome, Humber decided that its only recourse at this point was to sever ties with Ryerson as a matter of principle, and to take the risk of seeking another option.

Questions to Consider

At the end of September 2000, the president of Humber advised the provincial government that Humber was unable to conclude a mutually acceptable agreement, and while wishing to support the government in finding positive resolution for outstanding nursing issues, would not capitulate to the terms of Ryerson's constantly changing conditions. The other two colleges, while also having their reservations, continued to work with Ryerson. Humber also pointed out that so much damage had been done to the credibility, trust, and respect between the staff of the two institutions that even a last-minute compromise would not allow a long-term relationship to be sustained. Humber immediately initiated discreet discussions with Ministry officials to suggest that a different arrangement for Humber could still address the government's goals as well as preserve Humber's academic integrity. Several problematic questions required speedy response:

1. Given that almost all colleges in Ontario were also encountering problems in their collaborative relationships with university partners, would the government agree

that Humber was unique in being put in an untenable position and therefore should be allowed to seek a new university partner?

2. If the answer to Question 1 was yes, and considering that realistically a more flexible university nursing partner would not be available in Ontario, would the minister permit Humber to seek a partner outside Ontario? Further, given that there had been a moratorium on all Ministerial Consents for the previous six years, would the government lift that ban to allow a new potential partner access to Ontario? (It would not be feasible that Humber students travel to another province to complete their degrees; they had to be able to undertake the whole program at Humber).

3. If the answer to Question 2 was yes, could Humber then find a new university partner, quickly and successfully conclude an equitable, academically sound agreement, and establish a framework for a long-term (*e.g.*, five years) working relationship?

4. As 2000 had already turned into 2001, would Humber be able to recruit a critical mass of academically able nursing students for a September start?

5. Faced with the fact that all institutions offering nursing were simultaneously recruiting faculty, would Humber be able to attract talented, committed faculty for the new degree-level program?

Thoughts and Analysis

Resolving complex situations of educational public policy in a pragmatic, positive fashion relies at least as much on careful case management, persuasive diplomacy, and dexterity in working within the political system as it does on the seeming logic or educational value of any position. In that connection, here are some suggestions that emerge from this case:

• Before engaging in any activity likely to be controversial, assess and understand the educational and political environments.

• Always play from strength. Never overplay an institution's hand, which could lead to public embarrassment or humiliation. There are no long-term kudos for hubris, bravado, or mishandling sensitive situations.

• All risk taking should be structured in a calculated way that predicts success with reasonable confidence. Never knowingly set up failure by overestimating manageable goals.

• Know and cultivate political allies, who could well vary from issue to issue. Above all, make absolutely sure that the college board and faculty are on your side before taking the issue to the outside.

• Using your best available external political intelligence, know your opponents and neutralize their actions insofar as possible.

• Work hard to develop a track record for delivering on commitments and promises, so that decision makers can have confidence in positive outcomes if they support your case.

• Cultivate relationships and extend personal networks long before their intervention and help on an issue is required. No one likes being obviously used, and it is harder to ask for favors if no bond has been nurtured. No matter what the occupation or rank, remember that everyone is human and requires positive attention and feedback.

- Build credibility by always exhibiting integrity, honesty, and supportive behavior.
- Always take the high road, regardless of the outcome. Win without gloating; lose without moping. Above all, never slander others to further your own cause. Cheap shots can come back to haunt you, and negative behavior will only diminish you.
- Never try to force positive response by embarrassing the government into action; you will rarely win public relations contests with the government's ability to put a favorable spin on its position. Government officials can have long memories, so there is little value in winning a battle yet losing the war.
- It is very difficult to gain approval for your case if the action to be taken does not advance the government's agenda. Understand the government's point of view and needs on every issue. Focus on providing resolutions that help you and solve their problems. The goal is to have converging agendas produce mutually beneficial results.
- Never forget that in the final analysis, it is not only about education; it is also about perception and politics.

Outcomes

While there was no guarantee that answers to the preceding questions would all be positive for Humber, the administration was reasonably confident that it could come up with a workable plan and implement it effectively. For one thing, Humber already had strong links with the University of New Brunswick (UNB), one of the oldest and most respected institutions in Canada, and was already engaged in an active partnership, offering a degree completion Bachelor of Nursing – both at Humber and through distance applications, using faculty from both institutions – for practicing registered nurses who did not have degrees. This successful relationship provided the catalyst for discussions about offering a generic nursing degree at Humber. A team was sent to Fredericton, New Brunswick to work out details for offering a collaborative, integrated Bachelor of Nursing (BN) degree.

The fit between the two institutions proved excellent, not only because they respected and trusted the strengths of each other, but also because there was value added for each institution. Humber sought a partner that would allow Humber to teach most of the courses; grant the degree; monitor curriculum, evaluation, and teaching; and accept graduates to a master's degree without prejudice. For its part, UNB was eager to access the vast array of resources available at Humber and in Toronto (*e.g.*, teaching hospitals), and saw a new revenue stream and strong potential for qualified applications to its Master's in Nursing.

Equally important, UNB was not a fair-weather friend. It would not give in to the pressures of some of the Ontario university community to resist any arrangement with Humber. And it was able to circumvent major deal breakers that Ryerson could not. For example, UNB was already experienced in offering its degrees at off-site locations and did not believe that such arrangements would threaten its own residency and faculty hiring regulations. Within two months, a Letter of Understanding had been signed by both institutions, essentially allowing Humber faculty to teach all four years of the program, an arrangement that met Humber's needs and expectations for the delivery of a high-quality degree-level program. This helped immeasurably in recruiting students because they could remain at one location for all four years, and it helped in attracting faculty who were interested in teaching at the degree level.

While continuing negotiations with UNB, Humber attended with due diligence to other critical areas. Foremost was securing a signal from the government that this initiative would receive support. Humber's Board of Governors did its part by unanimously passing a motion supporting the administration's actions to procure Ministerial Consent for the proposed partnership with UNB. Also, as it approached the minister for support, Humber was always careful to couch its case in terms that stressed the integrity of the college and its faculty as it strove to offer high-credibility nursing education, which ultimately could only help Ontario address its nursing crisis.

Humber also leveraged the fact that it already had the largest nursing program in Ontario, graduating annually more than 10 percent of the province's total RNs. It also recognized that the government was somewhat disappointed with the manner in which the universities had handled nursing education with the colleges, who seemed more concerned about preserving their monopolistic territory than helping to solve a serious public-policy issue. In short, Humber tried to position itself not as self-serving, but rather as attempting to find a pragmatic solution to help government address the nursing issue. As one example, Humber stressed it could always take more students into the program if that would help solve the pending shortage of nurses.

Following several exploratory discussions with the minister, it was confirmed that if a sound, collaborative agreement with UNB could be reached, Ministerial Consent allowing UNB to offer its program in Ontario with Humber would be forthcoming, together with the funding that had already been made available for Ontario-based partnerships. Though this process provided some anxious moments as it worked its way through the government formalities, Ministerial Consent was given on March 9, 2001.

Humber still had to launch the program with a class of students in a scant five months. The college had passed the point of no return in Ontario; failure was not an option. Ontario's universities were upset that Humber had been allowed to deviate from the ground rules, while many colleges were unsympathetic because they had found no alternate route to improve their own relationships. More important, however, was the fact that the minister had spent considerable political capital in championing this issue within her government and had absorbed some political heat personally. Humber owed the minister no less than rewarding her faith by delivering on its own end of the bargain.

Although recruitment of students could not formally begin until consent had been received, Humber had been quietly lining up prospects and was ready with a focused campaign to market the nursing degree. Many potential candidates had already accepted offers from other institutions, but Humber was not without some significant assets, including the strategic location of the college in the western quadrant of the populous Greater Toronto area; the fact that no competitors offered nursing there; the availability of all four years at one campus; the established reputation of Humber in the nursing field, particularly with hospitals; and the fact that, traditionally, many nursing students enroll as adults, making late personal educational decisions. A respectable 89 qualified registrants began classes in September 2001. By September 2003, the program had come into its own, with 253. Humber's nursing program remains the largest in Ontario.

Humber sought to attract highly qualified faculty from a restricted field thoroughly combed through for months by other institutions. Again, Humber had some strengths, one being that some staffing could be deferred to subsequent years, since in September 2001, the college would only be offering the first year of the degree program. There already existed a large pool of qualified professionals working in this city of nearly six million. The trick was to attract some of the best to Humber. The combination of Humber's location (*i.e.*, suburban, with no commute to downtown); reputation of program and quality of working environment; and an optional research-publication requirement attracted a number of excellent candidates. For example, Humber hired some formidable people from hospitals. For these new faculty, college teaching was a way of continuing to use their expertise in a less stressful environment. By September, Humber was able to round out its faculty with outstanding people, while conversely, Humber faculty who had been teaching diploma nursing but did not wish to teach in the degree program found a satisfactory niche in the Registered Nursing Assistant Program. By January 2004, the degree nursing program at Humber had put down solid roots, the partnership with UNB had proven to be strong and harmonious, and, encouragingly, there were even signs that relations with Ryerson's program had begun to improve.

Robert A. Gordon is President of Humber College Institute of Technology and Advanced Learning in Toronto, Ontario, Canada.

3. Expanding Enrollments: Legal Ramifications for Widening the Open Door

Patricia Grunder

Context

Santa Fe Community College is located in a university community in rural north central Florida. The college offers a comprehensive range of programs and serves as the community's area vocational technical center. Over 30 years ago, the college was first in the state to successfully invite high school students onto the campus to participate in a wide range of vocational course offerings. One of the hallmarks of this innovative program has been the admission of students who may be considered marginal in terms of their academic performance. The success of the college's intervention with at-risk populations has served as the impetus for program expansion to include Associate of Arts options in general college-transfer studies as well as the fine arts and allied health programs. Students often find themselves in classes with college-age students (although a full range of high school courses is offered on campus for students not academically eligible or interested in the college track) and are held to the academic rigors of a college curriculum. The benefits accrued from this program have been immeasurable to the students and their families. Many graduate from the college with certificates and degrees that enable them to enter the workforce or transfer to a university as upper-division students. Others leave with one-third or more earned college credits. There is no cost for tuition associated with the program. It is a model for time-shortened degree opportunities that complement the national educational accountability imperative.

Historically, the counseling staff has managed Student Services for this program. A team of three counselors and the director of the program administer all facets of student life including discipline. This staff, according to stipulations in the district's articulation agreement, work in tandem with the student's high school of record to ensure that school-board policy as well as college policy is followed when an incident occurs. In the 30-plus years of the program's existence, these policies have evolved to include the more complex range of incidents that surround today's student populations. Considerations for federal legislation including the American Disabilities Act and Title IX as well as state legislation, as it pertains to felony crimes, have found their way into school and college codes of conduct.

An 18-year-old male was arrested outside a college building for severely assaulting his 17-year-old girlfriend during the course of an argument. Both individuals were enrolled full time in the college's High School Dual Enrollment Program. The college's police department responded and arrested the male student for felony battery because of the severity of the young woman's injuries. Eighteen-year-olds are considered to be adults in legal matters; however, if they are still enrolled in high school, important procedures surrounding adjudication must be followed. The young woman was transported to a local hospital for treatment. The young man was removed from campus and taken to the county sheriff's office for processing. The director of the High School Dual Enrollment program was notified of the incident, consulted with the police department, and then began the task of notifying the students' parents and their high school of record. Although the young man would face official charges through two law enforcement agencies for his actions, the college and the high school also reserved the right to adjudicate the student through the student-conduct process. In light of the fact that both students were enrolled full time at the college, the high school chose to adjudicate the matter according to the college's student-conduct code. The director of the High School Dual Enrollment program worked in tandem with the college's judicial officer to ensure compliance with the college's policy and procedure. Notification was made to both parties, and the date for a hearing was set.

During the course of establishing communication with each student's home high school, attention was drawn to the fact that the assailant had a Section 504 plan on file. The community college also had this document on file. Although the Section 504 plan dealt specifically with learning accommodations for student success, an interesting point was raised regarding the existence of such documentation for a high school student. A process known as Manifestation Determination must review any high school student with a Section 504 plan on file. This process reviews the facts of the case to determine whether the student's documented disability contributed to behaviors that resulted in judicial charges. A 10-day notification must precede the Manifestation Determination committee's deliberation. If the criteria are not met and the college or school proceeds with adjudication, then the Manifestation Determination process could be called into question, resulting in an appeal of the committee' decision or legal action on the part of the assailant. It should be noted that parents have the right to waive the 10-day notice. An interesting point surrounds the fact that the Manifestation Determination process only involves students in the K-12 system. College students are not required to follow this procedure.

Summary of the Case

Community colleges are welcoming high school populations onto their campuses by offering time-shortened degree opportunities as well as alternatives to the traditional high school environment. Community college codes of conduct historically have been written for an adult population, without consideration for students who still maintain high school status for institutional reporting purposes. Any action on the part of a high school student that brings the student into conflict with the college's code of conduct must be adjudicated with the understanding that certain extenuating circumstances may influence how a case can be prosecuted.

Two high school students attending a community college full time as participants in the college's high school dual enrollment program were involved in an altercation that sent one student to the hospital as a victim of assault. After the college communicated at length with each student's home high school, it was determined that the existence of a 504 was in place for the assailant at both the high school and the community college. Even though this plan did not specify any concerns or recommendations regarding violent behavior, it was determined that a hearing must first be held to determine whether any conditions stipulated in the 504 influenced the student's behavior in the altercation. It was imperative that this manifestation hearing be held prior to any judicial ruling in the case. If the hearing had not been held, it could have resulted in an appeal by the student in question, or legal action on the part of the student and parents or legal guardians, or both.

Questions to Consider

1. Should colleges modify their judicial conduct codes to consider the consequences of prosecuting students with Section 504 plans?
2. Should the applicant screening process be expanded to include an interview with a school counselor to explore the details of the student conduct history?
3. Should parents receive a special communication, independent of the student handbook, during the application process for the program about their rights, should a judicial hearing be required because of student conduct?
4. Should high school and community college officials receive additional training from in-house counsel on matters surrounding the legal rights of students who retain dual status as high school-community college students?
5. How should the director of the program and other college officials deal with the press, should the incident become publicized?

Outcomes

As a part of the information-gathering process, it was determined that the student was required to have a hearing establish Manifestation Determination. In other words, did anything documented as a part of the student's 504 have a bearing on the student's behavior? Although the 504 on this student only addressed actions that would affect learning success strategies – *e.g.*, must sit in the front of the room, must be given extra time during examinations, and so forth – it was determined upon a complete review of the student's record that violent behavior had been documented. This information was not admissible in the hearing to determine manifestation. Because the community college judicial board found no relationship between the recommendations in the student's 504 and his behavior, the student was allowed to proceed to the judicial conduct hearing as stipulated in the college's conduct code.

The college's legal counsel, along with the school board's legal counsel, had determined that if the Manifestation Determination hearing had not been held, then both the school board and the college could be open to an appeal of the decision and to a possible lawsuit. The judicial conduct committee ultimately adjudicated the student guilty for the assault charges. The committee recommended that the student be removed from the high school dual enrollment program at the college and be returned to the high school of record. Criminal charges are still pending against this student in county court.

The most important factor in this case surrounded the need to consider a high school student's relationship with the laws governing two academic entities. Even though an articulation agreement existed between the school board and the community college, special consideration was not given to Section 504 regulations as they pertained to student learning and student conduct. The lesson learned was that consideration for state and federal legislation must be factored into student participation – not as a deterrent to the open-door policy of the community college, but as a precautionary measure to ensure that equal protection is provided for every student.

Patricia Grunder is Vice President for Innovation and College Advancement at Santa Fe Community College in Gainesville, Florida.

4. The Sexual Predators

Bill Mullowney

Context

Valencia Community College, founded in 1967, is a multicampus public institution serving Orange and Osceola Counties in Central Florida. Annual credit enrollment was 41,620 in 2002-2003, which, combined with annual continuing education, conferences, and seminar enrollment, yields total annual enrollment of over 53,000. Valencia employs roughly 2,500 full-time and part-time employees who serve on four campuses and at various other sites throughout the two-county service area. The college is governed by an eight-member District Board of Trustees appointed by the governor of Florida.

In July 2002, new provisions of Florida law became effective that require registered sexual predators and sexual offenders to notify the state or the sheriff, as appropriate, of enrollment, employment, or the carrying on of a vocation at an institution of higher education in Florida. Each change in enrollment or employment status must be similarly reported. The state or sheriff must promptly notify each institution of the sexual predator's or sexual offender's presence and any change in the sexual predator's or sexual offender's enrollment or employment status. One major gap in the law is that the issue of what the institution is to do in response to the receipt of this volatile notification is completely ignored. Other than the basic federal requirement of advising the campus community where the information on registered sex offenders can be obtained (in many cases, a state law-enforcement website), institutions of higher education in the State of Florida responding to specific notifications now are on their own in balancing issues of educational mission and accessibility with issues of safety and liability.

Summary of the Case

Sure enough, shortly after the implementation of the new law, and three weeks into the academic session, Valencia received official notification from the state that three of its enrolled students were registered sex predators or offenders. Upon receiving the notices, the college requested and received from law enforcement and corrections authorities background information on the three students. Students One and Two were 21-year-old males who pleaded guilty to participating in the gang rape of a female high school classmate some three years earlier, as described in agonizing and disturbing detail in the arrest reports. They had both served a brief time in jail and were on probation. Student Three was a 37-year-old male who had pleaded guilty about seven years earlier to fondling and molesting a young female babysitter as she slept on his living room couch, she being engaged to watch his two children while he and his wife attended a late-ending event. This encounter was also described in discomforting detail in the arrest records. His plea bargain resulted in minimal jail time and probation. None of the students had any conduct records with the college, while they all were carrying full class loads for which they had fully paid.

Questions to Consider

1. What, if anything, should the college do in response to the receipt of the sex offender notifications from the state?
2. On what basis and by what process could or should the students be separated from the college?
3. If the students remain in classes, what are the obligations of the college to notify faculty, students, and staff of their presence? What other steps should be taken to minimize risk and disruption to the educational environment?
4. In a community college setting, how should or does one balance the health, safety, and welfare of the educational community with the part of the mission of the college to provide educational access – an open door – to those motivated to pursue higher education?
5. Which college officials should be notified, consulted, or involved in the decision-making process and the implementation of the decision?

Thoughts and Analysis

Given that the sex offender-predator notifications from the state as received by the college are the result of a statutory mandate, one would guess that guidance on what to do with the notification would also be found in statute. Shocking as it may seem, this is not the case. Looking further into Florida law for guidance only raises more safety concerns. Section 775.21, F.S., the Florida Sexual Predators Act, states in part,

"Repeat sexual offenders, sexual offenders who use physical violence, and sexual offenders who prey on children are sexual predators who present an extreme threat to the public safety. Sexual offenders are extremely likely to use physical violence and to repeat their offenses, and most sexual offenders commit many offenses, have many more victims than are ever reported, and are prosecuted for only a fraction of their crimes."

And Section 943.0435, F.S., states in part,

"The Legislature finds that sexual offenders, especially those who have committed offenses against minors, often pose a high risk of engaging in sexual offenses even after being released from incarceration or commitment and that protection of the public from sexual offenders is a paramount government interest."

This is strong and threatening language for a community college with an open door and a commitment to learning-centeredness, one that values, among other things, an accessible, supportive, and safe environment in which people learn and work, supporting a mission to reach out to potential students of diverse backgrounds to provide affordable, accessible learning opportunities.

Perhaps, we thought, a quick survey of other colleges and universities in the state would reveal a common pragmatic theme in institutional responses to sex offender-predator notifications that could form the basis for our emerging procedure. Again, this inquiry was unproductive. Florida higher education institutions had chosen extraordinarily disparate avenues of response, ranging from no action at all to admission with specific notification to students and faculty in the offenders' classes to instant dismissal (and many others). This review and analysis did afford the college an opportunity to consider the myriad factors involved in formulating our response, such as the rights of the offending students versus the rights of the academic community, the disruptive impact of notifying students and faculty that a sexual offender-predator was working in close proximity, and finally the assurance of a safe educational environment.

Our consideration suggested the beginnings of a process: instant separation with an opportunity for appeal to satisfy college due-process requirements. Further, reinstatement should not be easily obtained, and should require a rigorous evaluation of essential facts, including the nature of the crime, recency, mitigating circumstances, rehabilitation, and counseling records. Reinstatement, if it occurs at all, should be granted only when the specific facts overwhelmingly support a conclusion that the student poses virtually no risk to the community and that the student's presence would not be disruptive. There was a very good counterargument that this kind of approach defeated our mission and denied educational access to people who needed it most; besides, went the argument, where do you want these people, in jail or in school?

Mission is important, but at a very basic level, so is safety. It is clear that the college would have difficulty answering the potential question from the lawyer of a student or faculty member sexually assaulted by a registered sex offender allowed to enroll. "Let me get this straight: The state told you that this dangerous person was enrolled at your school, further detailed the danger in statute, and you thought it would be a good idea to let them stay and prey on my client…" In this case, the safety of students, faculty, and staff and freedom from disruption of the educational environment would generally overrule the arguments based on educational access.

With the procedure as outlined above identified, the search for guidance continued with a review of all college policies that possibly could provide the basis for implementing this procedure, and one policy in particular appeared to be relevant. Based on §1001.64(8)(a), F.S., one of our policies states that the college may consider the past actions of any person applying for admission or enrollment and may deny admission or enrollment to an applicant because of misconduct, if determined to be in the best interest of the college.

Outcomes

The college adopted a procedure, now contained on all college admission applications, that states in part,

> "The College has determined that the presence on campus of students officially designated as Sexual Offenders/Sexual Predators would be disruptive of the orderly process of the College's programs and/or would interfere with the rights and privileges of other students.… Accordingly, the College denies

admission/enrollment to students who are officially designated as Sexual Offenders/Sexual Predators. If an academic term has already begun at the time the College receives notification, the student's admission will be revoked, and an administrative withdrawal and refund for fees paid for the term in progress will be processed. The student may also receive a credit for required textbooks purchased for classes from which the student is withdrawn. This decision may be appealed to the Vice President for Student Affairs."

The college then notified Students One, Two, and Three that their enrollment was to be ended, in accordance with the procedure. None of the three students appealed the action.

Bill Mullowney is Vice President for Policy and General Counsel at Valencia Community College in Orlando, Florida.

5. Effective Political Advocacy at Kirkwood Community College

Steve Ovel

Context

Kirkwood Community College, located in Cedar Rapids, Iowa, serves a seven-county area in eastern Iowa with a population of 400,000 and an immediate urban area of 140,000. Last year, 15,000 students enrolled in college-credit classes and another 50,000 in noncredit continuing-education classes. Like the other 14 comprehensive community colleges across Iowa, Kirkwood serves as a core partner in Iowa's one-stop workforce development center system. The size of the college and the scope of its mission make legislative and political advocacy an important priority, especially in a time of declining state education and job-training resources.

Kirkwood and Des Moines Area Community College (DMACC), located in Ankeny, Iowa, are the two largest community colleges in the state. Both institutions have employed full-time governmental relations staff since the late 1970s. For many years, the state's other 13 community colleges depended on the efforts of these staff members and a small team of multiclient, professional lobbyists. Until the mid-1990s, a small handful of people thus carried the concerns of the state's 15 community colleges to 150 state legislators.

These efforts, however, yielded important results. In response to the recession and farm crisis in the late 1970s and early 1980s, and in recognition of the need to diversify the base of the state's economy with new technologies and businesses, the Iowa legislature for the first time made efforts toward stimulating economic development. The Iowa New Jobs Training Program, Chapter 260E of the Iowa Code, was established in 1983 to provide state funding support for training new employees in new business startups or the expansion of existing basic-sector businesses. This program uses a pregeneral fund diversion of employee state income tax withholding and is delivered by and through Iowa's system of 15 community colleges, which can issue tax-exempt or taxable bonds for up to 10 years on behalf of eligible businesses. Since 1983, Iowa's community colleges have issued $466 million in bonds through 1,800 training agreements, helping to support the pledged creation of 126,341 new jobs in Iowa. For projects finalized in 2002, the average salary per newly created job in the Kirkwood service area was $39,850.

In 1989, funding support was established for retraining of the incumbent workforce in the form of the Iowa Jobs Training Program, Chapter 260F of the Iowa Code. This program is designed to foster the growth and competitiveness of Iowa's business and industry by ensuring that Iowa's existing workforce has the skills and expertise to compete with any workforce outside the state of Iowa. This program is also delivered through the community college system and also uses a pregeneral fund diversion of employee state income tax withholding. Funding is made available through the

Workforce Development Fund, established in 1995, which has distributed nearly $40 million toward retraining Iowa's incumbent workforce. Since the inception of this program, more than 89,000 Iowa workers in 650 companies have participated in more than 1,000 training projects.

While celebrating these significant developments in job-training programs, Kirkwood leaders believed that a more cohesive link among community colleges across the state would more effectively impact legislative programs. The voices of business and industry leaders also needed to be enlisted to more effectively convey to state legislators the potential of partnerships between community colleges and business and industry to satisfy the state's competitive need for job training and economic development.

Summary of the Case

Iowa experienced significant progress in the 1970s and 1980s toward state-aided economic development programs that used the services of the state's community college system. Even so, by the mid-1990s, leaders of Kirkwood Community College recognized the need for a more cohesive effort toward political advocacy with other community colleges in the state. Further, Kirkwood leaders sought to partner with leaders from business and industry to raise awareness on the part of state legislators of the potential these partnerships had to positively affect the state's economic development efforts.

Questions to Consider

1. Why is political advocacy increasingly important to community colleges in today's challenging economic, budgetary, and political environment?
2. What role do the president, leadership team, and board of trustees play in ensuring an effective political advocacy system?
3. How can a community college and its state organization best coordinate to carry out an effective political advocacy program?
4. How does a community college use its students and business and labor partners as political advocates?
5. How does a community college build a strong case statement for promoting a specific legislative initiative?

Thoughts and Analysis

1. A community college needs to be aggressively and actively involved in the political process in order to expand its education and job-training funding base to meet the needs of its service area. However, community colleges must differentiate themselves from all other sectors of education and show how they can respond most effectively to the economic development needs of their region.
2. The president, board of trustees, governmental relations representative, and other members of the leadership team must share a vision for legislative advocacy that includes priorities and measures of success. They must also take an active, visible role in the legislative process. Efforts must be made by the whole team,

not just one or two individuals, to be known personally by all the elected representatives serving the region. Legislative leaders must be invited to campus but also supported off-campus.

3. The resources of smaller colleges are limited; even so, a cohesive effort by community colleges across the state ensures better communication among the colleges, business and industry leaders, and state legislators, resulting in more effective and uniform efforts locally and across the state toward improved workforce development initiatives.

4. Involving business and labor leaders in political advocacy not only cements relationships for the good of the local community, but also raises the bar for the state in creating better workforce and economic development programs.

5. Involving the voices of community college students, along with business and industry leaders, is an effective way to build strong cases for legislative initiatives. Partnerships are the foundation of successful program development. Successful programs lay the foundation for future program development.

6. Successful legislative initiatives can occur even in times of economic distress, but a strong political advocacy presence in the legislative forum is needed in both good and bad economic times.

7. Relationship building is at the heart of successful political advocacy for community colleges. The personalities, interests, and ideologies of legislators and of their staff must be known, and the legislative process must be understood from their perspectives.

Outcomes

Since the mid-1990s, Iowa community colleges have worked together more cohesively, with two organizations providing the structure for better communication: The Iowa Association of Community College Trustees (IACCT) and the Iowa Association of Community College Presidents (IACCP). The IACCP meets yearly to formulate the legislative framework for the IACCT board and, after receiving its endorsement, provides the legislative platform for the year.

In 1998, Kirkwood initiated a study of area businesses and their projected needs for employment and skills. The Skills 2000 Commission was formed. This group of area business and education leaders was enlisted to study employment needs of 33 major east-central Iowa companies. The study, resulting in the *Skills 2000 Report*, provided a strong case statement for approaching state legislators with concerns about losing workers to other states and countries.

The Iowa legislature responded to the *Skills 2000 Report* and to the more unified community college system's lobbying efforts by establishing the Accelerated Career Education (ACE) program in 1999. This program has since provided $13 million in operational funding via an income tax withholding diversion, and $23 million in infrastructure appropriations to community colleges for the creation or expansion of high-wage, high-skill technical degree education programs. Kirkwood and other community colleges have used this program to work with local employers to identify and meet workforce needs in emerging technology-based career fields. Kirkwood's ACE programs are also coordinated with new Career Edge Academies, which help local high school students gain real job skills and experience for employment in Iowa.

In 2001, after a significant decrease in the state budget and support for community college funding, and in response to a state senator's comment that legislators were not hearing from community college students and business partners, Kirkwood launched an aggressive statewide letter-writing campaign, asking community college students and employer partners to participate. Over a thousand business partners already serving on Kirkwood's vocational-technical advisory committees were also enlisted. These valuable voices served to increase the visibility of the community college system and its partnerships.

In 2003, the Iowa Legislature responded to the weakening economy by establishing an economic stimulus package called the Grow Iowa Values Fund. Once again, Iowa's community colleges were given a significant role in this new state initiative. Of the $503 million marked for Grow Iowa Values Fund distribution in the next seven years, Iowa's community colleges are projected to administer $75 million in support of their existing successful technical education and job training programs.

In 2003, Kirkwood conducted an update of the *Skills 2000 Report*. The Cedar Rapids-Iowa City Technology Corridor committee, of which Kirkwood is a member, sponsored the study. The committee was made up of representatives from chambers of commerce, economic development groups, higher education, and government. Using 10 industry sectors, more than 150 companies located throughout Kirkwood's service area were identified. The report produced by the committee, titled *The Skills 2006 Technology Corridor Report*, provides an assessment of employers' skill and employment needs. A common theme among employers in 1998 was still evident in 2003: Gaps in essential skills (team building, communication, customer service, and problem solving) and technical skills (math, writing, and computer applications) existed among job applicants and incumbent workers in the region. Kirkwood is using the report to lobby for increased funding for existing programs.

Across the country, there are few state-aided workforce and economic development portfolios like that found in Iowa. For effective state political advocacy, Kirkwood's leadership team has recognized the need to link more cohesively with the other community colleges in Iowa and to enable the voices of students and business leaders to be heard by state legislators. Throughout their experiences with political advocacy, Kirkwood leaders have found that three principles hold true: Partnerships are the foundation of success, success breeds success, and positive results can occur even in negative economic times.

Steve Ovel is Executive Director of Governmental Relations at Kirkwood Community College in Cedar Rapids, Iowa.

Part VII

What?

1. Leading a College and a Life Divided

David C. England

Context

Most presidents find unexpected challenges when they begin their tenure at a new institution. Like the candidates, boards of trustees and key administrators want to make the best impression possible during the interview process. Accordingly, I was expecting the unexpected when I assumed the presidency of the Des Moines Area Community College District (DMACC) in October of 2001. But the contrast between my initial experience and the reality I confronted was so extreme that leading the college stretched my abilities to the limit. In confronting the challenges I encountered, having a background in Continuous Improvement and Institutional Effectiveness proved to be of much more value than simply satisfying accrediting agencies. What I call databased management made it possible to unite the faculty and staff behind a set of common goals, and to transcend the lack of initiative and passive-aggressive conflict that had existed for over a decade and begin to develop more cohesive working relationships among cabinet members, board members, and the state's community colleges. I say *begin* because a serious mistake in my personal life prematurely ended my presidency.

Summary of the Case

At first, the situation seemed ideal. The former president, who, along with the chair of the board, was serving as search consultant, recruited me. He made it clear from the first that he was impressed with my work as president of North Lake College of the Dallas County Community College District in opening new technical programs, focusing on workforce development, forming numerous partnerships, and reaching out to previously underserved populations. Those accomplishments fit well with his own priorities, and he was obviously very supportive of my candidacy. I had never heard of DMACC, and neither had very many of my colleagues, but it was located in the state's capital city and offered most of the advantages of urban living without most of the problems. It was an ideal size, from my perspective (around 13,000 students), with six campuses – not too big to be manageable and not too small to have a significant impact. And it was known for having numerous high-quality and high-tech programs and for innovative workforce development programs.

The interview went well. There was no major turbulence at the campus forums, just the usual concerns about academic freedom, lack of adequate funding, and service-area needs. While I sensed competitiveness between different campuses and different functional areas, the conflict did not seem very intense. Dinner with the six vice presidents was pleasant, collegial, and, because of the stimulating conversation, lasted two hours longer than scheduled. The interview and dinner with the board went smoothly and reinforced the chair's assurance to me that "We want you to run it. We'll support you and stay out of the way."

From the first cabinet meeting, it became clear that there were two factions among the vice presidents. One faction, in private conversations with me, repeatedly accused the other of subverting my leadership and of being controlled by the previous president. The other faction maintained that its opponents were unfair to those they didn't like and accused them of saying one thing to me and doing another. Over time, I learned that my predecessor had favored the latter faction and had adopted a micromanagement style late in his presidency that discouraged the faculty and staff from innovation and risk taking, and that placed him as the arbitrator of most decisions. Because of the culture this style had created, I was bombarded daily by questions about the most mundane matters and was frustrated by the lack of initiative caused by the fear of making a mistake.

Early on, I had invited everyone on campus to contact me if they had suggestions on just about any issue. I soon learned that virtually everyone felt shortchanged. Academic faculty and staff felt they got less than their share of funding; after all, they had most of the students. The technical programs feared the academic programs were plotting to take over the technical math and English courses (I was surprised that in Iowa the technical students take different academic courses taught by different faculty). One campus was so paranoid that any change suggested by the central administration was viewed as hostile. One very remote campus had a perpetual chip on its shoulder. The most diverse urban campus felt discriminated against and misunderstood. The large main campus was protective of its history of controlling the district.

I soon found that most board members had a pet issue or staff member. And most felt that the vice presidents had evil intent toward their favorites. My predecessor had juggled all this turbulence by choosing winners and losers and by giving each board member the appearance of control over his or her chosen dominion.

In addition to these internal challenges, externally, I found a state that had historically underfunded, misunderstood, and underappreciated its community colleges. Even though it was clear that Iowa desperately needed economic development, the community college role in this important effort was not encouraged in state policies and priorities. While there was a shortage of technical workers in the state, community colleges were not rewarded in any way for growth, and expensive technical programs did not receive any supplemental funding. Because of the inadequate state funding, community college tuition in Iowa is one of the highest in the nation, effectively pricing who could benefit most from a technical education out of the market. Additional funding for training for business was available but did not address the need for new workers with technical degrees to attract new businesses. And the relationship between the state's 15 community colleges was characterized by a longstanding lack of trust and a fierce independence.

Questions to Consider

One of my friends once told me that the key to leadership was to "figure out which way everyone's going and get out in front." Obviously, there were too many fronts here for that to work. Maybe it's because I'm lazy, but my worst nightmare is to be solely responsible for everything on every level, which I began to think everyone expected me to be. Besides, I was addicted to accomplishing things, and we weren't going to accomplish much if everyone didn't take some responsibility and initiative.

1. How could I get the administration, faculty, and staff to transcend factionalism and work ambitiously toward accomplishing a common set of goals?

2. How could I make my vice presidents and executive deans into a cohesive team?
3. How could I encourage my board members to focus on policy and not administration?
4. How could I get the state to recognize the importance of its community colleges?

Thoughts and Analysis

Perhaps I am naïve, but I've always believed that if everyone is involved in identifying needs, in setting logical, data-based priorities, and then held accountable to making a contribution to advancing those priorities, incredible things can happen. I believe that a CEO's main job is to design and implement a system that, eventually, will make him or her irrelevant by embedding into the culture of an institution a cyclical process that results in continuous improvement with little or no intervention.

The system I have now implemented at four very different community colleges was particularly well suited to DMACC. The faculty and staff felt they had no influence over the direction of the college. I divided the college into functional work groups and appointed one representative from each group to the Strategic Planning Council, ensuring that each campus and each employee group was represented. It was each member's responsibility to gather input from his or her work group and report back on the activities and progress of the council on a regular basis. This strategy was designed to provide everyone on campus with an opportunity for input and to hear the points of view of different work groups and staff levels without the tedious and time-consuming process of endless forums and meetings. But I also used a number of other techniques to improve communication and involvement: attending division meetings, distributing a regular president's newsletter campuswide via email, hosting monthly luncheons with the president for randomly selected faculty and staff, and so forth.

I appointed tri-chairs of the council – an administrator, faculty member, and support staff member – but I initially led the council myself, because there was a history at the college of the work of task forces and committees being ignored by upper administration. Before the first meeting, I gathered and studied environmental scanning data myself including the results of a campus climate study, student outcomes data, penetration rates, demographic trends, workforce needs, and regional trends and issues, and prepared a thick notebook for each committee member. I brought in an environmental scanning expert to teach them how to use the data. I conducted meetings myself for a number of reasons. Not only did that strategy demonstrate my commitment to the process, because I was more familiar with the data than any of the members, but I could guide the goal-setting process toward the college needs and opportunities I had already identified. Not that I dominated the deliberations; many valuable insights came from the members. Since the college had a history of factionalism refereed by the president, I felt my leadership was necessary to move the process forward expeditiously. As conflicts arose, I could coach the combatants to base their positions on data, which led to the resolution of many longstanding disagreements and misunderstandings.

The council was able in six months to agree on a new mission statement, a discrete set of goals for the college, and the need for six new task forces. Each council member was assigned to work with a group leader to formulate work-group objectives based on the college goals and to help lead the development of individual action plans by each work-group member. At each level of this system, outcome measures were identified and tracked. I also used this system to develop a Facilities Plan, a process that had always been characterized by intense conflict. The Facilities Planning Council, through the use of objective data, was able to reach agreement on a plan to expend the funds raised through the local tax for capital expenditures for the next 10 years.

Concurrently, I attempted to decrease the intensity of the campaigns under way for my approval among the vice presidents and executive deans by forming a new cabinet that included the executive deans and that systematically met on different campuses every two weeks. I relied on these group meetings and on periodic individual meetings with each member to make it clear that opinions should be based on facts, solutions were needed more than problems, and that the past should be left in the past. I was making some progress, but it was slow and frustrating trying to change a well-established culture. And I made the mistake of listening to what I wanted to hear rather than what I needed to hear.

I now believe that I should have asked for members' resignation to be accepted or rejected after my first year to motivate them to abandon their conflicts and focus on what I was trying to accomplish. At the time, I was afraid that the paranoia such an extreme step might create would intensify the conflict. It might also have created more dissension on and inference by the board, because most board members had their favorite administrators.

Each month, one or more board members would offer administrative direction on some issue either by phone or, many times, during open board meetings. The chair who had hired me would be helpful in reminding board members that their job was policymaking, but he resigned after my first year to become a state senator. Without his leadership, I began to spend a significant amount of my time keeping individual board members happy and questioning whether I truly had the support of the board. I had planned a board retreat with a consultant on policy governance to facilitate a well-defined agreement with the board on our respective roles. Whatever that turned out to be, I hoped I would at least learn specifically what they expected of me. One major success with the board was gaining quick, noncontroversial approval of the 10-year facilities plan. In the past, individual board members had lobbied to increase their campus' share of the funds or to move their campus' project up in the timeline. At the board meeting where the plan was proposed, the lobbying started but quickly stopped when I explained that the plan had received unanimous approval from a committee with all campuses and functional areas represented and was based on a facilities-use study and data on regional needs and growth.

Externally, I horrified my fellow presidents by conducting an aggressive campaign to promote the importance of community colleges and gain recognition for their significant role in the economic development the state so desperately needed. I used data on the lack of technical workers in the workforce and comparisons with community college funding in other states in numerous speeches, meetings with legislators, and newspaper articles. The prevailing philosophy among the presidents had been that demanding too much attention would inspire retaliation from the powerful Regents universities, who received generous state funding and had one of the lowest university tuition rates in the nation, and would result in more state interference in the administration of the colleges. One often-heard excuse given by policymakers for not providing sufficient support and funding was that there was too much disagreement and conflict between the colleges. To help remove that excuse, we agreed to develop a common course-numbering system as a first step to becoming more unified; we were also seriously discussing, and began developing, a more centrally coordinated lobbying effort. The governor began making positive and supportive statements about community colleges in his speeches, and the newspaper ran editorials recognizing the importance of a technical workforce in economic development, as well as urging additional funding for community colleges.

Before my year-and-a-half tenure as president of DMACC so abruptly ended, I was proud of the work of the Strategic Planning Council and the Facilities Planning Council, but I was frustrated with my progress on other fronts, particularly with my cabinet and with state policymakers. One of my vice presidents had warned me that change was slow to happen in Iowa, if it ever happened at all, but I stubbornly and perhaps foolishly continued to follow F. Scott Fitzgerald's advice to develop "the ability to recognize that everything is hopeless and yet remain determined to make it otherwise." I was exhausted and needed a break. Be careful what you wish for . . . .

On March 12, 2003, approximately 20 narcotics agents tore my home apart and falsely accused me of being a drug trafficker. *The Des Moines Register* ran article after article, many on the front page, accusing me of drug trafficking. After an aggressive, multiweek investigation that included an audit of the college's finances, a review of all my emails, and interviews with scores, if not hundreds, of my colleagues and acquaintances, nothing was found to be out of order and no one who even knew I used marijuana, much less sold it, was discovered. I was, however, using marijuana to help me relax and go to sleep, and I eventually pleaded guilty to possessing marijuana and sharing it with my wife. It was a big mistake that has so far destroyed my career. I hope that no one else experiences what I have experienced over the past 10 months. However, in an article about my experience published in *The Chronicle of Higher Education*, "one well-known leader of a sizable college district remarked to a reporter: 'If all of us who hit one when we went home at night got busted, there'd really be a leadership crisis . . . .'"

Outcomes

My experience as a college president, my long-distance running, and my family have helped me survive this horrible ordeal.

As a college president, one learns to live one day at a time, one challenge at a time, because to deal with every issue and problem that confronts you is humanly impossible. One develops a thick skin, expects his or her privacy to be routinely violated, and expects the media to exaggerate anything negative they can find. One also must develop a confidence and faith in his or her ability to survive crises and to find solutions to complex and challenging situations. Without these qualities and skills, a college president would have a hard time getting out of bed in the morning.

I have run four to six miles every day since 1978. A long-distance runner has to learn how to pace himself and concentrate on each step of the run rather than think about the finish line. A runner has to learn how to endure pain and keep going when he feels like quitting. And for me, running has given me a lot of confidence. At the end of each run, I always feel like, "If I can do this, I can do anything."

I have a loving and talented wife, a daughter who graduated from college in December, and a son who is a high school senior who, I recently learned, shares my love of writing and literature. This experience has brought us much closer together and has made me realize what is really important in life. I spent much too much time relentlessly chasing my next accomplishment and then isolating myself to escape the stress and frustration that inevitably resulted from excessive impatience and ambition. I think this experience has taught me how to pace myself in life as well as in running.

I made a big mistake, but I've learned a lot from it. I believe I now have more to offer in my personal and professional life than ever before. I hope I get a chance to prove it.

David C. England is former President of the Des Moines Area Community College District.

2. Is an Employment Contract Worth the Paper It is Written On?

James S. Kellerman

Context

The North Orange County Community College District is a large multicampus district with colleges in Fullerton and Cypress, California. In addition, the district operates a large adult education center in Yorba Linda, California. The college district is governed by a five-member elected board of trustees with delegated responsibility for administering the district given to the chancellor (CEO).

Summary of the Case

In February 1986, the CEO became chancellor of the North Orange County Community College District. During his previous 25 years, he had established a state and national reputation of leadership and integrity. He was a member of numerous boards and committees of higher education and was the recipient of several national awards. In October 1988, the CEO was given a four-year written contract extension, which included a pay raise over the previous year. As chancellor, he earned $97,000 annually plus fringe benefits.

On March 2, 1989, the board, represented by two trustees, the chair, and vice chair, informed the CEO that his contract, which was to terminate on June 30, 1992, would not be renewed. They also stated that the board would encourage and financially support the CEO in his efforts to seek other employment. In addition, they said, "We'd like to keep this confidential, and we'll write you a good recommendation." In fact, the board chair called the CEO the next morning and used a phrase that he invoked frequently: "This was strictly a business decision." He then reinforced his pledge to support the CEO financially.

Then, on the afternoon of May 2, 1989, seven months after his contract had been renewed, and without notice or opportunity to be heard, the board president informed the CEO that he was on administrative leave, effective immediately, and that he should clear out his office by 5 p.m. The CEO was fired on May 18, 1989.

Two versions juxtapose as to why the CEO was summarily placed on leave and fired. The board's version is that the CEO had committed various acts of impropriety – none of these sexual or criminal in nature – and he was fired for cause. Violations included using district postage on two occasions without authorization; receiving a personal bill at work; asking a staff employee to hold a Home Interiors party; purchasing a personal computer at an educational discount; failing to promptly repay a travel advance of $500; and similar miscellaneous violations. The CEO's version is that due to a power struggle on the board of trustees (initiated by the retirement in December 1988 of the most senior trustee), the CEO's termination was political, as a new power team wanted its own man.

Although the CEO is normally present at all board meetings, he informed the board members in early January that he would be absent from several meetings during January and February while he attended to his daughter, who was in the hospital with a life-threatening illness. It was during these board meetings that the trustees secretly conducted their internal investigation. In fact, one of the trustees admitted that during board deliberations concerning replacing the CEO, the president of the board stated, "If we're not satisfied with the new chancellor, we will just do another witch hunt on him, like we did on the CEO". A subsequent year-long investigation by the Orange County District Attorney's office found no criminal wrongdoing.

During and after the investigation by the board, one of the trustees informed the press as to the allegations concerning the CEO: "The CEO may have misappropriated thousands of dollars." "The CEO may have coerced other employees to misappropriate money." "The CEO may have used district funds to purchase his computer." These comments made the front page of the *Los Angeles Times*, as well as many other local and national publications. Subsequent discovery revealed that each allegation was false. However, as a result of this publicity, the CEO was shunned by colleagues and was forced to resign from all his state and national boards and committees.

On May 1, 1989, the CEO's 7-year-old son underwent emergency surgery for a malignant brain tumor. On May 22, 1989, the board, by special vote – although informed of the recent surgery as well as the fact that the son was undergoing chemotherapy – voted to terminate the CEO's health benefits, effective immediately.

After four months, the CEO obtained a new job in Missouri at 60 percent of his previous salary, with no benefits. The new job is a relatively low-level administrative position with a budget of $250,000. The district budget was in excess of $70 million when the CEO was chancellor.

The CEO sued the district and the trustees for breach of contract, including lifetime health and retirement benefits he would have received had his contract been completed; emotional distress due to particular susceptibility to stress at that time and due to the fact that the conduct by the board, especially in the comments to the press, was an unexpected consequence of employment; defamation of character; and violation of Labor Code 1050, 1054 (blackballing), based on negative quotes to the press made by the board president after the CEO was fired (treble damages). In addition, the CEO asserted that malice would be proven, particularly in view of the fact that the trustees knew the allegations were pretextural, and that the firing was a witch hunt. Nevertheless, the board portrayed to the press that the allegations were serious and substantial. The CEO sought punitive damages from the district, whose assets exceed $70 million dollars.

Questions to Consider

1. Was the board of trustees obligated to provide the CEO with a meaningful opportunity to respond to the grievances before firing him?
2. Did the board of trustees breach the employment contract with the CEO?

3. What recourse did the CEO have when the board of trustees placed him on administrative leave and told him to clear out of his office?
4. How should the CEO deal with the press?
5. Should the board of trustees have given the CEO an opportunity to find another job?
6. Should the CEO have taken legal action against the district's board of trustees?

Thoughts and Analysis

1. The CEO is the only employee directly responsible to the board. However, boards should establish policy parameters to ensure that the selection, evaluation, and dismissal procedures for all employees are legal, fair, clear, and appropriate.
2. The success of the board-CEO relationship depends on a shared sense of purpose, open communication, honesty, and mutual support.
3. The relationship between the board and the CEO should be open, frank, and mutually supportive. Without a shared sense of purpose between the board and the CEO, and without mutual respect and trust, a college will experience difficult times.
4. The primary purpose of an evaluation is to bring the CEO and the board together to discuss how their performance and priorities affect the educational program and services to students. An evaluation process, written or otherwise, designed to get the CEO hurts operations and morale of the entire institution and the image of the college in the community.
5. When board members are at odds with each other and the board is split on most decisions, the CEO's job security is frequently at stake.

Outcomes

In May 1989, the North Orange County Community College District placed the CEO on administrative leave and terminated his employment without benefit of due process. Various members of the board of trustees chose to bring allegations of misconduct directly to the media, rather than to the CEO personally. In fact, the trustees refused to ever sit down and discuss the specifics of the allegations with the CEO. Instead, they instructed their attorney to bring the accusations before the local district attorney's office in the hope that a criminal action would be filed. After a bona fide investigation was conducted, the D.A. found no grounds to file charges and dropped the case.

The CEO felt compelled to bring a lawsuit against the district and various trustees for breach of contract, fraud, and defamation. In addition to the approximately $250,000 the district spent in public money in defense of this case, on October 26, 1994, it paid the CEO almost $400,000 to avoid a trial on the merits. Not surprisingly, since the entire episode was provoked by political infighting, the district trustees continued to be legally embroiled in an internal action over nonpayment of its own attorneys' fees.

In a prepared statement, the CEO said, "Occasionally, I feel I would rather have kept my reputation intact and my career on track than receive a name-clearing hearing in the form of their check to me five years after I was fired. On the other hand, when I consider that the incident presented me with the opportunity to relocate to a wonderful state

(Missouri), to work for a tremendous organization (Missouri Community College Association), and to have more time to enjoy my family, I realize that reputation and career climbing are meaningless ambitions compared with focusing on things that matter."

James S. Kellerman is the Executive Director and CEO of the Missouri Community College Association.

3. Between a Rock and a Hard Place

Larry W. Tyree

Context

The institution, a comprehensive community college with an enrollment of some 6,000 students, is governed by a nine-member board of trustees appointed by the governor of the state. At the time, many of the board members had considerable longevity, resulting from an absence of term limits and from the same political party controlling the governor's office for multiple consecutive years.

Summary of the Case

Chairing the board for more than a decade was a strong and powerful but fair and objective individual. During the initial part of his tenure, the young and inexperienced president was more than a little intimidated by the influential and wealthy board chair.

Not only were all the trustees politically well connected and community leaders, they were also good friends with each other. The camaraderie between them was such that after most board meetings, the trustees and the president would retire to a local watering hole and discuss any number of matters over a couple of adult beverages. This occurred without negative consequences in spite of state laws to the contrary.

In meetings, the business of the board was conducted quite informally, almost casually. While allowing for ample discussion of items and input from all trustees, when it came time for formal action on an item, the chair would, without exception, say, "Mr. Black moves, Ms. Brown seconds. All in favor?" During the president's 10 years of attending board meetings when that particular chair presided, he never heard a person actually make or second a motion, and because of their personal affinity for each other and enormous respect for the board chair, no one ever objected.

After years of determining the college's banking relationship based on political expediency and with no regard for financial efficiency, the board finally acquiesced to the recommendation of the chief executive officer and chief financial officer to bid out its banking business. A request for proposal (RFP) was painstakingly prepared so as not to make any of the district's banking institutions ineligible to respond to the RFP.

Between the time the RFP was issued and the deadline for the interested financial institutions to respond, one of the more senior trustees, a respected professional in the district, found himself in need of a substantial personal loan. He went shopping for the lowest interest rate he could find, visiting virtually all of the banks in the district who had requested a copy of the RFP.

The problem with the trustee's interest-shopping excursion was that he promised to vote for the proposal to the college from the bank that offered him the lowest interest rate on the personal loan he was pursuing. He also promised to persuade enough of the other trustees to support that proposal, indicating that he could control the outcome of the vote. Perhaps it could be called a form of bartering. Certainly, it was a breach of board ethics.

As one would expect, calls came pouring in to the president's office from the various lending institutions. That the local newspaper, an archconservative antigovernment publication, was never tipped off is astonishing. The editor would surely have seen to it that the story appeared in his newspaper on Page One, above the fold.

Fortunately, the college was spared a public relations nightmare. The reason none of the banks chose to contact the news media could have stemmed from the respect they had for the college coupled with a desire not to embarrass it.

After confiding in and conferring with the college's chief financial officer, it was determined that the president was between a rock and a hard place, for all the obvious reasons.

Questions to Consider

1. Should the president have directly but privately confronted the bartering trustee?
2. How should the president have responded to the irate banking institutions?
3. Should the RFP process have been immediately terminated and started anew?
4. Should the president's first response have been to seek the advice of legal counsel?
5. Should the issue have been discussed at a cabinet meeting in order to gain staff input?
6. What was the president's duty, if any, to inform other trustees of the controversy?
7. Should the matter have been discussed in an open, public board meeting, inviting representatives of the various banks to appear and offer their versions of what had transpired?

Thoughts and Analysis

It was deemed inadvisable by the president to directly but privately confront the bartering trustee. Besides potentially damaging his relationship with that board member, the decision was made that this was a board matter.

The president should have assured the banking institutions that this was clearly an exception to the values, standards, and operating procedures of the college and that the matter would be dealt with promptly and decisively.

The answer to the question as to whether the RFP process should have been terminated and started anew is, "Maybe; maybe not." Had the eventual ultimate solution not materialized, the process probably should have started afresh after a lapse of several months.

Whether to seek the advice of legal counsel in a matter like this is determined by a number of variables. As it turned out, the decision was made not to do so because of the closeness of the relationship between the involved trustee and the board attorney.

The president determined that the sensitivity of the matter involving a board member precluded a discussion at a cabinet meeting, given that the cabinet was composed of student, faculty, and classified staff representatives. Committed to the practice of no surprises, the president felt he did have a duty to apprise the other trustees of the controversy. How he chose to honor that duty is revealed in the outcome of the case.

The president and the college's public information officer were adamantly opposed to the matter being discussed in an open, public board meeting. Protecting the image of the college as well as the reputation of the involved board member was their reasoning.

Outcomes

Fortunately, the college dodged a bullet! Immediately upon learning about the issue from the representatives of the banks, the president did not call the board chair, but paid him a personal visit. He explained all he knew about the situation, admittedly with trepidation. The seasoned, powerful board chair said something like, "Worry no more. I will handle it."

So how was it handled? For starters, the chair read the offending board member the riot act. That they were close personal friends made no difference whatsoever in the chair's reportedly explosive conversation with and direct remarks to the trustee. His next course of action was to personally call the chief executive officers of each of the banks where the bartering had occurred. During his conversations with the banking officials, the chair reiterated the president's assurance that this was an exception to the college's values, standards, and operating procedures. He assured them that no such situation would ever again occur and that the trustee in question would not attend the board meeting at which the banking relationship decision would be made.

If the chair had not had close relationships with the banking executives, and had he not enjoyed their enormous respect, this approach likely would not have been successful and may even have backfired.

The banking contract was eventually given to the bank that – in the collective opinion of the trustees save one who was not at the meeting when the vote was taken – was in the college's best interest, and this happened without event or incident.

So how did the president comply with his no-surprises duty to inform the trustees? At the social gathering of the trustees after the meeting at which the banking decision was made, the board chair asked the president to reveal all the details. Amazed though they were at what had transpired, the trustees were profuse in their praise of and appreciation to the chair for his adept handling of a potential powder-keg situation.

Larry W. Tyree is a professor in the College of Education and Director of the Institute of Higher Education at the University of Florida in Gainsville, and Executive Director of the National Alliance of Community and Technical Colleges. He is a Senior League Fellow, League for Innovation in the Community College.

4. The Arrested Vice President

Alice Villadsen

Context

Brookhaven College is the second largest of the Dallas County Community College District colleges, located in the northern suburbs of Dallas. The student population has been in rapid transition from what was a predominately Caucasian demographic to one that is reflective of the rich diversity of the county. The fastest growing minority group is Hispanic, at 20 percent; African Americans and Asians comprise 13 percent each; and international students make up the remainder of the 50 percent minority population at Brookhaven. Students represent more than 100 nations and collectively speak 85 languages.

The president reports to the district chancellor, who answers to an elected board of trustees, several of whom have strong agendas to represent the needs of minority communities. The president had served for six years. On her arrival, she had inherited a seasoned cabinet of vice presidents. She led Brookhaven through an analysis of strengths and weaknesses during her first year, moved the college to select and endorse a new focus on student success, and prepared the college for its 10-year reaccredidation study and visit. During her six-year tenure, the college grew 30 percent in credit and stayed steady in noncredit enrollments even during the downturn of the economy following 9/11. Student credit headcount each semester exceeds 11,000.

Summary of the Case

A young Hispanic administrator was on the fast track to leadership at the college when the president arrived. Bilingual, energetic, and smart, he was known for his entrepreneurial approach. He was dean of business and continuing education. During the third year of the president's tenure, the long-serving vice president for instruction took a year's sabbatical, and with the support and encouragement of the chancellor and board, the president appointed the young administrator as acting VPI.

During the year, he became a strong and vocal member of the president's cabinet. Willing to tackle hard issues such as an instructional budget shortfall, inequity of faculty loads within some divisions, and data-based evaluation of instruction, he impressed all with his insight and forcefulness. He initiated a partnership with a university in Spain and developed teaching contracts with his country of origin and with Mexico. He traveled extensively in establishing the international programs. Upon the return of the VPI, and with that veteran's strong support, the president decided to promote the young administrator to a vice presidential position; she named the returning VPI as executive vice president, and she engaged the returning administrator in mentoring the younger man further as a possible successor.

Mentoring and correction of the young man had been required several times both before and after he was named vice president. He had a reputation for taking risks and testing college policies. On many occasions, the president and the vice president had privately counseled the young man over unplanned and unexpected absences and over his arrogant manners. Twice, the internal district auditor questioned his travel paperwork and requests for reimbursement. However, work assignments were always completed well and mistakes were not repeated, once addressed.

During the second year of the young man's tenure as vice president, the president began to note more instances of unexplained absences, odd illnesses, or emergencies at home, as well as distractions at work. Confronted by the president about these issues, he indicated that he was re-examining his intention to seek further community college leadership options and an eventual career as a community college president, an intention that he had confided several times previously to the president. He was instead "examining other options," perhaps in his home country. Finally, the young man indicated that he was flying home for an interview within the national education department. The president felt some relief over that possibility, having decided that her best efforts at mentoring were not helping.

The next day, the president was contacted by a reporter who indicated that the young administrator had just been arrested in Florida and was accused of money laundering, visa fraud, aiding criminal activity, and other charges. Arrested with an associate of questionable reputation who had aided the young man upon his arrival into the United States years before, the vice president had been caught in a sting operation by the FBI. The reporter asked the president for a comment.

As the facts became clearer, it was evident that for months, the young man had been planning a major investment in his country of origin, had bragged that he could get foreign students into the country through F1 visas at Brookhaven College (for a large fee, of course), and could manipulate the legal system in his home country through relatives and friends in high places.

The president was faced with these immediate challenges: managing the huge media interest in the story (front-page news in three states, daily calls from print and television news reporters, interest from higher education publications); dealing with the visa fraud allegation and the possible breach of international student admissions to the college; anger, disbelief, and resentment among college personnel concerning the young administrator and his actions; college reputation issues in the local community, the state, and on the national scene; legal issues including employment status, open-records requests, security of equipment and communications access; possible ramifications for upcoming SACS reaccreditation visitors; and notification of the board of trustees.

Questions to Consider

1. What means could the president use to discover the facts about the arrest?
2. Should the president speak to the press? When? If so, what should be the message?
3. What should the president's first actions be once the facts of the arrest were confirmed?
4. Should the president terminate the young administrator? If so, when and how?

5. How should the president deal with the internal community? The board? The external community?
6. What actions should the college take to ensure the legality of the college's processes with international student admissions and visas? What operation might be compromised?
7. What should the president report to SACS? Why or why not?
8. What should be the role of the campus police? The information technology director? The public information officer? The cabinet officers?

Thoughts and Analysis

The president was committed to the growth and development of young administrators, particularly minority ones, in that she was well aware of the dearth of well-prepared leaders to take over strategic positions at hers and other community colleges. She had been encouraged in the mentoring of the young man by her supervisor, her board, and other highly placed leaders in the community college movement who also were hoping to find future minority leaders. And yet her own instincts told her that shortcuts to leadership seldom worked, that the young man's lack of real teaching and student-development experience was obvious, and that his troublesome unwillingness to attend to the details of policies was a bad sign. She sought counsel on several occasions about ways to steer the young man or the advisability of terminating his relationship to the college.

Outcomes

Following the arrest, the president's natural tendency and willingness to be open about details within the bounds of legality worked well. Through wise counsel and reliance on the college's public information officer's contacts with media and law enforcement out of state, the president was privy to as much information as possible as early as possible. The public information officer became the primary contact and confidante to the president during the crisis. The college was kept informed, as were the local communities and national community college publications. The approach of sharing information also helped to heal the brokenness that the college felt about the administrator's betrayal of the college trust. However, the president's openness resulted in one misquote that caused her to appear rather naïve and foolish. Her own professional reputation suffered as a result of the incident and the misquote. She eventually wrote an article about the incident. Others in community college leadership came to aid her, citing similar incidents at their own institutions.

Securing all records that might be needed by police and FBI and by internal auditors was a quick decision that proved to be important. Whenever any legal authority produced requests, the college was in a position to provide documentation that had not been tampered with in any way. Such quick action, immediately upon notification of the arrest, was one way that the college president could take control and show good-faith efforts at disclosure. The same was true for initiating a call to the Southern Association of Colleges and Schools followed by a letter requesting that the visitors pay particular attention to admissions issues. As a result of these actions, no college personnel were ever called to testify in the trial. Materials were already available to lawyers, law enforcement, and the media. The SACS visitors arrived two weeks after the incident and confirmed that all was in order at the college. And the external auditing firm hired to examine the multicultural center found no breaches in the international admissions processes.

Termination of the administrator proved impossible until after either the end of the young man's contract or his indictment and plea, scheduled for months away. Therefore, the president used paid leave and then a formal separation agreement with the administrator in order to move as expeditiously as possible toward closure. Working with the college lawyer to provide guidance in both employment and disclosure issues was crucial to the smooth conclusion of the whole affair. The young administrator resigned quickly. He eventually chose to plead guilty to one count out of the four in his charge and to provide testimony against his former associate. At the time of this writing, he is serving time in federal prison.

The college survived the incident, completed successfully its accreditation visit, and has continued to grow in student enrollments and in staff hires. However well handled, the truth of such incidents is that they shake the foundations of an institution and test a president's leadership capabilities. Once is quite enough to have to deal with an arrested vice president.

Alice Villadsen is President of Brookhaven College in Dallas.

Part VIII

Fundraising

1. Re-Energizing Your Board

Brenda Babitz

Context

Monroe Community College (MCC) in Rochester, New York, was founded in 1961 to help address a critical shortage of nurses regionwide, and opened in September 1962 with a first-year enrollment of 720 students. Since then, MCC's enrollment has grown steadily, the curriculum has been greatly broadened, and new programs are continually being developed to meet changing demands in both the private and public sectors. Now the largest college in upstate New York, MCC offers 83 degree and certificate programs and annually enrolls more than 36,000 full- and part-time students.

The Monroe Community College Foundation (MCCF), an institutionally related 501(c)(3) public foundation, serves as a repository for all private support and nongovernmental gifts received on behalf of the college. Since its inception in 1983, the MCCF has raised millions of dollars in private-sector funding for scholarship aid, faculty enrichment, program innovation, new learning technologies, classroom resources, and student life.

The foundation is guided by a 40-member board of directors that meets quarterly and whose members are drawn from Rochester-area business, civic, and charitable organizations. One-quarter of the current directors are MCC alumni. All alumni activities are integrated within the foundation. Twelve operating committees report to the foundation's 10-member Executive Committee, which meets six times a year. The foundation completed its first capital campaign in 1996, exceeding the $4 million goal by more than one-third, and is now in the final phases of a second campaign, Building on Success, which is fast approaching the campaign's $10 million funding goal.

Summary of the Case

With a mature, energetic board of directors, the Monroe Community College Foundation has forged new ties with the region's public and private sectors; raised substantial funds; and developed broad community support for the college. Yet, as Building on Success nears completion, foundation leadership has sensed that some board members are experiencing fatigue and are uncertain of postcampaign expectations. With these factors in view, foundation leaders planned and conducted a two-day retreat largely focused on developing ideas and strategies that would (1) create an effective bridge from the current capital campaign to a larger, wide-ranging postcampaign program; and (2) strengthen the board's overall capacity to determine and direct the foundation's future course.

Questions for Consideration

Recognizing that a successful campaign results in changes and tensions as well as in sustained growth, the foundation's retreat agenda included four basic questions: As a board, what must we do

1. to best prepare ourselves for tomorrow's opportunities and challenges,
2. to maintain our focus on fundraising,
3. to refine relationships between board and staff, and
4. to partner with the college most effectively?

Thoughts and Analysis

During two days of frank and fruitful discussion, board members considered the college's educational, social, and economic impact upon the Greater Rochester community. They looked at the forces driving change, especially in the corporate and academic cultures, and sought to anticipate what resources MCC would need to best serve the people of upstate New York in the years ahead. What they found were compelling needs for a workforce with strong skill sets, industry-tailored curricula, workplace-compatible learning resources, and community outreach to underserved populations throughout the region. Within each, though, was a rewarding opportunity for the foundation to benefit Greater Rochester, and by the retreat's end, board members emerged not only recommitted to the MCCF's core values, but even more passionate in their resolve to further the MCC cause through fundraising and friendraising.

Approving a five-year plan to strengthen linkages with local business and industry, dramatically increase the number of MCC Foundation-funded scholarships, and encourage large-scale participation in foundation initiatives and fundraising, board members began mapping broad routes and specific roadways to each objective.

The essential first step: a communications plan to assess educational priorities, develop the MCC/MCCF response, and provide a basis for updating the foundation's own strategic plan from the bottom up. A second prerequisite: re-evaluating the board's composition and preparation, employing such yardsticks as communitywide representation, accountability, roles, and participation. In the longer term, the board would seek to build new staff competencies; expand partnerships with the private and public sectors; strengthen revenue streams, principally the unrestricted funds generated by annual giving and special events; and increase both participation and the income derived from planned giving.

Outcomes

In developing postcampaign activities that will align fundraising goals with community strategic initiatives, strengthen revenue streams, and highlight MCC's newly emerging centers of excellence, the foundation now looks to appoint a transition team of four board members plus one representative each from the faculty and administration, who can help guide the MCCF toward 2008.

The members of this transition team will center their agenda on four critical issues: (1) successfully completing the current campaign, (2) determining best approaches in support for MCC's centers of excellence, (3) identifying community-based opportunities for foundation involvement, and (4) evaluating unmet priorities and future special initiatives.

With the transition team activated, a subcommittee to the Committee on Board Development will develop and construct an action plan for invigorating the board itself. Recommendations may include but not necessarily be limited to member orientation and preparation, group and individual performance benchmarks, board self-management, and structural and organizational changes that may be necessary to carry out the board's strategic plan and the transition team's action plans.

To create an ongoing dialogue with those on the campus and beyond, a foundation task force will look to design and implement an MCCF Community Forum. With guidance from the college, the Community Forum will be a catalyst and resource for developing a joint communication and marketing task force.

To assess the effectiveness of committee actions planned and undertaken in concert with the strategic plan, the foundation's Executive Committee will review the portfolio and performance of the foundation's 12 existing committees in order to effect and implement the changes recommended by the transition team.

Even as the MCCF transition team is in formation, we will begin measuring the foundation's progress toward 2008, from achieving the capital campaign funding goal and increasing both annual-fund and planned-giving involvement to energizing the board; improving and broadening communications, marketing, and public relations; and furthering appreciation of MCC as a community asset worthy of community support.

Success in each of these endeavors remains predicated on the commitment of MCCF Board members, individually; through their roles in advocacy, donor cultivation, and solicitation; and as a group, working to provide wise counsel and leading by example.

Brenda Babitz is President of the Monroe Community College Foundation in Rochester, New York.

2. A Firm Foundation

Allen Edwards

Context

Pellissippi State Technical Community College is a multicampus comprehensive community college located in Knox County in East Tennessee. The college operates from a main campus near Knoxville, and, as this case began, operated two satellite campuses that served a two-county area of about 450,000 people. Pellissippi State is part of the Tennessee Board of Regents System, which governs 13 community colleges, 6 universities, and 27 technology centers. The college receives its funding from state appropriations and from student tuition and fees. Local governments provide no financial support to Pellissippi State. The college president had been at the college for eight years at the time of this project.

The main campus of the college is relatively new, having been built on a technology corridor on the western edge of Knox County 15 years ago. The rationale for the move was to provide space for growth on a 125-acre site and to provide technical training for industries projected to move into the technology corridor. When the new campus was completed and the college moved most of its operation from downtown, many citizens, particularly those among the minority community, felt that the college had abandoned them in order to be closer to the affluent western suburbs. In fact, the college kept its downtown campus and subsidized bus service to the new campus in an effort to pacify those who objected to the move.

Ten years after Pellissippi State moved its main campus to the western edge of the county, another long-time east Knoxville educational institution, Knoxville Catholic High School, decided to build a new facility and chose the western part of the county for its new site. Their rationale was that most of the current and future students would come from west Knox County, and that the move was fiscally sound for them as a private institution. This move angered and frightened many of the business people and residents of east Knoxville. They were concerned about the many buildings on the east side that were already vacant. They expressed feelings of abandonment and felt neglected by most of the mainstream organizations in the city.

The president of the college had visited the Catholic high school a few years earlier and had expressed interest in acquiring the facility if it ever became available. Remembering this, the bishop of the diocese called to let him know that the church would prefer that the campus remain an educational facility; he wanted to know if the college would be interested in purchasing it for $2.15 million. Furthermore, the bishop wanted an answer within two weeks, because the mayor of the city had expressed a desire to purchase the building for use as a police training center. The mayor had the money and was anxious to close the deal. Neither the college nor its foundation had cash in hand to purchase and renovate the facility.

Summary of the Case

Pellissippi State had a rare opportunity to fulfill a commitment to serve all of the people of the community by purchasing and renovating the Knoxville Catholic High School building for use as a satellite campus. The college had only two weeks to develop a plan and secure substantial financial commitments from the community in order to move forward with this project. The college could not commit funds from the Board of Regents to this purchase. The college's foundation was new and did not have money for this acquisition. A big player in the community, the mayor, was against the college's purchasing this building because he wanted it for a police training academy.

Questions to Consider

1. Given the short time frame, how should the president proceed?
2. How can the college use the bishop's influence, since his desire is that the facility retain an educational function?
3. How can the president use the foundation board most effectively?
4. Can the president involve the media in some positive way?
5. What should the president report to the Board of Regents office during the process?
6. How can the mayor's disapproval be dealt with in order to avoid having him oppose the college's position on future projects?

Thoughts and Analysis

1. It was important for the college finally to fulfill its commitment to providing access to education by locating a campus in the heart of a minority neighborhood.
2. Because of the bishop's influence, other support for helping the building remain an educational facility should be available among Catholic organizations and individuals.
3. The mayor's desire to put a police training facility in the heart of the minority community was not a popular idea with many.
4. The short time frame given to move ahead with this project might actually make it an attractive idea for the foundation to embrace, since busy board members would know in a very few weeks whether or not this goal was going to be accomplished.
5. There was a great deal of sentiment in the government and business sectors that the college would be a good partner and a possible source of pride for the east Knoxville community.

Outcomes

The Pellissippi State Foundation decided to move forward with the campaign. Within two weeks, the college had secured a silent partner that guaranteed the bishop the money if Pellissippi State could not raise it during a capital campaign. This gave the bishop an incentive to work out a plan with Pellissippi State and to turn down the mayor's offer to purchase the facility.

The silent partner who came to the assistance of the college was a local Catholic hospital foundation. Several factors contributed to the hospital foundation's willingness to provide this quick assistance. First, the bishop had publicly stated his desire that the facility remain an educational institution. Second, the hospital foundation had several key board members who were friends of the college. Third, the college president and the CEO of the hospital were well acquainted, having worked on several community projects together. When the president called the hospital CEO to ask for help, the hospital foundation board needed only a few days to decide to back the college. The arrangement was kept secret in order to avoid interference with the college foundation's fundraising efforts. The Catholic hospital foundation's intent was to assist the college, not to purchase the property for the college.

The college's foundation board took up the challenge immediately. A principal member of the board stepped forward to lead the project. Within a week, several major prospects had been contacted. When approached by the president and the foundation chair, the county executive committed $500,000 to the project. When asked for $500,000 to meet the county commitment, the city mayor declined, saying that this project was not a priority for the city. (Later in the campaign, the city did commit $500,000 when minority leaders approached the mayor about becoming involved). Another major contributor in the campaign was a recently formed local foundation that committed $500,000 within days of being asked. Another local foundation committed $500,000 over five years, and the Catholic hospital foundation committed $200,000. In the final accounting, the college raised almost $3 million, allowing the college not only to purchase the facility but also to upgrade rooms and equip many of the laboratories. The campaign was completed six months early, and the campus opened six months early as well. The campus has become a center for many community activities and has been recognized by local community groups as one of the most important assets in their neighborhood.

Allen Edwards is President of Pellissippi College in Knoxville, Tennessee.

3. Creating a Comprehensive Foundation

Cheryle Mitvalsky and Sue Hawn

Context

In this era, called by some the Golden Age of Philanthropy, it is estimated that of the $11 trillion in personal wealth, 77 percent, or $8.5 trillion, resides in assets held by people 55 years of age or older. John Havens and Paul Schervish (2003) recently asserted that in spite of the recent economic downtown, wealth totaling $41 trillion is expected to be transferred by the year 2052. This projection, combined with the reality of declining state aid, means that a planned giving program can only enhance a community college foundation's efforts toward annual and major giving.

Planned giving solicitations have become increasingly emphasized at Kirkwood Community College in Cedar Rapids, Iowa. The college serves a seven-county area in eastern Iowa with a population of 400,000 and an immediate urban area of 140,000. Last year, 15,000 students enrolled in college-credit classes and another 50,000 in noncredit continuing-education classes.

The Kirkwood Community College Foundation, Inc. executes its work through the college's Resource Development Program, which includes 6.5 staff members and the foundation board of directors. Until 1990, the Kirkwood foundation ran modest campaigns yielding average donations of $100,000. In 1989-1990, with a newly hired chief development officer, Kirkwood undertook a $5 million major gifts campaign. At the end of the two-year campaign, $6.5 million was raised. To everyone's surprise, the telling of the Kirkwood story of open-door accessibility prompted a few members of the community to make bequests to the college. These generous donors raised the awareness of the Kirkwood development staff about planned giving. The staff now sought to build a comprehensive foundation that included planned giving along with annual and major gifts. However, it was realized that planned giving solicitations could not be handled haphazardly; rather, the approach must be structured and deliberate.

Summary of the Case

By the mid-1990s, foundation staff, board members, and other Kirkwood leaders were considering implementing a planned giving program. A major gifts campaign in 1989-1990 had yielded an unexpected spirit in the community toward planned giving bequests. This, along with knowledge of an unparalleled intergenerational transfer of wealth across the country, prompted leaders to begin to consider creating a planned giving program. The challenge was how to move the foundation from a fundraising arm focused on annual giving and major campaigns to a more comprehensive foundation that included structured efforts toward planned giving.

Questions to Consider

1. What steps should the foundation take to ensure the commitment from the

president and the board of trustees when establishing the need for a planned giving program?

2. How can the need to build an endowment be defended with the decline in state budget funding and the projection of no new revenue for at least three to five years?
3. With a growing percentage of adjunct faculty, because of budget reasons, how can a new position dedicated solely to planned and endowed giving be justified?
4. How can awareness be built in the community and with professional advisors of the college's planned giving program?
5. With limited resources, what items need to be addressed in a planned giving budget?
6. What is involved in staff training?

Thoughts and Analysis

Since the gifts are deferred, there is no immediate cash for a planned giving budget. A planned giving program is technical and challenging, requiring a designated staff person, an account specialist, investment committees, board members experienced in business, and money-manager consultants. These challenges make it difficult to convince a president and board to embrace the idea of a planned giving program. However, the foundation must have not only the support of the administration and board, but also an allotment of resources and a complete understanding of the nature of planned giving. Given the projections of intergenerational wealth transfer, planned giving not only enhances both annual and major giving; it can help establish permanent financial security for the college, ensuring that its mission is fulfilled. Low interest rates can be beneficial for planned giving programs: If the college invests wisely, donors can potentially earn better interest on charitable gift annuities than from other investments.

When state funding declines, there may be no better time to begin building an endowment, which will soon help provide a buffer against traditional funding uncertainty. The need for immediate funds cannot be ignored, of course, but comprehensive foundation efforts enhance all levels of giving in annual gifts, major gifts, and endowments, and revenue generated from endowments eventually can be used to meet current needs.

Since planned giving programs generate substantial gifts within five to seven years after the inception of the program, a commitment of resources now to support a planned giving staff member allows the foundation to realize a significant return on investment in a relatively short time. Colleges and donors may wish to designate the returns for creating more permanent faculty positions or addressing other financial concerns endemic to community colleges.

The perception and the importance of the planned giving program in the community can be increased through targeted marketing efforts, cultivation, solicitation, and stewardship. Strong relationships with professional advisors can be built by positioning the college as an educational resource in planned giving. College planned giving specialists can become advisors to professionals by sharing information on planned and charitable giving in a variety of formats, from seminars to interactive websites. Relationships with these professionals help bring in new community involvement with the college.

A planned giving budget must include a knowledgeable planned giving officer, marketing materials, software, events, and staff development and training. Within just a few years, this investment is minor compared with the yields that begin within five to seven years.

Planned giving staff members must understand the technical side of planned giving and how the program fits into an integrated development effort. They need to attend local and national seminars, join professional organizations, and subscribe to appropriate periodicals. At the same time, allied professionals such as attorneys, CPAs, trust officers, and insurance underwriters also provide expertise by helping edit contracts, giving timely updates, and offering other advice.

Outcomes

The Kirkwood Foundation planned a second major campaign in 1995-1996, setting a goal of $2 million from planned giving endowments and $8 million from cash gifts. The college moved a staff person from annual to planned giving who became licensed to market charitable gift annuities. The campaign was a success, with both goals met and exceeded. The planned giving contributions totaled over $3 million.

In the nearly 10 years since these first structured efforts toward planned giving, the college has found that planned gifts are often much larger than immediate cash gifts and that donors often give multiple gifts, combining cash gifts with gift annuities, bequests, and endowments. The college currently has 89 endowments, totaling $6 million, with 99 percent of the yields directed to student scholarships and other forms of direct student assistance.

The importance of the team effort has become apparent in Kirkwood's planned giving program. The planned giving officer is only one member of the team, with the college president, vice president of resource development, college trustees, and foundation board members also contributing by identifying donors and being present at solicitation visits and appreciation events. In addition, board members and community advisors serve on a planned giving committee that lends critical guidance in all aspects of the planned giving programs. Part of the success is building the team of internal people who will become students of planned giving and partners of allied professionals who will embrace the college's mission and help attract donors.

Planned giving donors are associated with Kirkwood for the rest of their lives and thus become a part of the college family. However, foundation staff members bear in mind that the hallmark of a good planned giving program is that the gift is best suited first for the person, then that person's family, then the college. Further, Kirkwood leaders take seriously the importance of stewardship in the form of thank-you notes, a wall of honor, recognition in newsletters and annual reports, recognition dinners, membership on special committees, and campus tours. Stewardship is all about building relationships with donors and showing them how students of the college thrive because of their gifts.

Kirkwood recently lost two beloved friends, a husband and wife, who epitomized the success of a structured planned giving program. The wife, as the initial donor, served on the foundation facilities board. After she died a few years ago, her husband, who had accompanied his wife on many visits to the college and was a friend of Kirkwood President Norm Nielsen, continued the spirit of giving. At an annual recognition dinner, the husband handed President Nielsen a check for $100,000. This donor later created a $500,000 charitable gift annuity, telling the foundation staff member who delivered his monthly annuity checks that, while he did not have a history of giving until after his wife died, he had come to experience the joy of giving. After he died unexpectedly last year, Kirkwood was notified that he had left a large portion of his estate to the college. The couple's combined giving during their lives will total over $1.8 million. The college has taken the opportunity to express appreciation of the philanthropy of these dear friends by naming a new performing arts wing after the couple.

These people were quiet givers who understood the college's mission of open-door accessibility. The way the couple grew with the college truly evidences the power and strength of planned giving. Once potential donors understand how they can benefit society with social capital after their deaths, they are truly happy to engage in the joy of giving to their communities. Community colleges can benefit students tremendously by implementing comprehensive foundations with planned giving options.

Cheryle Mitvalsky is the Vice President of Resource Development at Kirkwood Community College. Sue Hawn is the Director of Planned Giving at Kirkwood Community College, Cedar Rapids, Iowa.

Reference

Havens, J.J., and Schervish, P.G. (2003). "Executive Summary: Why the $41 Trillion Wealth Transfer Is Still Valid – A Review of Challenges and Questions." *Boston College Social Welfare Research Institute Newsletter*.

4. Performing for Friends and Funds

Cash Pealer and Mary Ann DeSantis

Context

Central Florida Community College (CFCC) is a fully accredited, public two-year community college located in Ocala, Florida, with a branch campus in Citrus County and an educational center in Levy County. Established in 1957, the college has a current enrollment of 6,100 credit students. The average age of the student body is 28. Ocala is a diverse community and has seen a phenomenal growth in the number of retirees who have relocated to the area.

CFCC is governed by a seven-member appointed board of trustees with delegated responsibility given to President Charles R. Dassance, who came to the college in 1996. The CFCC Foundation was established in 1959, and is a public, tax-exempt, nonprofit corporation whose sole purpose is to provide support to help the college carry out its community mission. Major directions for the foundation board are to create public awareness of the college and foundation, to provide funds for restricted scholarships and endowed chairs, to provide unrestricted funds for the college, to manage the assets of the foundation for the college, and to secure foundation operational funds that ultimately support the college. *Guidestar* ranks CFCC sixth among Florida community colleges in total foundation assets, with $26 million.

Cash Pealer is president of the CFCC Foundation and vice president of institutional advancement for the college. He leads a 10-member executive committee and a 30-member volunteer board that is separate from the college's board of trustees.

Pealer became the foundation president in 1989, after serving in several other positions at the college since 1969. When he took charge of the foundation, he had a two-person staff; he now has eight full-time and three part-time employees. In 1989, the foundation had $600,000 in endowments; in 2004, the amount had grown to $12 million.

The CFCC Foundation sponsors a Performing Arts Series, currently in its 16th year. The Performing Arts Series is by far the best fund-raising event for the college. Over the past 16 years, income from the Performing Arts Series has created a $70,000 endowment, with earnings used to support future performing arts programs and activities as well as scholarships. On an annual profit-and-loss basis, the series in most years has made a profit.

Summary of the Case

Established in 1989, the CFCC Foundation's Performing Arts Series serves as an outreach to both the Ocala and Lecanto communities. The series provides an opportunity for community leaders to be introduced to and become involved with CFCC's main campus in Ocala and the Citrus County campus in Lecanto, where an identical performance is also held the same week. Individual donors have made sizable and ongoing contributions to the foundation after they attended their first Performing Arts event.

In 1989, the CFCC Foundation took over the Lyceum Series from the college, which was losing funding. Pealer saw an improved performing arts series as a way to increase visibility for the college, especially among the area's retirees, who rarely visited either campus.

Entertainment in the series has ranged from one-man shows such as *An Evening with Gershwin* and *The Witty World of Will Rogers* to concerts by saxophonist Boots Randolph and jazz singer Banu Gibson.

A volunteer committee of patrons works with the foundation to select acts showcased and exhibited by the Southern Acts Exchange and other similar organizations. The committee looks at trends, shows, prices, and marketing strategies. The members have attended the Performing Arts Series for years and understand what kinds of performances will work in the Ocala and Lecanto areas. The foundation commits to programs approximately 15 months in advance and up-fronts the costs of the series.

The CFCC Performing Arts Series must pay for itself, and usually does so thanks to season ticket sales. The 435 seats available at the CFCC Fine Arts Auditorium sell out, as most season ticket holders buy for the next year as soon as season tickets become available. This also enables the foundation to have some operating cash for the series seven or eight months before the performances are held. The quality and reputation of the series is such that many folks who cannot get tickets for the Ocala performances make a 45-minute drive to Lecanto for the performances at the Curtis Peterson Auditorium, which has 1,140 seats. In addition to a professionally designed flyer describing the series, the foundation creates many of its own advertisements for the individual performances and sells tickets online through its website at www.cfccfoundation.org.

The season ticket pricing structure is arranged in levels reflecting an academic environment, from High Honors at $60 to Summa Cum Laude at $3,000, which includes limo service to the theatre. All season ticket holders get membership benefits and tickets to other CFCC events such as band concerts and student drama performances. Any patron who pays above $500 also receives tickets to the CFCC Foundation's Annual Dinner Theatre, now in its sixth year and also a sell-out event.

Anyone contributing at the $130 Deans List level or above is listed in the program distributed at each performance. Donors are often recognized at some point during the event, which is another friendraising activity that bonds them to the college. A display table about the CFCC Foundation and the college contains information that patrons can peruse during intermissions.

Questions to Consider

The Performing Arts Series can be replicated by other community college foundations. However, the following questions should be asked:

1. Is the foundation board committed to establishing a performing arts series on an annual basis?

2. Is there a strong commitment from the college president and the foundation board? The foundation staff will have to spend a significant amount of time on the event.
3. How much time can you give to this project?
4. Do you have the staff and volunteers to handle the bookings and to deal with performers when they arrive on campus? The CFCC Friends of the Foundation is a vital component at CFCC. Does your college have such a volunteer group?
5. What kind of ticket prices will audiences pay in your community?
6. Know your market. Can you find a niche? For instance, big bands and jazz appeal to retirees. Who is your target market? Retirees? Baby boomers? Career Professionals?
7. Can your foundation handle the outflow of cash or up-front money at the beginning of each season?
8. How will you market the events? You must be able to build your budget to include advertising and professional-looking flyers.
9. What else is going on in your community? What are the other arts or entertainment programs available?
10. Finally, can you juggle a performing arts series with other foundation responsibilities? You have to find a balance with other fundraising activities.

Thoughts and Analysis

Getting people on campus is a powerful way to build relationships and bond with potential donors. One of the reasons for the success of the CFCC Performing Arts Series is that it brings in folks who have never been on campus before. In addition, the CFCC Foundation has been able to grow other events as off-shoots of the Performing Arts Series, primarily the annual Dinner Theatre that is held every January and has become another successful fundraising event.

Outcomes

The visibility to the college and the foundation from these events is well worth the effort to produce them. Approximately $4 million in donations to the college have come from donors who are or have been performing-arts patrons. Many people have noticed the need for scholarships just by reading the program and have called the foundation to see how they could help. Some have even established ongoing relationships with the students as well as the college.

Events such as the Performing Arts Series are friendraising as well as fundraising. Every time patrons attend functions on campus, they are cementing their relationship with the college.

Cash Pealer is President of the CFCC Foundation, and Mary Ann DeSantis is Coordinator of Marketing and Public Relations at Central Florida Community College in Ocala, Florida.

5. Building a World-Class Community College Foundation

Peter A. Spina

Context

Monroe Community College (MCC) is a large multicampus community college located in Rochester, New York's third largest city. A bulwark of the state's economy, Rochester's industrial fortunes are tied to the manufacturing sector and thus began to ebb in the early 1990s as manufacturing jobs were lost, first to the American South and West, then to offshore firms. While workforce out-migration and job-sector transformation from manufacturing to service and high technology were jarring to Rochester, the area generally fared better than the rest of the state, which struggles to retain business and stem the outflow of its well-educated young adult cohort. As far back as the 1980s, MCC anticipated the state's economic problems and began to develop strategies to compensate for potentially reduced state aid. MCC set out to maximize resources by increasing enrollment and retention of students (the college's funding formula is enrollment driven), and to raise money from external sources. MCC created a foundation in 1983 to accomplish the latter initiative.

Community philanthropy has long flourished in Rochester due to the enlightened leadership of luminaries like George Eastman (Kodak) and Joseph P. Wilson (Xerox). The area's United Way campaign has ranked at the top of United Way giving nationally for decades. On a per capita basis, Rochester residents and corporations are among the most generous in the country.

Yet even in a giving-oriented community like Rochester, the college encountered several challenges during the foundation's formative years. First, Rochester considered itself a private-college town, with many influential constituents harboring strong allegiances to long-established private institutions and expressing the sentiment that public colleges should not compete and raise private money. Second, even MCC's own trustees were tepid about creating an auxiliary fundraising apparatus. Since the inception of the college in the early 1960s, the trustees had raised and managed a modest amount of money for scholarships and to fund college initiatives unlikely to receive state support. A few trustees were disappointed that we wanted to engage outsiders to raise money for the college. Several of our board members served in similar capacities at private colleges (interlocking directorates were once *de rigueur* in Rochester), and they found it awkward to endorse another fundraising player in the community. Third, when MCC joined the board of the League for Innovation in 1984, membership brought with it some unintended consequences. When we participated in the sharing and showcasing of innovative programs and services – a League hallmark – we realized that for MCC to have a prominent national presence, we would need significantly more capital to bolster our programs and services. With the long-term state fiscal picture dim, new revenues would have to come from private sources. Our final challenge was finding a competent fundraiser. We needed a sophisticated, experienced fundraiser who understood community colleges and who could galvanize a skeptical internal community and mobilize an indifferent or mildly unreceptive external community to support the college – an elusive amalgam, we discovered.

Summary of the Case

MCC's long-term strategic planning produced several propositions. The college projected that state aid, adjusted for inflation, would likely plateau or regress. To elevate its programs and services to world-class levels, a significant infusion of new capital leveraged from the private sector was necessary. Raising private money required changing attitudes both within and outside the institution and finding the right people and fundraising vehicles to do the job.

Questions to Consider

1. To direct its foundation, should MCC hire a local, someone conversant with the idiosyncrasies of Rochester giving but with limited familiarity of community colleges; or an outsider with relevant fundraising and community college experience?
2. How can the college overcome the deeply held sentiment by individuals and corporations that public colleges should not raise private money?
3. How can the college find its fundraising niche and set appropriate fundraising goals?
4. How does the college avoid being a victim of its own fundraising success, especially with state and local politicians who might limit public funding should the college yield significant private resources?
5. What strategies can be used to convince internal stakeholders that the costs of investing in fundraising will ultimately result in additional net revenues for the college?

Thoughts and Analysis

1. MCC's previous fundraising was low key and reactive; changing its profile to a more planned and aggressive one would produce a sea change with both positive and negative consequences, on and off campus.
2. A comprehensive fundraising program requires appropriate staffing and research support; spending public money to staff the program will generate negative reactions, internally and externally.
3. The president's work schedule would be considerably affected to accommodate participation in an expanded fundraising program; ramifications of this work-schedule change would be both personally and professionally significant.
4. Since MCC relies on close cooperation with local senior colleges to fulfill its transfer mission, finessing the issue of competition and joining the fundraising community was very important.
5. Inculcating fundraising into the college culture, especially among the faculty, would be both important and difficult; faculty would have to be convinced and included.
6. The relationship between the college trustees and the foundation board must be delineated very carefully with sensitivity over mutual roles gradually eliminated.

Outcomes

After two false starts, which created several additional challenges, MCC hired an experienced local fundraiser from the hospital sector. She conducted an internal audit that formed the basis for a strategic fundraising plan. The plan called for expanding and diversifying the foundation board, developing and communicating a compelling case for support, hiring qualified personnel, and engaging the college and larger community.

By hiring a Rochester professional, we gained some credibility with local fundraisers who knew and respected her, and we lost little to the learning curve. She articulated MCC's desire to develop a fundraising niche and to focus first on raising scholarships for needy community college students who paid the highest tuition in the country. By taking a measured and nonconfrontational approach, she was able to convince the Rochester higher education community that MCC's fundraising success would be a rising tide elevating all ships.

A case support document was professionally prepared after integrating focus-group outcomes, and it proved compelling to both donors and prospective foundation board members. In time, MCC was able to attract a diverse and productive board and, interestingly, several new board stars followed our foundation director from the hospital to the community college.

The sensitive issue of making MCC's two boards – its trustees and foundation directors – complementary and harmonious was achieved by initially including several respected trustees on the foundation board. Once the trustees were ensured that the foundation was developing appropriate programs and strategies, they considered the foundation as an asset. The college faculty was more difficult to convince, but the strategy of offering board membership to two faculty leaders and empanelling a faculty-staffed college spending priorities committee gradually engaged them; at least, it diminished their resistance to the concept.

Our concern that local and state politicians might attempt to cut college funding if MCC enjoyed robust fundraising success never materialized. Once the foundation received several well-publicized major gifts from individuals and corporations, local politicians, many of them business people, looked positively on the foundation – people love a winner! Likewise, the issue of using public money to raise private funds never rose to the boiling point.

The president's work schedule changed markedly as the fundraising program expanded and the foundation became successful. Formerly, fundraising represented an inconsequential portion of the president's schedule, but by the end of the last decade he spent between 25 and 30 percent of his work week planning for or doing fundraising. The foundation's growth represented an add-on to the president's workload, since none of his erstwhile duties could be eliminated.

Currently, the MCC Foundation raises millions of dollars annually to support a wide range of academic, cultural, scholarship, and professional development programs. Few community colleges in the nation have reached this level of private support.

Peter A. Spina is President Emeritus of Monroe Community College in Rochester, New York. He is a former Two-Year College Trustee, Council for the Advancement and Support of Education (CASE).

Part IX

Media

1. Media Relations in Good and Bad Times

Augie Gallego

Context

The San Diego Community College District operates three comprehensive colleges and six adult education centers located throughout the city of San Diego. The three colleges serve about 50,000 students each semester and the adult education centers an additional 50,000 students. The district also offers military contract education programs operating in 10 states, serving some 56,000 U.S. Navy recruits each year and an additional 35,000 military personnel in technical training programs. In San Diego, the colleges and centers serve ethnically diverse populations, including several thousand recent immigrants. Approximately one-third of the classes in the adult education division are English as a Second Language. To get a sense of the diversity, consider that the district enrolls more Hispanics and twice as many African Americans as all eight undergraduate campuses of the University of California combined.

Summary of the Case

The CEO of the multicampus San Diego Community College District had developed good relationships with members of the local print and broadcast media. The CEO and other members of the district community were excited to learn that a long-time adjunct faculty member in the adult education program offered to bequeath more than $8 million to the college district for a new adult education center. The offer was welcome news to faculty, staff, and students because the existing center was in a crowded, leased facility in disrepair, and state funds are not provided for new adult education facilities. The district was also in the midst of state budget crisis, so the $8 million was particularly welcome news.

The education center's dean had recently retired, and plans had been announced to transfer a senior dean from another site to head the center. The incoming dean is an African American who worked her way up the ranks to dean of student services at a college and was dean of an adult center with 9,000 students. Several faculty members, including the instructor who planned to donate $8 million, objected to filling the vacant position, arguing that the two administrators at the site were sufficient, particularly in these difficult financial times. The donor told the district's chancellor that his offer to bequeath $8 million would be withdrawn if the position were filled. He further stipulated that no "immigrant classes" shall be conducted in the new center. These classes include English as a Second Language and citizenship.

A columnist for the local daily newspaper learned about the generosity of the faculty member to bequeath $8 million for a new center and called the CEO to interview him. A story that should have been very positive in the local newspaper now had the potential to turn very negative.

Questions to Consider

1. What should the CEO tell the reporter?
2. Should the CEO state that the arrangements for the donation have not been completely worked out, or should he explain the turn of events?
3. Should the college district accept the $8 million offer?
4. Would the decision be easier to make if the only stipulation was to not fill the vacant position?
5. What would you decide if the only stipulation was to not offer "immigrant classes"?

Thoughts and Analysis

The CEO had already made the decision not to accept the $8 million with the strings attached before the reporter called. The CEO has maintained a position of trust and integrity with the local media in times of both good and bad news, and informed the reporter about the developments that made it impossible for him to accept the $8 million on behalf of the district. The story on the incident ran in the column's normal location, the front page of the features section, as the first story in the upper-left corner. The headline: "Lessons in give and take (back) of philanthropy." Instead of reflecting negatively on the college district, however, the story portrayed the integrity of the district, including a quote from the CEO that "I am not going to compromise the district's policy and procedures, whether it's 8 cents or $8 million." The article opened with the following words:

"Ethics 101, from the Community College of Hard Knocks: Suppose you are asked to do the 'right thing', for the wrong reason. Suppose the 'right thing' is a matter of opinion, not fact. Suppose the 'wrong reason' is, as a matter of fact, $8 million. What do you do?"

Several years later, the CEO led a $685 million facilities bond measure that passed with almost 69 percent voter approval. The daily newspaper and television stations ran editorial endorsements of the bond. The very first facility funded under the bond was the new adult center that the adjunct faculty member had planned to contribute $8 million to build. The daily newspaper that ran the story about the $8 million incident wrote a glowing editorial on the opening of the new center with the headline, "Civic Showcase," and adding, "A brand new continuing education center being dedicated today should be a boon to revitalized City Heights. But it wouldn't have happened without considerable effort by the San Diego Community College District." In addition to praising the valuable contribution to "transforming a once-blighted community into a civic showcase," the editorial also called for more state funding for adult education programs.

Outcomes

That kind of coverage comes from cultivating news media general managers, editors, reporters, editorial writers, and others before you need them. In leading up to the passage of the $685 million bond, the CEO met with print and television owners, general managers, reporters, and editorial boards to gain support from the media. In 2001, when the California governor disproportionately cut the community college budget, the CEO of the San Diego Community College District (SDCCD) met with the editorial board of the daily newspaper, resulting in a series of editorials demanding that the governor restore the funds. *The San Diego Union-Tribune* editorials began a statewide movement that resulted in every major daily newspaper in the state, as well as weekly publications, running editorials urging the governor to restore community college funds. The campaign was effective and the governor restored $98 million.

Another example of the influence a community college CEO can wield through the media is through the candidates the media support for locally elected boards of trustees. As a result of the SDCCD CEO's good relationship with the daily newspaper's editorial board, when three board positions were being contested in 2000, the newspaper supported candidates that the editorial said could work well with the CEO.

Community college CEOs also have a responsibility to speak out on issues that affect their communities, even if they have only an indirect connection to the colleges. As an example of this type of community involvement, in 2000, when there was an initiative on the statewide ballot to shift state funds from public K-12 schools to private schools through vouchers, the SDCCD CEO joined the campaign opposed to school vouchers by writing an opinion piece for the daily newspaper and speaking out on television public affairs and news programs in opposition to the voucher initiative.

The key is to develop relationships with the media before you need them. However, sometimes no matter how much effort and thought you put into good media relations, there will be some individuals who won't be persuaded by the positions you take. Others will act at times irresponsibly in the rush to report the news. As a general rule, the more honest and helpful you are with the media, the more likely they will respond with fair coverage, and perhaps even champion some of your causes on their editorial pages.

Augie Gallego is Chancellor of the San Diego Community College District.

2. The Media and the Gainesville Student Murders of 1990

Lawrence D. Keen

Context

Santa Fe Community College (SFCC) is a multicampus, comprehensive community college located, along with the University of Florida (UF), in Gainesville. In May 1990, SFCC named as its third president Lawrence W. Tyree. Approximately two-thirds of 12,000 SFCC students were enrolled in programs typically taken to transfer to the UF. High school graduates arrived in Gainesville to be roommates and socialize together; some entered the university as freshmen, and others attended SFCC in order to transfer to the university. Almost all SFCC students were from Florida, and 55 percent of its enrollment was from the college's two-county service district.

Gainesville was a city of 85,000 residents in 1990. SFCC's Northwest, or primary, campus is five miles from the UF and six miles from Archer Road, which borders the south side of the UF campus. Most off-campus housing for the university and SFCC students was located along Archer Road. SFCC does not have on-campus student housing. The UF has extensive residential on-campus housing. The UF received significant local, statewide, and national media coverage. SFCC received extensive local media coverage but was mentioned less often statewide and seldom nationally.

SFCC was founded in 1965 with the philosophy of the "whole student." Great attention was given to psychological factors relating to student success. A poster advertising the college in the late 1960s displayed the words "warm, friendly, and peaceful."

In 1990, SFCC continued to emphasize its student-centered philosophy. The college offered services to improve retention, grades, and career outcomes and to help resolve personal problems. SFCC students generally had an expectation that they would be served and educated in a personal manner.

Summary of the Case

On Sunday, August 26, 1990, shortly before the beginning of fall semester classes, the bodies of 17-year-old UF freshmen Sonja Larson and Christina Powell were discovered in their apartment on Archer Road near the university. Both had been stabbed repeatedly, mutilated, and positioned to shock whoever discovered the bodies.

As the police investigated, the body of 18-year-old SFCC sophomore Christa Hoyt was discovered in the Archer Road apartment where she lived alone near the UF. Hoyt had been decapitated and otherwise mutilated. Evidence indicated to law enforcement officers that the murders were related.

On Monday morning, the Gainesville Police Department and Alachua County Sheriff's Office initiated a combined task force that soon included the Federal Bureau of Investigation and Florida's Department of Law Enforcement and Highway Patrol. The

GPD and ACSO held their first joint press conference Monday evening. The story was the lead item in the local media, which had reported some details about the brutal nature of the crimes and raised the question of whether a serial killer was in the community. Telephone lines to the GPD were jammed. Rumors about the slayings were rife locally.

The bodies of 23-year-old Tracy Paules and Manuel Taboada were discovered Tuesday morning in the Archer Road apartment they shared near the UF. Paules was a UF student, and Taboada had finished classes at SFCC in spring and was prepared to enter the UF. The apparent linkage of these murders to the others engendered a panic in the university city. SFCC and the UF were overwhelmed with telephone calls from students, family members, and others. Law enforcement agencies from elsewhere in Florida provided officers to enhance the police presence in the city, particularly along Archer Road.

Media interest grew to statewide, national, and international proportions. The quantity of media telephone calls to SFCC was unprecedented. Reporters from distant news outlets arrived in Gainesville, many with large satellite trucks. Media competition became heated. Reports were about news, rumors, and speculation.

The GPD and ACSO established a press center at a central location in Gainesville one mile from the UF and five miles from SFCC. The UF established a press center on its campus five miles from SFCC.

SFCC implemented measures to assist students. The college offered crisis counseling, added security patrols, provided escorts for night students, allowed students to make free phone calls home, established a hotline for parents to contact their children who were SFCC students, suspended grading and financial penalties for students who left school, provided self-defense training to students, and contracted for a student safe house off campus. The college CEO called the parents of Christa Hoyt to express condolences and offer any appropriate college service.

Questions to Consider

1. Should SFCC hold press conferences and establish a press center?
2. Should the college president act as spokesman?
3. What is the extent of the college's obligation to students in this case?
4. Should all media be treated equally?
5. What is the college's obligation to the media?
6. Should established media-relations procedures be followed?

Thoughts and Analysis

1. Models for crisis media management call for proactive measures such as press conferences or availabilities and a dedicated communications center where reporters obtain information and make inquiries. However, the fact that such measures were taken by other agencies near the locus of the crimes raised the question of whether it was necessary for SFCC to do so.
2. The president is the most credible spokesperson for a college and the most

stabilizing presence in the event of a crisis. Countervailing considerations are the amount of time the president should spend with the media and that the president would be subject to unhelpful surprise questions.

3. *In loco parentis* is a weakened doctrine in education, and SFCC does not have resident housing, which would have raised the level of its legal obligation to students. However, SFCC had a tradition of personalized attention to students, and the moral obligation to assist them was powerful.

4. A maxim of public relations is to treat all media equally, taking into consideration deadlines and the kind of medium. During the crisis, it was observed that members of the local media were upset by the murders, reflecting in coverage that was more factual and described measures taken by agencies. Media from outside the region, in particular out-of-state media, gravitated toward sensational rather than solution-oriented coverage. In addition, the majority of SFCC students were from its service district, and almost all of its students were from Florida. If media were to be evaluated for their ability to communicate to the college's students, families, and constituents, the local and state media were of great value and the out-of-state media were of much less use.

5. The accepted approach to press relations is to affirmatively serve the media to achieve balanced coverage and, if a story is negative, to have it told quickly. In the present case, the college had to decide whether to emphasize all stories or those that were solution oriented.

6. SFCC had a local-media response plan prepared by the public information officer (PIO). It entailed telephone, personal, fax, and email contact. It did not have procedures for distant media outlets, although the PIO was prepared to contact them.

Outcomes

A survey of student reactions to the crisis was not taken. The strong anecdotal consensus was that the ambience at SFCC was much calmer than it was at the UF. It seems certain that a partial explanation is SFCC's distance from the locus of the murders, the UF campus, and the press centers. However, it is suggested that the state of SFCC's campus was partly attributable to the calibrated response by the college.

For example, the college decided not to host a live outdoor taping on campus by the "Donahue Show," a pioneering television program in confrontational journalism. The show's producers said the taping would be conducted in a professional and sensitive manner. However, the college PIO believed no one could manage emotional comments, criticisms, and speculation in such a setting. Similarly, the college president did not conduct regular press conferences, with their free-ranging and uncontrolled content.

Conversely, the PIO immediately relayed all ameliorative measures taken by the college to all local media and specific statewide media. These were cooperative in announcing or printing this information. In doing so, they aided the college in its communications with students, their families, and other target audiences. The college CEO was made available to local media on a selected basis. In one instance, *The Gainesville Sun* reported about the president and other college employees serving as nighttime security escorts on campus.

Many media outlets deflected attention from SFCC when they named the slayings the UF Student Murders. There was no intent at SFCC to have the university manage the media burden. The PIOs from both institutions were in contact daily. However, a decision was made to lower the level of media attention after realizing its tendency to concentrate on the university or law enforcement.

Reporters did visit the SFCC campus, including those in large satellite trucks. In these instances, the PIO acted as spokesman and gave interviews quickly in order for reporters to depart for the activity in central Gainesville.

The suggestion is that it may be advisable in certain instances to lower the public profile of the institution. Such a decision is counterintuitive; therefore it should be made with full knowledge about media relations.

Lawrence D. Keen is Associate Vice President for College Communications at Santa Fe Community College in Gainesville, Florida.

3. Engagement: It's More Than PR

Carole Lapensohn

Context

Established in 1957, Gulf Coast Community College (GCCC) in Northwest Florida serves approximately 6,000 credit students each year, with another 25,000 students served through continuing education. The main campus is in Panama City, with centers in the northern part of the Bay County, at nearby Tyndall Air Force Base, and in another county some 50 miles away. Although originally governed by the local school board, in 1968, the college came under the governance of a District Board of Trustees. This board, appointed by the state governor for staggered three-year terms, has nine members who represent the three counties in the college service district. Leadership of the board has been consistently strong and politically powerful. Chairs have included land developers, entrepreneurs, the millionaire widow of the first board chair, a bank owner's wife, and a nonpracticing Harvard-educated attorney. What has been remarkable is that, despite the political nature of board appointments, trustees have largely put aside both personal and political agendas in order to advance the college.

In its more than 40-year history, Gulf Coast has had only four presidents: the first, its founder and president for only two years; the second, its builder, who led a strict autocracy for 16 years; the third, a charismatic visionary who led the college to excellence over his 12-year term; and the fourth, an alumnus of the college and a true believer, who has raised millions of dollars for the GCCC Foundation's endowment during his long tenure. At this writing, consensus is that he will retire by age 65.

The second president established the college's direct support organization, selecting affluent opinion makers to be the foundation's initial directors. Beginning modestly in 1967 with $21,000 in assets, the foundation at the end of 2003 had assets greater than $16 million and awarded more than $530,000 in scholarships for the 2003-2004 academic year.

Summary of the Case

From its founding, Gulf Coast has been considered the community's college. Deeply embedded in the community, it was established by citizens who traveled 90 miles to the state capital at Tallahassee to request that a junior college be located in Panama City. Although there is no way to scientifically gauge penetration of a college into the community, it's likely that a significant percentage of Bay County residents have attended the college themselves, either in degree programs or as students of continuing education or enrichment courses, or members of their families have done so. A consistently high level of both academic and occupational education has created a belief in the integrity and substance of the college.

The establishment of a Citizen Leadership Institute, funded initially by the Kellogg and Kettering foundations, has served to position the college ever more clearly as the space where citizens gather, not only for leadership training, but to discuss issues of significant relevance to the community and the nation.

Political appointment to the District Board of Trustees is prestigious, as is election to the Board of Directors of the foundation. The history of integrity and productivity has made strong advocates of community members and particularly of community leaders. Trustees, foundation board members, the president, and mid- and upper-level college management have engaged in a substantial amount of volunteer support. The United Way, the Chamber of Commerce, social service agencies, churches, and civic organizations have drawn support from college ranks.

The strength of the college's relationship with the community is mirrored and even measured by its relationship with local media. While a number of reporters and producers themselves are alumni of the college, the CEOs of local print and broadcast outlets have also taken the college to their hearts, providing enviable free advertising time and space for events and major fundraising campaigns. Strain between the college and the media has been rare.

Although state standards of accountability have strengthened Gulf Coast's reputation for academic excellence, faculty and staff commitment to student success has operated on a word-of-mouth level. Two major advertising campaigns supported the position of the college at the end of the 20th century. In the early 1990s, the college initiated a Just Ask campaign that won a national first-place Paragon Award for marketing campaigns from the National Council of Marketing and Public Relations. With approximately eight different television ads spotlighting the accessibility of employees and the experiences of students who had achieved success, that campaign was replicated at other colleges. The second campaign featured the slogan Start Here. Go Anywhere. It resonated in the community, on campus, and even at the national level, where Maine's L.L. Bean retailers began using the same verbiage. The slogan has been used in local editorials; more importantly, it is used often by members of the community, students, faculty, and staff, who apparently believe it is more than a slogan. To them, it's the truth.

Questions to Consider

1. Given the eventual retirement of a long-term popular president, what type of leader should the trustees select to sustain positive, proactive, and successful connection with the community?
2. Could anything be done to ensure the continuing high quality of leadership on the gubernatorially appointed District Board of Trustees?
3. What should be the most effective response to a crisis of confidence, should one arise, either with the long-tenured president or his successor?

Thoughts and Analysis

1. Sustaining viable connections in the community is obviously critical to the continuing success of relationships with local citizens. The person selected for the presidency must become deeply and positively engaged in the community

and must be accepted and respected as a member of that community. A new president also must show true belief in what the college does for the community. An individual with these qualities will help sustain the college's reputation, will continue in the critically important presidential role of fundraiser, and will allow the college to work effectively at the state level to enhance funding.

2. The relationship between the president and the trustees must be synergistic, growing out of mutual understanding of the history, culture, and values of the college. Assuming the trustees understand these critical aspects, the new president should clearly support and then enhance the college. As trustees continue to achieve political appointment, the president and the body politic of the community should help shape the work of the District Board of Trustees, to help sustain a long-established culture, ultimately putting aside personal agendas for the greater good of the college.

3. Because the current president has the advantage of long-time service, and because his age puts him close to the accepted timeframe for retirement, were there to be a crisis of confidence during his tenure, retirement would be both expedient and practical. If such a crisis were to occur during the term of the fifth president, a whole new set of options would appear. Despite the long-term enviable relationship the college has enjoyed with the community and the media, a major crisis could abruptly end that relationship. The saving factor, however, will remain the political clout of the gubernatorial appointees to the District Board of Trustees. Because the trustees sit at the pleasure of the party in power, they well could weather whatever storms arose. It is probable that they would support the president they selected. If, however, the storm played serious havoc with relationships in the community, the trustees would likely relieve the new president of his duties. It has been done before, when a crisis of confidence eroded the environment in several of the other 27 of Florida's community colleges. Essentially, then, response to a crisis of confidence at a Florida community college will continue to relate directly to an entrenched and supportive political system.

Carole Lapensohn is Executive Director of the Gulf Coast Community College Foundation, Inc., and Director of Institutional Advancement at the college in Panama City, Florida.

4. Dealing With the Student Press

J. William Wenrich

Context

At virtually every community college that has a student press publication, there will be some times when there will be some tension, if not conflict, between the student press leadership and some other elements of the college community – administration, faculty, the board of trustees, college employees such as financial aid and registration staff who provide direct services to students. Dealing with the tension or conflict in a way that fosters student learning and development without unfairly endangering the image or reputation of the institution can be a challenging task for college leaders.

Summary of the Case

This case occurred in a middle-size college (7,000 students) that is one of three separately accredited institutions in a multicollege district serving an entire county with a largely urban-suburban population. The new, young, first-time college president reported to a district chancellor who was directly responsible to an elected board of five trustees. The student newspaper was published weekly during the academic year and was funded by the college budget. It operated under the guidance of an academic division and dean who assigned the function of journalism advisor to a full-time English faculty member who had professional journalism experience. The advisor worked directly with the student editor in chief and associate editors. The quality of the paper was generally acceptable, and there were only minor disagreements among the dean, the journalism advisor, and the student editorial team during the president's first year at the college. General editorial control was given to the student editor, but the advisor and the dean had the right to restrict material or articles based on journalistic quality or legality. Occasionally, they felt it required the review of the president, as the representative of the publisher – the board of trustees, who had legal and financial responsibility for the publication.

During the second year of the president's tenure, the new editor in chief was a middle-aged woman who returned to college after her divorce. Her advocacy for women's liberation causes was understandable and did not unduly affect the editorial position of the newspaper. Her relations with the journalism advisor and academic dean were generally positive, although there was occasional disagreement about some of the reporting assignments she wanted her staff to pursue. There were no disagreements with the president or critiques of the board of trustees or other college constituencies.

The conflict came when the editor wrote an article that the advisor thought was really an editorial, and an inappropriate one at that. Her piece took the position that liberated women really did not need men and could successfully meet their sexual needs through masturbation. The article was not a review of a study, a conference, or some other event. It was basically a position statement advocating female masturbation. In reviewing the copy, the faculty journalism advisor told the editor that it was inappropriate as an article and as an editorial. The academic dean concurred with the advisor's position, and they both consulted with the president, who supported the journalism advisor. The editor appeared to accept that position.

On the Friday of that week when the paper came out, there was a two-column blank space on the inside third page on which was printed, "Censored by Your College President." Inserted in each copy of the student newspaper was a yellow sheet of paper with the editor's article/editorial printed on it. The administration made no attempt to restrict the distribution or availability of the newspaper. Copies were routinely sent to the chancellor and board members directly from the student staff, and this edition was no exception. The reactions came fast and furious. Student body members seemed somewhat amused, but not necessarily upset by the censorship allegation. Several board members and the chancellor were upset that this had happened. There was criticism of the journalism advisor that this had been allowed to happen. Some wanted the student editor expelled and the advisor removed or fired. As the news of the conflict disseminated into the community, there were threats of litigation in favor of the student editor by the local American Civil Liberties Union chapter. The faculty senate was concerned about academic freedom implications but supportive of the faculty member who served as the journalism advisor.

Questions to Consider

1. Was it really a case of censorship of the press or simply an application of the rights of the publisher?
2. Is the college district really the publisher?
3. Where had there been a failure of communication or dissemination of policy?
4. Should punitive action be taken toward any of the players?
5. If so, which one(s)?
6. What actions could be taken to make this conflict a positive learning experience for the people involved and for future student journalists?

Thoughts and Analysis

The conflict caused student and faculty discussions with the administrations at the other two colleges in the district and, ultimately, a dialogue with the board of trustees. What became clear was that neither at the college nor at the district level was there a policy statement that the board of trustees, through the chancellor and the college president, had the legal and financial responsibility as the publisher of the newspaper. Nor was there a written policy about editorial appropriateness, or who determined that. There was a need for students to grow in the journalism profession and to understand what was censorship and what was legitimate control by the body with legal and financial responsibility for the publication. This seemed like a teachable moment.

Outcomes

The president took no punitive action against the student editor, the journalism advisor, or the division dean who supervised them. He asserted that ultimate editorial review was still his prerogative, in concert with the editor, the journalism adviser, and the dean, but that he would form a community journalism council comprised of editors, publishers, and professional reporters of the daily and weekly newspapers in the communities served by the college. This council would be convened only if the student editors felt there was censorship that would not be tolerated by the public media. The journalism council would review the specific issue and give feedback to both the president and the student newspaper staff about how this would be treated in the professional media to which the students were aspiring.

While the president could restrict material from the student newspaper, if he did so against the advice of the journalism council, he opened himself to censorship criticism from all the local print media. On the other hand, material deemed inappropriate by the profession would be clarified for the student journalists so that they had a realistic understanding for their future careers. Everyone felt this was a workable solution to prevent future conflicts of this nature and to more effectively involve the local media with the college student journalists. During that president's tenure, there was never another issue about alleged censorship.

J. William Wenrich is Chancellor Emeritus of the Dallas County Community College District.

Part X

Technology

1. Implementing and Sustaining a Technology Management Plan

Jan Bullard

Context

Santa Fe Community College (SFCC) serves over 16,000 students from north central Florida locations in Alachua and Bradford counties. Courses are provided at the largest campus in Gainesville, at four strategically located centers, and by web access. Although SFCC is a comprehensive community college offering transfer, vocational, and adult education programs, it serves over 77 percent of its students in credit university transfer courses.

Approximately 2,000 students per year transfer to the University of Florida, and many more transfer to other state universities and to colleges out of state. Vocational program graduates excel in licensure pass rates and in securing jobs in their field. The college consistently places in the top 10 in the nation in the number of associate degrees awarded.

Students attend SFCC from all counties in the state of Florida, all but one of the United States, and from 83 foreign countries. Over 72 percent of the students are under age 25, and almost 83 percent are under 30.

SFCC is a charter member of the League for Innovation in the Community College. Its membership on the League's board was reaffirmed in 2003, following the transition in the presidency to Jackson N. Sasser from Lawrence W. Tyree, who had been president since 1990. Vice president for administration and finance Jan Bullard was hired in 1994. The long-time chief academic officer, Bob Myers, and the current chief technology officer, Tim Nesler, had been employed by the college since 1972. Budget and technology advisory committees have been active since 1996.

Summary of the Case

Santa Fe Community College's student demographics, organizational culture, commitment to quality and innovation, program mix, and history of student success present a challenge in setting institutional priorities to sustain past successes and provide for expansion and improvement. Of particular concern in the period 1994 to 1996 was the state of the technology infrastructure. Given the speed in the advancement of desktop computing and the coming bubble of high school graduates with their increased expectations for technology support, the need for available, current, networked desktop computers was expected to increase exponentially in the near future.

Adding to the challenge was the cost of technology and the limitations of the college's operating budget, both internally and externally imposed. In 1994-1995, SFCC's operating budget totaled $35,944,936, with allocations for all operating capital outlay at 1.4 percent. Similarly, the 1995-1996 budget was $36,698,650, with 1.8 percent going toward operating capital outlay. The amounts allocated to operating capital outlay were insufficient for the normal replacement of instructional equipment, much less to make advancements in the desktop computing and support infrastructure. Throughout its history, SFCC has chosen to make the allocations for its faculty and staff as its most important first new-dollar investment, leading to an allocation of almost 84 percent of its budget to personnel costs in 1994-1995. Under the leadership of then-President Tyree, the college sought a plan for a realignment of its operating budget to balance the traditional valuing of its faculty and staff with the need to advance its technology infrastructure. Externally, it had become clear that state revenue support was waning and increases could not be expected to provide new funds to improve the allocation to operating capital outlay.

The existing technology infrastructure was suspect. Fortunately, the college had just completed and equipped a new instructional technology building with several dedicated student labs for IT instruction and one large open-access lab. Unfortunately, no recurring budget had been allocated for future upgrades and replacements. No detailed inventory existed of the number and type of desktop computers in use in other dedicated student labs or by faculty, but it was believed that distribution by program was inequitable, and some labs contained computers of various generations of hardware and software. Budgeting and acquisition of new or replacement computers was decentralized to the departmental level. No standards had been institutionally adopted for hardware and software.

Questions to Consider

1. What precisely was the state of the college's desktop computing infrastructure? Would the academic departments be supportive of a centralized effort to gather the needed data and adopt college standards for desktop computing?
2. How was the current need to be determined? The future need?
3. What level of college faculty and administrative support would be needed to adopt the plans? To implement them? To sustain the long-range plan?
4. How much funding would be needed for the initial upgrade of existing student and faculty desktop computers? How much recurring budget would be needed to sustain the plan? How would the support be obtained to sufficiently increase the proportion of the recurring budget allocated for the plan and other capital outlay?

Thoughts and Analysis

Whatever the ultimate outcome, it was clear that a desktop computing replacement plan, later named PC Replacement Plan, could not be centrally implemented and sustained without broad support within the college. Traditional college processes were not supportive of securing an accurate, centralized database of hardware and software; determining and adopting standards for hardware and software; planning for future replacement and refreshing; and budgeting for the plan.

With the leadership of the president firmly in support, the administrative and finance and academic vice presidents and the chief technology officer needed to seek input and support from key college constituencies while translating the input into a plan.

By early 1996, the college's equipment inventory and departmental records had confirmed informal observations that except for the labs in the new technology building, desktop computers were inadequate for instruction, inequitably distributed, and incompatible in both software and hardware configurations. Department heads and many faculty and support staff became early allies. The system and organizational skills of the chief technology officer and his staff guided and documented the effort.

Translating the information on the current state of desktop computing into a plan for immediate upgrades and a long-range replacement naturally fell to the chief technology officer. Through his staff and his leadership of the Technology Advisory Committee, PC replacement planning was incorporated into the broader College Technology Plan in 1996. The Technology Advisory Committee membership was broadened to include academic and administrative users. The initial goal of a three-year replacement cycle was accepted. During the years from 1996 to 1998, hardware and software standards were established. Policies and procedures were adopted within the revised Technology Plan.

In the short term, it was critical to upgrade the existing labs and faculty PCs. Redirection of a sufficient portion of the college's operating budget to fund the immediate need would have been a hardship on other programs and services and would have undoubtedly lost the support gained for PC replacement planning. Agreement by effected constituencies was secured for a three-year commitment of a portion of discretionary, nonoperating capital funds. A local bank through a master lease agreement offered the best option for the three-year payout. The computers and related network equipment and printers were purchased and installed in 1996.

With the replacement of the newly purchased computers and those in the new technology building scheduled for 1999, the college enthusiastically joined the community college system effort to secure a vendor for a Technology Refresh Program. (See case study on Technology Refresh Program by Rand Spiwak.) SFCC technology staff participated in the evaluation and brought the advantages it sought into the College Technology Plan.

In order to fund the PC Replacement Plan, SFCC calculated it would need $1.1 million of operating capital outlay in its annual operating budget. Beginning in Budget Year 1997-1998, more dollars from new revenue and cost efficiencies were added proportionately to capital outlay than to other needs so that by budget year 1999-2000, the budget goal for the PC Replacement Plan had been reached. Support for the shift in the proportion of the budget going to capital outlay was won gradually, and, although not unanimous, it was broad based. The pricing and standards of the TRP were essential to sustaining the PC Replacement Plan.

Outcomes

The college described its PC Replacement Program in its 2002 League for Innovation Institutional Self Evaluation:

> The PC Replacement Program equips the college with up-to-date technology, reduces the total cost of ownership, and improves learning and productivity. The

college replaces all desktop PCs, file servers, and network electronics on a four-year cycle to ensure that academic programs and administrative services have the IT equipment required for their specific needs. Centralized purchasing and collegewide hardware and software standards help to better manage costs for PCs, servers, and networks. . . . Since 1999, the number of PCs and network electronics has increased by 44 percent and 57 percent respectively, but the resources to purchase and support the hardware and software have remained the same. The PC Replacement Program has also improved student learning and staff productivity. Since the program was implemented, hardware failures and software incompatibilities have been reduced by 50 percent, and the time to repair hardware failures has been improved by 30 percent. Standard desktop hardware is repaired within 24 hours. The network is operational 99 percent of the scheduled available times. With fewer hardware and software problems, students can focus on learning and staff can become more productive.

Jan Bullard is Vice President for Administration and Finance at Santa Fe Community College in Gainesville, Florida.

2. Sex, Cyberspace, and the Pursuit of Academic Freedom

Suzanne L. Flannigan, Thomas G. Greene, and Barbara R. Jones

Context

Southlake Community College (SCC) is a large urban campus in the Midwest serving over 10,000 credit students from diverse backgrounds. Pat Thompson, one of the college's most popular instructors, has been teaching sociology at SCC for 17 years. Each fall semester, a waiting list forms for students wanting to enroll in Thompson's class, The Sociology of Sex (SOC 104). Taking an avant-garde pedagogical approach to the subject matter, Thompson uses a variety of instructional methods to enhance student learning, including the requirement that all students read *Playboy* and *Playgirl* magazines and view and discuss sexually explicit videos.

Although Thompson's approach to SOC 104 has been questioned by some members of the administration, the college has upheld all challenges to academic freedom, and the faculty association unanimously supports the actions of its beloved sociology professor. In fact, Thompson was granted the Outstanding Faculty Member of the Year Award, which recognizes full-time faculty members who have contributed significant research to their field of study and who consistently receive high satisfaction ratings from students. Thompson has published more books and articles than any other faculty member at SCC. Furthermore, as a leading sociologist in the field of sex, Thompson is often sought out by other professionals and has received an open invitation to teach courses on sexuality at the local university.

Summary of the Case

Recently, Pat Thompson chose to incorporate internet erotica into the curriculum of SOC 104, requiring that students view a minimum of three adult-only websites and conduct a five-page analysis of what they find. Approximately half of the students worked on the assignment from home during this semester, while the others used the college's computer labs to conduct their research.

SCC has strict rules about the appropriate use of computers and the internet. Until now, however, the rules had not been tested, and there had not been an overt case involving pornographic websites that necessitated the enforcement of the rules or associated penalties. The specific rule relating to this case states,

> It is expected that the use of computing resources by the individual user, whether employee or student, requires that the individual act in compliance with college policies and procedures, as well as state laws. Criminal and illegal use may involve, but is not limited to: unauthorized access, intentional corruption, or misuse of computing resources, theft, defamation, obscenity, and harassment based upon race, ethnicity, national origin, disability, age, religion, or sex.

Three incidences occurred in quick succession soon after Thompson assigned the internet research project. The first occurred in the college's main computer center, where a group of female students became irate when they noticed the screen content on one student's computer as he surfed a website for his SOC 104 assignment. The women immediately informed the lab proctor, who removed the young man from the room. Soon thereafter, the women sent a complaint letter to the college president. One of them suggested that she might consider charging the SOC 104 student with sexual harassment.

The second incident occurred in the home of a female SOC 104 student. She had completed her research project on the family's home computer the previous day, during which time, and unbeknownst to her, she had downloaded a computer pop-up program from one of the adult sites. Unfortunately, this particular program popped up as the student's 7-year-old brother was surfing the Disney website. Hoping to get rid of the ad, the boy clicked on it, not realizing he had just activated a web page displaying pornographic photos. It was about this time that his mother entered the room, glanced at the computer screen, and nearly fainted. After figuring out what had transpired, the SOC 104 student's mother called the college president, demanding a face-to-face meeting.

The final incident concerned the daughter of a board member. She was working on her project at home one night when her mother noticed and was quite disturbed by the internet site her daughter was viewing. The student explained the project to her mother, who was horrified that any professor would subject students to such content, and who called the president of the college immediately. She then called the rest of the board and a number of other people she knew at the college. She was adamant that the SOC 104 assignment be stopped and that the Professor Thompson be fired immediately.

Word quickly spread throughout the college. The students were very angry. A large representative group of Thompson's current and past students went to the president and threatened to go to the media if he was suspended or prevented from teaching the class. They thought Thompson was an excellent teacher, and they believed that the subject matter was dealt with in a professional and appropriate way.

SCC President Harden was inundated with letters, emails, phone calls, and visits from a variety of stakeholders, each one having very definite opinions on the rightness or wrongness of Professor Thompson's methods. Some focused on his approach to teaching the class; others spotlighted the issue of appropriate and acceptable internet exposure in public institutions. Questions were raised about the impact of the content of the course on individuals and the overarching impact of allowing general access to pornographic sites.

Questions to Consider

1. From President Harden's perspective, what are the most critical issues?
2. How should the president respond to the angry board member and the constituents who want to fire Professor Thompson?
3. What approach should Harden take in responding to the faculty association? The students? The angry mother whose 7-year-old son was exposed to the pornography?

4. How will the president ensure that these complaints are not followed by lawsuits?
5. Should Harden seek a compromise, allowing Thompson to remain at the college but assigning someone else to teach SOC 104? If so, how will the president respond if Thompson and the faculty association elect to pursue legal action?
6. In reading this case, did you assume that Thompson was a man or a woman? How, if at all, does the gender of the professor impact your view and opinions of the situation?

Thoughts and Analysis

President Harden was concerned that this issue could create irreparable divides among the board, the students, administration, and faculty. The president knew that a decision on how to proceed must be made quickly. Harden contemplated the many issues involved; the responsibilities of public institutions to the public in terms of morality and ethics (*i.e.*, the appropriateness of allowing access to pornographic sites); the stakeholders and their polarized positions, which were not conducive at the moment to reflective dialogue for the betterment of the college as a whole; and, most important, the issue of academic freedom and the all-too-tenuous board policy on appropriate use of computer technology. How does the institution ensure that an academic environment is free from censorship and at the same time accountable to the public?

Outcomes

The first action taken by President Harden was to contact the college's legal counsel regarding the existing policy on the use of computer technology and to seek information about any court rulings involving academic freedom and the internet.

The legal representative did find a statement issued by the American Association of University Professors:

> *Freedom of expression and academic freedom should be limited to no greater degree in electronic format than in printed or oral communication, unless and to the degree that unique conditions of the new media warrant different treatment. While expression in cyberspace is obviously different in important ways from print or oral expression – for example, in the far greater speed of communication, and in the capacity to convey messages to far wider audiences – such factors do not appear to justify alteration or dilution of basic principles of academic freedom and free inquiry within the academic community.*

A Virginia law prevents state employees from using state-owned or -leased computers to "access, download, print, or store. . . . sexually explicit content." Claiming that such restrictions compromise academic freedom, five Virginia state college and university professors filed suit.

Based on advice from the college lawyer, President Harden came to the conclusion that any dissemination of information accepted in the print environment should be accepted in the digital environment. As long as material is not unlawful, a faculty member is within rights to request that students research any relevant information on the web. However, Harden realized that the college's policy on the use of computer technology was not specific and resulted in misinterpretation. She assigned a task force, under the guidance of the legal staff, to research appropriate policy ensuring that academic freedom was not jeopardized.

Harden issued a statement acknowledging the importance of academic freedom, recognizing the contribution and success of Professor Thompson, and indicating specific steps that would be taken to ensure the college was compliant with laws and policy.

The following decisions were made within two weeks of the original complaint:

- Professor Thompson was not fired, and will be allowed to continue teaching SOC 104. However, based on the new policy, Thompson may be asked to restrict internet research to in-class only.
- The students, board member, and parent were each sent letters from the president apologizing for the events that transpired and indicating that new policies would be developed to more closely address computer use.
- The task force was assigned and given charge to rewrite the computer-use policy, ensuring the integrity of academic freedom.
- All syllabi will be required to have a liability statement that introduces the college's positions on academic freedom and the use of the internet.

Suzanne L. Flannigan, Thomas G. Greene, and Barbara R. Jones are doctoral students in Community College Leadership at The University of Texas at Austin.

3. Technology Refresh Program (TRP)

Rand S. Spiwak

Context

In 1994, Pensacola Junior College (PJC), a state community college, attempted to address the challenge of maintaining state-of-the-art personal computers (PCs) in its laboratories and offices. Technology was advancing so rapidly that equipment was becoming obsolete in two to three years. PC technology was being integrated into all aspects of the college, thus demanding more resources, support services, and technical expertise. Four major PC manufacturers were contacted to attempt to determine a solution to this four-part problem: affordable acquisition, attractive financing, lifetime maintenance, and equity recovery upon replacement. The outcome was no takers, and the initiative failed. Both PC manufacturers and retailers were happy to sell the equipment but weren't interested in the multiple maintenance options the colleges desired or in tax-exempt financing; there was definitely no interest in guaranteed equity recovery (trade-in or salvage value). The college then attempted to solve this problem piecemeal, less effectively, with marginal success.

Then, in the summer of 1997, an opportunity arose to address this problem again. In an attempt to politely dismiss the sales efforts of a representative of a local governmental nonprofit financing brokerage firm, the representative was offered the opportunity to propose a solution to the previously failed four-part problem. Much to our surprise, the representative returned in a few weeks with a proposal that included a potential partnership with a PC manufacturer, a major lending institution, and an electronics recovery company. If this salesman could create a potential solution, then surely the college could do the same. PJC would contact interested PC manufacturers and retail companies to determine that this time a real solution could be created. Thus began the Florida Community College Technology Refresh Program (TRP).

Summary of the Case

The college continued to expand its use of PC technology throughout the institution. Faced with limited resources, PJC's administration was concerned that its attempt to maintain state-of-the-art technology might not be possible. The true cost of the technology far exceeded the acquisition of PCs. It included technical staff to install, maintain, and upgrade both hardware and software; financing needs; lease versus purchase concerns; related recurring costs; training; replacement costs; and expansion. A real solution to this technology refresh dilemma was a high priority faced by colleges and universities across the nation. How best solved?

Questions to Consider

1. How important was the infusion of PC technology in the instructional and administrative functions of the college? If significant, would this be a short-term or long-term need?

2. What were the variables in this problem that would make a solution possible? Were there key issues or special circumstances that would make the solution attractive?
3. How should the college attempt to seek a solution to this problem?
4. Since the PC replacement need was cyclical, (a three- or four-year obsolescence), would the solution be a short-term fix or long-term marriage?
5. Would any major PC manufacturer or retailer give serious consideration to one college, even if it had 2,500 PCs to be refreshed?

Thoughts and Analysis

1. PJC is one of 28 public community colleges in Florida, comprising approximately 3 percent of the state's community college enrollment.
2. The state government offered statewide bid pricing on PCs and related peripherals. While available to the college, the state procurement and bid process was too lengthy and offered nearly obsolete equipment and minimal cost savings.
3. State-bid PCs did not address either tax-exempt financing, varied maintenance options, or equity recovery.
4. The college needed access to future technology today. That is to say that knowledge of the next generation of PCs would make today's expenditures better timed and a more effective use of limited resources.
5. If the college were to pursue this project, should it ask for the moon and attempt to solve a myriad of technology concerns or just address its obvious needs?

Outcomes

Staff from PJC's information services department, purchasing department, business office, and computer labs met to formalize this Tech Refresh Program (TRP). Something was missing; some concept or idea to make this plan work was lacking. It finally dawned on us what we were seeking: numbers, large numbers of PCs that could be offered to the vendors as a potential market. Why not invite all 28 of Florida's community colleges to join us at no risk, no obligation? It was done; the TRP was begun.

In February of 1998, a meeting was held in the state capital to discuss the Florida community colleges' interest in jointly implementing a statewide TRP. Attendance included more than 60 members of Florida community colleges' business officers, information systems staff, purchasing staff, and information technology staff. It was agreed upon at this meeting to pursue the development of a cooperative request for proposals (RFP) that could result in a master contract to control the terms and conditions of this venture and standard financing documents for institutions requiring financing (lease-purchase) assistance. The intent of this RFP was to establish stable and attractive pricing, trade-in values, and tax-exempt financing options, allowing participating colleges to refresh technology on a cyclical basis.

To acquire the information needed to begin the development of this RFP, a survey instrument was developed and disseminated to collect data on the PC inventories, future PC expansion, PC configurations, maintenance practices, information technology capabilities, and financing needs of the 28 colleges. The data were compiled and incorporated into an RFP that was forwarded in April 1998 to more than 30 precontacted, interested PC manufacturers, retailers, and financing organizations. A pre-RFP conference was held the first of May with more than 20 potential proposers and an equal number of college representatives. This conference resulted in three RFP addendums clarifying the intent and certain issues of the RFP.

Proposals (two stacks' worth, each more than four feet tall) were publicly opened three weeks later and formally evaluated within a week by a team of college personnel from eight of the colleges. The evaluation was conducted in the sunshine, with more than a dozen of the proposers in attendance, strictly as observers. This resulted in a short list of four proposers and six proposals. Formal presentations were given by the finalists in early June, resulting in one proposer and two proposals being eliminated. The remaining finalists then delivered the proposed equipment (preconfigured, bundled computer systems, as specified in the RFP) to each of three colleges for technical testing and evaluation. The TRP evaluation committee then considered RFPs, formal presentations, and technical evaluations. It was evident to the committee that a number of the proposers were very interested and serious in their response to our RFP and were clearly capable of conducting a successful partnership with us. In the end, the committee unanimously selected Dell Computer Corporation's proposal and Dell as our TRP partner. We continue to receive inquiries from vendors not selected who are now aggressively pursuing other potential consortia of colleges and universities.

The subsequent contract with Dell resulted in the following benefits to our colleges:

- PCs discounted at no less than 22.5 percent under list price, this discount applicable to all future PCs and future list price reductions; the percent discount has been as high as 34.5 percent
- Peripherals at 5 percent over Dell's cost
- Three-year on-site maintenance included in the price of purchase, lease, or lease-purchase, with other maintenance options offered
- Very aggressive tax-exempt lease-purchase financing
- Eleven percent trade-in values guaranteed at 36 months and *Orion's Blue Book* values for older trade-ins;
- Dedicated website access for preconfigured bundles, ordering, bulletin boards, and so forth
- Same PC/peripheral prices available to faculty, students, and staff
- A formula-based process for future determination of PC configurations
- Access to Dell long-range road-mapping plans
- Numerous other beneficial services and features

The colleges formed a steering committee and technology committee to govern this venture. Volunteers appointed to these committees are responsible to the Council of Business Affairs, made up of 28 Florida community college chief business officers.

The steering committee, jointly with Dell, has reconfigured our PC bundles five times since September of 1998, when the contract commenced. These new bundles have resulted in lower costs; faster chips; more memory; flat-screen options; the addition of laptops, servers, and workstations; and other improvements. Most of these improvements were initiated by Dell through the quarterly road-mapping meetings we have jointly held. Our community college system is clearly taking advantage of the advances in technology and not spending our limited resources on soon-to-be-obsolete equipment.

In September 1998, there were 62,000 PCs in use among Florida's community colleges. Based on a three-year refresh cycle, the colleges could save an estimated $33.1 million, or $534 per PC (RFP price versus state contract price or discounted list price of comparable PCs). With the inclusion of the state universities and the 37 public and private colleges and universities in Florida, an estimated 75,000 additional PCs could be purchased for an additional savings of more than $40 million. Savings would also be realized in purchasing software, printers, and scanners at 5 percent over cost to Dell or 7.5 percent under Dell's list price for other PCs and servers (estimated savings at $3 to $5 million over three years).

The community colleges had been expending approximately $17 million per year for PC technology in each of the last four years prior to TRP. The savings on maintenance, labor, parts, and so forth will be significant. PJC alone estimated a $50,000 savings, as less time would be spent maintaining the equipment and more time could be devoted to training, enhancements, and expansion. The 28 community colleges could generate $1.4 million annually in savings in maintenance costs. From 1999 through 2003, the community colleges and universities acquired in excess of $161 million of PCs, peripherals, and software through this contract. The savings is estimated to be over $98.2 million when compared with previous negotiated pricing or state contract pricing.

Dell and the Florida community colleges and universities have entered into a long-term relationship held together solely by Dell's providing high-quality equipment, services, and financing at these low costs. This TRP gives our colleges and universities direct access to Dell's decision makers and in turn provides our institutions information to best use the limited resources we have available for technology. The Technology Refresh Program and the process designed to create it can be replicated by other groups of colleges, universities, and school systems, with any number of interested PC manufacturers or retailers. Florida's colleges and universities, as a system, have been thrilled with the relationship with Dell and the benefits gained from this program. The implementation of such a program in any system or consortium of educational institutions is strongly encouraged – how else can you maintain current technology and save a bundle?

Rand S. Spiwak is Executive Vice President of Daytona Beach Community College and the former Vice President for Business Affairs at Pensacola Junior College.

Part XI

Workforce, Partnerships, and Outreach

1. Reforming Workforce Preparedness

Donald W. Cameron and George M. Fouts

Context

Guilford Technical Community College (GTCC) is located in Guilford County, North Carolina, and serves a large urban county that contains two of North Carolina's eight largest cities, Greensboro and High Point. GTCC was opened in 1958 as one of North Carolina's first industrial education centers, which evolved into the present North Carolina Community College System. The industrial education centers were established to prepare people for jobs created by the rapid movement of North Carolina's post-World War II, agrarian economy to a new economy dominated by manufacturing, especially furniture and textile manufacturing. Guilford County was home to many of the nation's best-known textile and furniture industries. High Point, which hosts the International Home Furnishings Market, is still known as the Furniture Capital of the World.

In 1965, the Guilford County Industrial Education Center was granted the authority to award associate degrees and became Guilford Technical Institute. In 1983, following considerable opposition at the local and system levels, GTI added a college transfer program and became Guilford Technical Community College. Because of its long history of providing vocational and technical education, and to demonstrate their continuing commitment to that aspect of its expanding mission, the trustees insisted that "technical" remain a part of the institution's name.

Today, GTCC operates on four campuses and annually enrolls over 12,000 (unduplicated) students in curriculum programs and 30,000 (unduplicated) students in continuing education programs. More than 50 percent of the curriculum students are over 24 years of age, and 75 percent of those students work full or part time. GTCC is the fourth largest community college in the North Carolina Community College System. More than 90 percent of GTCC graduates remain in the area following graduation. Guilford County is also the home of two branches of the University of North Carolina, four private colleges, and numerous proprietary educational enterprises.

The CEO of GTCC is in his 14th year of service and served for 10 years as the college's chief academic officer prior to his selection as president. He is widely respected locally and at the state and national levels as an advocate for the traditional community college role of training and retraining citizens for work. In 2002, he received the State Board of Community Colleges' first Outstanding President's Award. Throughout his tenure and the college's history, GTCC has consistently been viewed by community leaders and the public at large as the principal player in the county's workforce training and economic development. GTCC has been frequently recognized and applauded for its technical degree and diploma programs and for its customized worker-training program for new and expanding industries. During its history, the Guilford County Board of Commissioners, which has statutory responsibility for the construction and maintenance of facilities, has provided what is considered to be one of the best local operating budgets in the North Carolina Community College System. Furthermore, the citizens of Guilford County have approved all seven bond issues proposed during the college's history.

In the late 1980s, the economy of North Carolina and of Guilford County, in particular, began to change. Traditional, locally owned textile and furniture companies began to be acquired by national and international conglomerates, and nontraditional industries – manufacturing, financial, and service – began to locate in Guilford County. The passage of NAFTA accelerated this change as many of the textile and furniture companies moved their manufacturing operations offshore. Newspaper headlines of plant closings and loss of jobs became weekly events.

Local business leaders, chamber of commerce officials, and economic development groups at first privately and then openly expressed their concerns about the quality of the county's workforce and the ability of those workers to successfully move to a new economy. The themes mirrored those of several national reports, including the U.S. Department of Labor's Workforce 2000 study. Furthermore, at the state level, the Governor of North Carolina had appointed a blue-ribbon task force on workforce preparedness. The work of this task force, which held public hearings across the state, generated considerable publicity, not only about North Carolina's changing economy, but also about the lack of both basic skills and technical skills in the state's workforce.

The concerns expressed by local leaders in many ways reflected the rhetoric at the state level, but one issue distinguished the Guilford County situation. Guilford County was one of the last North Carolina counties to merge its public school systems (K-12). That merger of three systems in 1993 was very controversial, at least in part because it was accomplished not through a vote of the people, but through legislative mandate. Prior to merger, most observers would agree that the existing systems' chief mission was preparing high school graduates for four-year college work. There was little focus, except in very traditional terms, on vocational education. Only one of the three previous systems and its superintendent had given much attention to the growing tech-prep movement. An analysis of the movement of the county's high school graduates to GTCC confirms this conclusion.

GTCC's trustees and its CEO had long expressed concern that a smaller percentage of local high school graduates enrolled at the local community college than did so in other North Carolina counties. While praising GTCC's technical and vocational programs, many leaders also questioned if some programs needed to be revised or even deleted in favor of new programs to respond to changing employment patterns.

But the growing discontent of local leaders about the state of workforce preparation in Guilford County began to focus on the newly merged public school system. Several members of the new Board of Education began to talk with trustees of GTCC and with its CEO about how to address this problem. In many respects, GTCC was being called upon to develop a plan which would impact not only how GTCC delivered workforce training, but how the public schools could be more effectively involved in that process.

Summary of the Case

Although GTCC enjoyed widespread respect and support for its technical programs, the CEO was now challenged with involving a recently merged and large (65,000 students; 8,000 employees; 14 high schools) public school system in a coordinated effort to improve the skills of the workforce for a rapidly changing economy. While relationships with the previous three systems and their superintendents had historically been cordial, only a few high schools belonging to one of the previous systems had actively promoted a tech-prep program of study. Because so many business leaders, chamber of commerce officials, and economic development leaders were involved in the daily life of GTCC (several as members of its board of trustees, many of the college's foundation board, and hundreds on the college's program advisory committees), the CEO was at least unofficially asked to develop a plan of action.

Questions to Consider

1. How should the community college president respond to criticism from local employers that the college is not graduating enough students with the necessary skills to meet present and future needs of their companies?
2. How can the community college president encourage the public schools to develop tech-prep partnerships that will channel more high school graduates to the community college?
3. How can the community college president effectively develop support from local business and industry leaders to strengthen existing programs and create new ones?
4. How can the community college build public awareness of the workforce preparedness issues in order to build support for the community college and its initiatives?

Thoughts and Analysis

The president decided to approach the newly appointed superintendent of the merged school district to discuss a possible joint tech-prep initiative. The superintendent, who was a community college graduate himself, was interested. Indeed, he had already sensed from community leaders and at least a couple of his board members that more needed to be done. Together, the president and superintendent, with strong support from chamber of commerce officials, launched a study of workforce preparedness issues in Guilford County. Each appointed key staff members to be involved in the process.

One of the first joint decisions was to employ an outside marketing group to analyze the workforce issues in the county. The president, who had frequently spoken in public about his views, felt that an outside voice was needed to confirm, deny, or refine the positions he had already taken. A nationally respected marketing firm was employed to conduct a workforce preparedness assessment.

The study, which included more than 700 people in focus groups and telephone interviews, was one of the most comprehensive ever done in the county. Employers, chamber of commerce officials, managers of employment agencies, and high school guidance counselors were asked for their perceptions and opinions regarding the quality and preparedness of the local workforce and the workforce needs of the future. In addition, questions were asked of employees, recent high school graduates, and recent college graduates about their perceptions of their preparation for the workforce. Finally, unemployed citizens were researched to determine reasons for their unemployed status. The research involved analysis of existing employment data, telephone and mail surveys, and focus groups.

The combined research identified a long list of skills needed in both the existing and future workforce, including technical skills and soft skills (what came to be called employability skills). Several recommendations emerged:

- To promote a public awareness campaign about the findings;
- To create more extensive participation by local businesses, aimed at enhancing workforce preparedness;
- To give students relevant information and help in seeking employment; and
- To provide more job shadowing experiences, internships, and cooperative education programs.

Outcomes

Over the next year, the president and the superintendent (and key members of their staffs) worked with their boards and principal business leaders to develop short- and long-term strategies to respond to these recommendations. A comprehensive plan developed under an umbrella that became known as the Partnership for Guilford County Workforce Preparedness. With oversight by a Workforce Investment Council (composed of education and business leaders), 10 program-specific business councils were formed.

Considerable publicity surrounded the research, the development of strategies, and their implementation. Local media continue to focus much attention on the joint effort. In addition, the *Wall Street Journal* did a front-page story on the effort.

To date, local businesses have contributed over $2 million to fund the tech-prep initiative, to provide scholarships for tech-prep graduates, to provide for faculty return-to-industry experiences, and to provide for instructional equipment.

A comprehensive tech-prep program was implemented in all Guilford County public schools, beginning with a career-awareness curriculum in the elementary schools, a career-exploration program in the middle schools, and a career-preparation focus in the high schools. The commitment by local business owners to this program has moved well beyond financial. Each year, scores of private business leaders attend tech-prep orientation sessions held in the public schools for students and their parents.

Not only has there been increased awareness of the need for sound workforce preparedness; there have also been tangible and welcome results. The percentage of Guilford County high school graduates enrolling at GTCC has increased substantially. In 2000, the first year that tech-prep scholarships were available, 10 were awarded. In

2003, 85 were awarded. In 1999, GTCC had 160 students enrolled in cooperative education programs; in 2003, there were 313 students enrolled.

The tech-prep program has earned many awards, including the Magna Award for Outstanding Programs in Student Achievement, given by the *National School Board Journal*, and the Dale Parnell Award, presented by AACC.

Most amazing, perhaps, is that eight years after the partnership was born, it continues to live and thrive. The former school superintendent was replaced by one equally committed to tech prep, school board members and community college board members have come and gone, the landscape of the local economy has continued to change, but the partnership remains strong. Both of the county's two chambers of commerce continue to support positions titled as directors of workforce preparedness. These people work to keep the chamber memberships focused on education and workforce issues.

The public schools have enjoyed new respect from the business community, and the community college's prior support has been broadened and strengthened as a result of the partnership. Since the implementation of the tech-prep program, the public schools have overwhelmingly passed two bond referenda, and the community college has also passed two issues with similar support. In addition, the community college's foundation has successfully launched a $6 million campaign to support endowed teaching chairs, scholarships, and instructional technology. Support of the business community for both the community college and the public schools has never been stronger.

Donald W. Cameron is President of Guilford Technical Community College in Guilford County, North Carolina. George M. Fouts was Executive Vice President of GTCC prior to his retirement in 2001; he currently teaches part time in the college's developmental studies department.

2. The Little Initiative That Could

Charles J. Carlsen

Context

Johnson County Community College (JCCC) is one of 19 community colleges in the State of Kansas. It is the only public two-year postsecondary institution providing transfer, career, and continuing education in Johnson County. Of the 3,066 counties in the United States, Johnson County income is among the highest, ranking in the top 1 percent in per capita income. Johnson County is also ranked among the nation's most educated counties, ranking first in high school graduates at 93 percent and ranking fourth in college graduates at 41 percent.

In 1969, classes opened in storefronts and a church basement in the northern part of the county. Enrollment was 1,380. The college moved to its current campus in 1972; nearly 100 full-time faculty taught more than 3,600 students in transfer and career programs in six new buildings. Currently, JCCC has more than 34,000 credit and continuing education students attending classes in 17 buildings on the present campus and at more than 40 off-campus sites in the community, including 20 area high schools.

JCCC's main educational programs and services have two focal points:

- A primary focus is on credit courses, including those that form the first two years of most undergraduate college curricula and segue to more than 100 transfer agreements with regional colleges and universities. In addition to transfer courses, credit curriculum includes more than 50 one- and two-year career degree and certificate programs that prepare students to enter the job market in high-employment fields.
- A second major focus is continuing education that includes professional development opportunities through courses, workshops, and contract training for individuals who seek workforce training and skills enhancement. In addition, continuing education includes personal enrichment opportunities via educational and recreational programs and cultural events in the visual and performing arts.

Summary of the Case

The CEO, in his sixth year of leadership at the college, initiates a partnership that he believes has potential to strengthen the college's reputation on both a local and national level.

Key players include the college's president and CEO, the president's administrative cabinet, the board of trustees, Burlington Northern executives, the mayor and city manager, college faculty, community members, and attorneys for the college and Burlington Northern.

The college provides training for Burlington Northern Railroad through its continuing education branch, and initial discussions involve welding training. Upon hearing that Burlington Northern is exploring the relocation of their offices to another city and state, the president proposes an idea to encourage the railroad to stay in the city. Specifically, he proposes a joint venture to build a training center that could become a national model. After meeting with Burlington Northern executives, the president meets with his administrative cabinet and the board chair. Neither supports pursuing the program. Of the reasons cited, the major concern is that the new program would impinge on the academic integrity of the college. Rather than succumb to the faculty complaints of "Choo Choo U," the President believes that the programs need not be mutually exclusive, and sees the merits of each as two very separate entities.

In addition to the academic concerns, there is the compounding issue of a year-end deadline that would provide potential tax benefit for the railroad. That said, the leadership issue for the president, for the purposes of the case study, is to determine whether or not moving forward with the potential partnership is a risk worth taking.

Questions to Consider

1. Should the president pursue the partnership without initial approval from his administrative team and board chair?
2. What are the factors that could cause this venture not to succeed?
3. What are the consequences if the partnership does not work out and is dissolved?
4. What is the best approach to address financing and how to pay for the building?
5. Could the college intervene in the city's right to tax Burlington Northern?
6. How should the public-private partnership trust issues in developing the proposal be navigated?
7. How does the president build a bridge between the two legal counsels to create a win-win situation?
8. Considering all potential options, the president must work to develop best-case and worst-case scenarios. What would they be?

Thoughts and Analysis

Beginning with the end in mind, the CEO begins to explore the win-win proposals that would bring all partners to the table.

The financing issue is explored with the city mayor and city manager, and the president begins to negotiate a $2.9 million building to be constructed on the college campus, financed with city revenue bonds. Compounding the financing is a moratorium on revenue bonds that could be addressed by the city council. Ultimately, the college proposes to assume one-third of the construction cost while the railroad assumes two-thirds of the cost. The president and his team propose a contract to receive ownership of the building in 10 years, giving Burlington Northern an option to renew its lease on a five-year basis.

Burlington Northern receives a training center, in which it establishes the National Academy of Railroad Sciences. Additional benefits include the built-in infrastructure of the surrounding campus – parking, food service, maintenance, and additional educational opportunities for which trainees can receive college credit.

The college gains nine classrooms, laboratory access for technical training, and warehouse space. The college also accepts maintenance responsibility for the facility.

The city and community gain the annual economic development impact of 14,000 hotel and motel room rentals plus restaurant and shopping revenues. Civic engagement of employees is an additional gain for the community.

Additional stakeholders are the faculty. The president decides to follow his protocol of meeting with individuals and then departments to assure them that the Burlington Northern partnership would not have a negative effect on academic programs, nor would funding be diverted from academic programs to support the training programs. In addition, the CEO proposes a distinguished service award for faculty that is funded by Burlington Northern, awarded by outside jurors, to recognize and promote excellence in instruction.

In meeting with the attorneys for both the college and the railroad, the president encounters potential roadblocks in the zeal from legal counsel to gain, in their opinion, the best legal document for their stakeholders. The president proposes a meeting of the administrative teams to reach a win-win compromise outside of legal counsel.

Outcomes

The college was awarded a presidential citation by Vice President George Bush in 1987, recognizing the effort as a successful national model of cooperation between education and industry. This success continues today. The ultimate results of the Burlington Northern partnership were the creation of the National Academy of Railroad Sciences and the nation's first associate degree program in railroad operations.

Charles J. Carlsen is President and CEO of Johnson County Community College in Overland Park, Kansas.

3. ESL Ice Hockey Facility

R. Thomas Flynn

Context

Monroe Community College is a multicampus, comprehensive community college located in Rochester, New York. The college serves approximately 36,000 students and is governed by a 10-person board of trustees: 5 appointed to a nine-year term by the local county executive, 4 appointed to a nine-year term by the governor of the State of New York, and a student elected to serve one year by the student body.

The local county funds approximately 25 percent of the college's operating budget, and in New York State, capital construction costs are equally shared by the county and the state.

Summary of the Case

As this case unfolds, the president has a very positive relationship with the county executive and the county legislature, and significant progress is being made for the county to approve $40 million worth of capital projects, including a new campus center and the college's first residence-hall complex.

The college receives a request from a private developer, who represents several influential individuals, to build an upscale four-rink hockey facility on campus. Shortly after these discussions commence, the CEO receives a call from the county executive strongly encouraging the college to go forward with this request.

This information is discussed with the board of trustees. It is agreed that under the right circumstances, the project will be a valuable asset to the college. However, the college administration and the board of trustees recognize that other rink owners in the greater Rochester area will object strenuously to the competition and to the prime location this rink will have. In addition, other rink owners will claim unfair competition because of this private firm being able to build on the college campus.

Prior to any decisions being made, information leaks to the community, and other rink owners in the greater Rochester area do object strenuously to the aspects of unfair competition. The minority political party takes up the banner with the private owners and objects strongly in the legislature as well.

The college's CEO and CFO meet to discuss these concerns with the county executive and other parties interested in building the ice hockey facility. The concerns are dismissed as being short-term issues.

Following several discussions between the board of trustees and the college administration, the college agrees to go forward with the project. Without question, there is great advantage to having an outstanding ice hockey facility located on the campus. An appraisal determines that a fair lease price would be $168,000 per year.

As the project unfolds, it is to be financed with approximately $12.5 million of tax-free bonds and $2 million of taxable bonds. When the college reviews the financial *pro forma*, we note with significant emphasis that we do not believe the facility could generate the income to retire the debt service and operate the facility effectively. For the most part, our concerns are ignored.

Fast forward about five years. The facility was built and is recognized as one of the finest ice hockey facilities in the Northeast. The college hockey team in this short time has become a national power, and the community absolutely loves this facility. Not only is it attractive, accommodating, and useful; it provides needed additional rink facilities for our community. From the outside view, it appears to be a huge success.

However, as operated, the facility has never generated the necessary income to meet financial obligations and is on the brink of bankruptcy. The owners approach the college to buy the facility. The college refuses in light of the outstanding bond debt and the loss of revenue potential. In addition, the facility is behind on many financial obligations and, as of November 2003, owes the college $700,000 in lease arrears.

One of the current owners decides to attempt to buy out the bonds at a discounted rate. As he is doing this, he requests that the college take a considerable reduction in the lease payments and other obligations the facility has to the college, including outstanding debt. The college recognizes the value of this facility to the community and to the college. Thus, it agrees to attempt to work with the potential new owner and find ways to adjust the financial obligations without losing an unacceptable amount of revenue from a valuable piece of land.

However, any changes in the lease arrangement will have to be approved by the county legislature, which will inflame the opposing political party, thus reopening the issue of the dubiousness of locating this private facility on the college campus.

Unfortunately, from the beginning of negotiations, it has become clear that the new owner expects the college to take a reduced financial arrangement – much lower than the CEO will consider. In discussions with the county executive, who is now going out of office, he makes it clear the college should not take a loss and we should protect the original financial agreement. He does not want the negative publicity, nor does the college.

In summary: (1) The college is strongly encouraged by the county executive to lease land to a private developer for building the ice hockey facility on our campus. He believes this would be a great recreational facility for the college, and more importantly the community at large. (2) Although the college notes concerns with the financial *pro forma* for operating the facility, the project goes forward and an outstanding facility is built. (3) The facility is a great benefit to the college and the community. (4) Unfortunately, the predictions of the college come true and the facility cannot be operated under the current debt and operating expenses and has accrued significant debt for not paying financial obligations, *i.e.*, $700,000 in lease payments to the college.

The college is faced with gaining some sort of cooperation in reducing the debt and operating expenses, or the facility will go bankrupt and close. The college would then have 12 acres of its land tied up with a nonoperating ice hockey facility – a facility that would readily deteriorate. The college board of trustees and administration determine that the worst of all situations would be for this facility to close.

The college CEO – the former CFO, who has been with this project from the beginning – begins to personally negotiate with the individual attempting to take over the facility. The CEO offers an arrangement whereby the annual lease would be reduced from $168,000 to $118,000, with the college accepting new signage on the outside and inside of the facility appropriately advertising the college and its ice hockey team. In addition, the CEO insists that the college CFO serve on the board of directors and have full access to financial information. The CEO further demands that if the facility begins to turn a profit, a percentage of that profit will go to the college. As part of his offer, the CEO demands the college ice hockey team receive all practice time at one-half non-prime-time rates and game time at regular rates. The projected owner suggests that these conditions are unacceptable and wants the college to reduce its lease payment to $65,000 per year, with no other considerations.

It is the CEO's opinion that this will be resolved with additional discussion in view of the significant investment of this private individual and the importance of the facility to the college and community. Of course, it is just for these reasons that the private investor believes the college will reduce its requirements. As of this time, December 2003, negotiations are still under way.

It might be important for one studying this case to project what the outcome will be. Should the CEO reduce the college's lease payments further or hold tight? Don't forget public perception, legislative interest, and the fact that this is valuable land. Also, the rink is a great facility, serving college and community needs.

Following, are some of the legal, political, and policy questions considered during the proposal, building, operation, and renegotiation for this facility.

Questions to Consider

Political. The college has a very positive relationship with county government. There is no question this facility would be a great asset to the college and the community.

1. What political risks does the college have with local government if it does not agree to build this facility?
2. What political risks does the college have with influential individuals in the community – all of whom are strong supporters of the college foundation – if it does not agree to build this facility?
3. What political risks are there in the community if it is perceived that the college is part of undue favoritism to these rink owners verses other private rink owners?
4. What are the potential upside and downside in the decision in this case?

Legal

1. Can the college lease land that has been purchased by public tax dollars to a noncollege entity for the purpose of a private business?
2. What liability issues does the college have with a sports complex not owned or operated by the college on our campus?
3. Do other rink owners have a legal challenge of unfair practice?
4. Are there tax and zoning issues that could stop such a project?
5. Could this be construed as a gift of public funds to a private entity (leasing public land)?

Policy

1. The college obviously needs to develop policies for the use of excess land (land not needed for educational purposes).
2. Should the college consider a policy that permits leasing land to noneducational entities for the purpose of raising revenue for its operating budget?
3. If so, what safeguards does the college have to take to assure that any such leased land does not become an eyesore or infringe on college operations?
4. Does the college want to lease all of its available land, not having any open spaces as it now does?

R. Thomas Flynn is President of Monroe Community College in Rochester, New York.

4. Taking the Wheel of a New Economy

James L. Hudgins

Context

The South Carolina Technical College System is composed of 16 technical-community colleges that served over 90,000 credit students and in excess of 126,000 continuing education students last year. The system's mission is comprehensive, with an historical emphasis and priority on economic development. Like community colleges in many states, the system must compete with many interests for state funding, which currently comprises approximately half of the colleges' operating budgets. Over the past three years, funding for higher education has declined by almost 20 percent.

Historically, the technical college system has been recognized as a primary partner with state and local economic development agencies and organizations in promoting and supporting economic development, and has an ever-increasing value in setting state priorities. The technical colleges have made efforts to project future employment needs and have established new developments in order to be positioned for meeting the future needs of the state. However, these efforts have been hampered by a shortage of funding.

The slowdown in the national economy and the expansion of world markets have been especially difficult for South Carolina. During 2003, South Carolina lost 41,000 jobs, with a large percentage of those losses being in manufacturing. The deportation of jobs to Mexico and other parts of the world has exacerbated the impact of the economic slowdown on this employment sector. In addition, a large segment of the state's adult population is rural and undereducated. Finally, South Carolina does not have a top-tier research university to foster development of entrepreneurial startups.

However, since about 2000, the state's three research universities have wisely recognized the priority that state leaders place on economic development. This recognition has prompted a coordinated response to criticism that the research universities have not applied teaching and research resources to the economic benefit of the state. The research institutions have been effective in persuading state businesses and elected leaders to accept the premise that the development of a knowledge or innovation economy for South Carolina depends on the leadership and success of the research universities.

Summary of the Case

A private-sector group comprised of some of the state's most prominent citizens heavily supported South Carolina's governor, elected in 2002. He proposed a bold vision to raise the per capita income to at least the national average (South Carolina is currently 80 percent of the national average) by having the state attract more knowledge-based businesses and industries. The knowledge-based economic development concept is centered on a belief prevalent around the nation that research universities are the engines that will drive a new economy. Efforts to install this economic development strategy are being propelled by the private sector. As this strategy emerges in legislation and policy, the research universities have been targeted for priority in state funding – for example, establishment of a specific funding program to support the creation of an endowed chairs program, along with legislation to effect regulatory relief, bond funding, and comprehensive merit scholarships.

With the current focus on a need for funding and regulatory relief for the state's three research institutions, there exists a critical problem for the state's two-year colleges: anonymity. While praised as a critical resource for the residents and businesses in their communities, technical colleges seldom have received any priority in state funding. Many have observed that this disparity is in part due to the historical success of the technical colleges; they are not perceived as needing attention because they are working well. In addition, in the current effort to shift the state's economic development strategy, current policymakers do not view the technical colleges as critical to the state's future success.

To evidence this, a prominent leader in the current movement to elevate the capacity of the state's research institutions has stated publicly that the technical colleges have been "historically important." The message is that the technical colleges drove the old economic strategy; the research universities are the sector that will drive the new strategy for economic development. Current policymakers have failed to recognize the vital relationship between research universities in stimulating knowledge-economy businesses through research and community colleges by providing skilled technicians to produce new concepts in the marketplace.

Policy leaders employed the Monitor Group, led by Michael Porter of Harvard University, to develop a strategy for South Carolina to participate in the new economy. The steering committee managing new strategic planning is primarily composed of research proponents. Consequently, the initial strategy has focused primarily on the necessity for South Carolina to invest in its research capacity, while ignoring the critical need to deal with workforce issues that can only be addressed by the state's two-year colleges. Despite repeated attempts to include workforce as a strategic issue, there has been little success at this time.

After four months of study, the Monitor Group report proposed a cluster-based economic strategy led by the research universities for South Carolina. The report commented on the strengths of the state's technical college system, but failed to expand on how the system would be a partner in preparing the state for the new economy.

Questions to Consider

Against this backdrop, the South Carolina Technical College System faced a number of issues:

1. What is the role of technical education in the new economy?
2. How does the technical college system make its case for participation without offending well-intentioned and influential state leaders?
3. What is the best strategy for developing partnerships with the research universities, who have been granted the leadership role in the new economy?

Thoughts and Analysis

The Technical College System, led by its Presidents' Council, has carefully organized a response to this issue:

- The system has analyzed characteristics of the new economy to demonstrate the necessity for skilled technicians. It found that 75 to 85 percent of all future workers will need education beyond high school, with at least 65 percent of the workforce composed of skilled technicians educated at two-year colleges.
- To develop understanding of the need for a common agenda, a position paper was developed and distributed to all leaders in the system and to friends of the system.
- The State Office organized a Summit on the New Technician and included the leaders from private policy groups, research universities, and the state's Department of Commerce.
- The system developed a coalition of business leaders who understand the need to include workforce issues in future strategic plans for the state. This group's focus is to influence the state's move to a new economy. The group is composed of policy and business leaders who belong to organizations such as the South Carolina Policy Council; South Carolina Manufacturer's Alliance; South Carolina Business and Industry Policy Education Council (SCBIPEC); South Carolina Small Business Chamber; South Carolina Chamber of Commerce; and South Carolina Department of Commerce.
- This coalition has begun working with the internationally recognized think tank Research Technology Strategies to develop a white paper highlighting the critical role of two-year colleges in supporting a research-based strategy to spur economic development. This effort is funded by college and private foundations.
- The coalition will use its resources to influence future policy and legislation to ensure that workforce needs in South Carolina are a priority.
- Concurrently, the system has developed a legislative plan to demonstrate roles of technical colleges.
- The system has organized a method to leverage its grassroots support through a web-based grassroots management system. Each college can use the system to engage consistent information locally.
- The system developed a model to demonstrate the need for collaboration among K-12, technical colleges, and research institutions.

Outcomes

The experience has taught the Technical College System several significant lessons:

- The potential strength of 16 colleges working in collaboration to use statewide influence to address a system problem
- The wisdom of avoiding a knee-jerk reaction to a problem and rejecting the option of allowing hurt feelings to seek sympathy, rather than focus on the actual value of the system's contributions
- The value of looking internally at the way the technical colleges are organized and providing services to identify new paradigms for the future

- The value of using organizations and agencies whose support has been earned by years of effective service
- The importance of using national research data to illustrate the importance of engaging community colleges in a state's plan to build a knowledge-innovation economic development strategy
- The value of learning from the experiences of other states that have adopted the cluster-based economic development concept

James L. Hudgins is President of the South Carolina Technical College System in Columbia, South Carolina.

5. Partnering for Change

Edwin R. Massey

Context

Located on the tropical Treasure Coast of Florida, Indian River Community College (IRCC) is a multicampus institution dedicated to serving the educational, career-training, and cultural needs of Indian River, Martin, Okeechobee, and St. Lucie counties. The area's comprehensive educational provider and designated vocational-technical center, IRCC offers a wide range of two-year degree and shorter-term certificate programs, with more than 40,000 people enrolling in classes each year.

The college offers programs for students who plan to transfer to upper-level colleges or universities and students who wish to pursue careers immediately upon completion of their IRCC programs, as well as a full curriculum for students who want to expand their interests and enhance their job skills. Additional programs include dual-enrollment and early-admissions programs, adult basic education, general educational development (GED), English as a Second Language, and the Adult High School.

The educational landscape of the Florida Treasure Coast includes the presence of several universities; four school districts, including 11 public high schools; and one community college.

Summary of the Case

Prior to 1991, problems and deficiencies affecting education were dealt with by the individual educational sectors in isolation of one another, yet many of the issues were bigger than any one system could manage. Ownership of these problems resided with no one in particular and no formal means of communication existed between the K-20 educational systems on the Treasure Coast. This exchange deficiency among leaders led to a lack of the same between faculty and counselors. Lack of awareness led to a lack of understanding. Lack of understanding of intent led to a lack of trust and support among sectors. Duplication of efforts and disconnected attempts to resolve issues resulted in an educational system that was far less effective then it might have been. Postsecondary didn't understand what secondary was doing, and secondary didn't understand what postsecondary wanted. Global issues and sector issues were compounded by the isolated approach to resolution.

No one was more aware of the need for improving communication between educational sectors than the community college president. Independent operation was limiting the potential sphere of influence, causing him to question how a quality educational environment could be created without effectively working together.

Other problems in need of attention included

- the need to reduce the postsecondary remediation rate;
- the need to reduce the high school dropout rate;

- the need to improve academic performance and formulate higher standards in all sectors;
- the need to produce students prepared to enter the workforce and continue their education at the postsecondary level;
- the need to restructure curriculum to reflect the contemporary workplace;
- the need to improve instructional delivery to include the use of technology and contextual learning;
- the need to emphasize math, science, and technology;
- the need to address economically disadvantaged students in the community; and
- the need to increase baccalaureate degrees available to students.

With the shift to the information age, the region was faced with the necessity to alter the educational system to accommodate training for the "skilled" category of occupations. The Treasure Coast is heavily dependent on agriculture as a major industry. The change toward a high-performance workplace demands high-performance workers. Changes in the workplace necessitate changes in the preparation of the workers. Leaders of the four-county educational institutions must be responsive to the societal and cultural shifts that affect student training and preparation. A few of the dynamics driving the labor force include

- the proliferation of new occupations with a technical and scientific core;
- declining employment among the ranks of the semiskilled and unskilled;
- the infusion of analytical and technical content into jobs that have not traditionally been considered technical (National Center on the Educational Quality of the Workforce,1992); and
- 4 million more jobs – soon to be 10 million – without qualified, trained people to fill them (*Impending Crisis*, 2002).

Questions to Consider

1. Should the community college president take the lead in creating an effective way to address these problems and deficiencies?
2. Should he bring together the Treasure Coast educational sectors to determine how to improve and strengthen the quality of education at all levels or continue to conduct business as usual?
3. What type of collaborative group could he create that would transcend the parties involved and remain strong with long-term continuity despite changes in personnel?
4. Could he successfully lead this group to identify common themes significant to each sector that, if pursued collectively, would result in positive legislation, funding, and performance outcomes?
5. When organized, how could this group expand partnerships with area businesses and industries to produce workforce-ready students?

Thoughts and Analysis

It became increasingly evident that a united four-county effort could accomplish far more addressing the challenges facing the educational sectors than any one sector could accomplish alone. Initial intent would not be about solutions but about identifying the issues. Essential practices needed to be embraced and implemented to provide students at all levels the best possible opportunities to prepare for the future. Forming a group to address the challenges would merge the individual sectors in thought, discussion, and action in an effort to benefit the whole educational environment.

Yet, to be truly effective, this system would have to transcend the membership. Sustainability would require a long-term commitment to pre-established goals and the prevention of domination by special interest. Connecting these educational leaders would send a powerful message to all educators that the district leadership is committed at the highest level to provide for students, with a whatever-it-takes stance, and for them to do likewise. Creating a shared vision and the means for achieving it also demonstrates to all stakeholders, parents, teachers, principals, businesses, and legislators that working together is the answer to strengthen efforts to enhance access, funding, and completion rates while resolving problems and challenges through a united and informed position.

Through a coalition, the sectors could work together to maximize both state and local resources. Joint-use facilities, joint-use programs, and co-located institutions would allow flexible and effective delivery of education. Partnering with the area universities could provide associate-to-baccalaureate opportunities; cooperative efforts could advocate for increased educational funding and use of lottery dollars, along with the development of joint grant applications and pursuit of joint funding for programs. Bottom line: Working together would improve all facets of education on the Treasure Coast.

Outcomes

In 1991, invitations were issued to superintendents, provosts, and board members representing all school districts, colleges, and universities in the service district. On the day of the initial meeting, with the response rate unknown, the president was delighted when all sectors were represented, with almost 100 percent in attendance. After a brief welcome and introductions, the president gave a presentation that outlined his vision, identified common areas of interest, and proposed a few initial goals for the group to consider. As expected, the dreaded moment of silence followed, that predictable moment that occurs after you've taken a major risk with no guarantee of acceptance, and the deafening silence in the aftermath creates a gut feeling of doubt, and you can't help but ask yourself, *What in the world was I thinking? What have I done?*

After a few seconds, which felt more like several minutes, one of the participants spoke up and enthusiastically addressed one of the overlapping concerns, offering several constructive ways for the group to work together for better outcomes. This led to one of the most positive, engaging exchanges of ideas the president has experienced in his professional career. This freewheeling discussion continued well beyond the predetermined point of adjournment. When the dialogue concluded, one of the participants made a motion to name this partnership the Treasure Coast Educators Coalition, voting to meet on an annual basis, thereby solidifying the alliance and assuring continuity of future activities. Today, 13 years later, a unified K-20 educational system exists on the Treasure Coast, anchored by a common purpose and goals and supported by mutual respect, constructive communication, and active partnerships.

Because the leadership came together in that initial meeting and demonstrated a willingness to address issues together, the stage was set – without pointing fingers – for employees of all sectors to do the same. The creation of additional partnerships has now extended to administrators, counselors, grant writers, curriculum leaders, and, most important, secondary faculty working directly with postsecondary faculty. This process has been time consuming and at times even a bit painful, but the return on investment has far exceeded expectations, resulting in remarkable, measurable outcomes. Coalition members realize they are change agents, making an immense difference. As a unified group, they monitor results and establish new short- and long-term goals at their annual meeting each year.

Response time addressing issues has been greatly reduced because the coalition has created a fiber that connects critical personnel within the educational system. This identification of key players has resulted in quick action in response to mandated legislative changes, funding challenges, curriculum reviews, and business and industry needs in the community. There has been immense external impact of this coalition as well:

Legislative – The coalition sends a strong message to the local legislative delegation, stressing a willingness to work together to solve issues through a single common Legislative Position Paper signed by representatives of each entity within the coalition. The paper is then submitted to all members of the Treasure Coast Legislative Coalition, the governor, and the commissioner of education.

Grants – The coalition created the environment in which all relationships could flourish, including the creation of a grant procurement collaboration that has resulted in the coalition receiving more than $156 million worth of state, local, and federal grants over the past 13 years.

Two-plus-two-programs – With the community college providing efficient and cost-effective means of offering lower-division education and the universities offering the upper-division education, this has resulted in 26 A.A.-to-B.A. or -B.S. degree opportunities now available to citizens on the Treasure Coast.

Curriculum – The coalition has led the way in a 10 percent reduction of the remediation rate that has been maintained over the past 13 years. That success is only one of many:

- Reduction of the high school dropout rate
- Dramatic increase in the number of students taking grade-level work in secondary to prepare for postsecondary
- Common curriculum guides for students and their parents, Grades 9-14
- Quick response to curriculum changes to address emerging industries, *e.g.*, biotechnology
- Enhanced development of math, science, and technology through programs such as the Living Science Program, Smithsonian Marine Science Instructional Partnership, and the Cisco Network Training Program
- Successful funding of programs for economically disadvantaged students, including Gear Up, Upward Bound, Talent Search, College Reach-Out, and KAPS programs

- Quad County Tech Prep School-to-Work Consortium, winner of the Parnell Tech Prep Award (1993); U.S. Department of Education Excellence in Tech Prep Award (1993); Selection by USDOE as the Tech Prep Demonstration Program Site (2003); and placement in the National Clearinghouse for Career Pathways (2003)
- NSF/Johns Hopkins Career Transcript Project focused on the SCANS competencies
- Development of a charter high school on one of the community college campuses and creation of a high-tech Advanced Learning Center for Grades 11-12 on another campus
- Programs providing faculty and staff development opportunities, including the Annual Counselor's Conclave, Annual Principal's Meeting, Faculty Symposium, and the Bridge to Teaching Program (Alternative Teaching Certificate)

The Treasure Coast Educators' Coalition has provided effective leadership for enhancing the quality of education on the Treasure Coast of Florida.

Edwin R. Massey is President of Indian River Community College in Fort Pierce, Florida.

6. A Focus on Learning and Serving

Margaret Spontak

Context

Based on trends, the United States Census predicts that the population 55 years of age and over will increase from 64.5 million in 2004 to 102.8 million in 2025 as baby boomers reach retirement age. Central Florida Community College (CFCC), serving Citrus, Marion, and Levy Counties with the main campus located in Ocala, Florida, already reflects the future demographics, with 24.5 percent of Marion County's current population at 65 years of age or over, compared with the national average of 12.4 percent.

The college is located in one of Florida's fastest-growing areas. To the west and south of the college's main campus in Ocala lie gated communities that have attracted thousands of retirees. What better area to pilot cutting-edge programs focusing on the needs of current and future older Americans?

Summary of the Case

Innovative developer Ken Colen of On Top of the World Communities planted a seed with college staff several years ago regarding a concept called the Life Options Center. The centers are designed to help adults make the transition from full-time work and family responsibilities to a new stage in life. A mix of programs includes life planning services, community engagement opportunities, lifelong learning, social interaction, information and referral, and other optional elements such as employment assistance.

The Life Options Center concept, hatched by author of *Prime Time* and President of Civic Ventures Marc Freedman, caught the attention of CFCC's President Charles R. Dassance. Shortly afterward, Dassance was invited by the American Association of Community Colleges (AACC) to meet with Freedman's associates in Washington, D.C., along with leaders from a few other community colleges. Dassance and his staff embraced the idea of launching two centers in CFCC's service district. Other community colleges have begun planning Life Options Initiatives, including Portland Community College (OR); Kingsborough Community College (NY); Cuyahoga Community College (OH); Columbus State Community College (OH); and several colleges in Maricopa Community Colleges District (AZ).

Questions to Consider

1. Should community colleges become involved in volunteer and social service programs?
2. Why should community colleges serve older residents when the traditional market for degree and certificate programs is much younger?
3. How can public-private partnerships and sponsorship arrangements affect community colleges?
4. What are the benefits and downsides of strong advisory groups and self-directed community work groups?

Thoughts and Analysis

1. It is critical that organizations stay focused on their mission. CFCC's mission and values include community and workforce development and service. The college plays an important role in volunteer recruitment and training, both for its own students through service learning and for area residents.
2. Citizens 55 years of age and older are a growing market. Author Peter Drucker states that continuing education will be one of the fastest-growing industries in the next decade. Designing new services for this market is important to maintain a trained workforce, meet community needs, and serve a market that is eager for learning opportunities. Such programs also have the potential to encourage giving to community colleges.
3. With national and state funding not keeping pace with community college growth, colleges must become creative in attracting funding for new programming. Linking with private partners who can mutually benefit from visibility in the targeted market is an effective way to develop long-term program funding. Grants often provide start-up funds, but other strategies need to be used to provide long-term program sustainability and to keep such programs revenue neutral.
4. In order for programs to succeed, community colleges need direct involvement and input from the users. In the case of the CFCC Senior Institute, the group is very self-directed in selecting programming and instructors. Pathways coaches meet monthly to develop midcourse improvements to the new service. The Pathways Advisory Board developed the mission, vision, and goals for the program and provided overall direction on service delivery.
5. It is important that advisory boards do not supplant college governing boards' roles and responsibilities and stay consistent with the college's vision and mission.

Outcomes

The planning for the centers, now called Pathways to Living, Learning, and Serving, has been completed at CFCC, with the first center opening in January 2004 at the new Ewers Century Center, a multimillion-dollar complex for business and community learning. Another center is scheduled to open at On Top of the World Communities' new development during 2005. Services are already being piloted in a temporary site. The two centers meet critical college and community needs.

In 2001, CFCC's Public Policy Institute completed a Senior Issues Study revealing that information and resources for older residents were lacking. CFCC's response, Pathways to Living, Learning, and Serving, incorporates the basic concepts of the Life Options Initiative and brings together information and resources that focus on volunteer service, lifelong learning, work options, wellness, and social engagement.

As part of the new program, the college and its partners launched one of the first life-planning services of its kind, targeting residents 50 years of age and over. A dozen trained volunteer peer coaches assist residents in developing a personal life plan and identifying the resources needed to make their dreams become a reality.

In addition to the life-planning program, community leaders involved in the Public Policy Institute study pointed out the lack of connection between the residents of the gated communities and the cities. In response, CFCC, now sponsor of the Retired and Senior Volunteer Program (RSVP), stepped up efforts to engage more volunteers from the communities. Within the first year of planning, CFCC, On Top of the World Communities, United Way of Marion County, and other partners launched Volunteer 200, a volunteer recruitment event that attracted almost 700 attendees and resulted in more than 100 people signing up for service opportunities. The event, hosted by On Top of the World Communities, is now in its second year.

A second volunteer recruitment, training, and placement program is under way in partnership with University of Maryland and Atlantic Philanthropies. The Legacy Corps for Health and Independent Living links college service learning students with RSVP volunteers for an intergenerational approach to providing respite care services. Members, as the volunteers are called, receive support and a paid stipend to help achieve personal college and career goals related to health and human services.

In order to meet the needs of the expanding pool of volunteers, the college's RSVP program and United Way of Marion County are assisting in building community capacity in agencies to more effectively manage volunteers. A monthly volunteer manager networking meeting, facilitated by RSVP staff, allows agencies to share best practices. A new CFCC Nonprofit Institute provides workshops on critical issues such as volunteer management, fiscal responsibilities, grant writing, public relations, and strategic planning.

Meeting workforce needs, both from the employers' and job seekers' viewpoints, is a critical component of the Pathways Centers. In spring of 2003, a large conference featuring best-practice presenters from the community and the nation kicked off a focus on creating new opportunities for mature workers. Area employers are being asked to provide more part-time and flexible opportunities, consider bridge positions for existing employees wanting to downshift, and assist employees in making positive transitions from work to retirement or "rewirement." The local workforce board and CFCC are conducting monthly workshops for mature job seekers and have planned a job fair for this audience.

As for lifelong learning, the changing needs and desires of the marketplace have led to rethinking educational programming for older adults that traditionally focused on fun and recreation. The CFCC Senior Institute, Munroe Regional Medical Center's Prestige 55 program, and On Top of the World Communities' Master the Possibilities program have collaborated on new lifelong learning programs that touch on significant issues, stimulate discussion and community action, help with career exploration, and lead to personal renewal.

As with most new community college programs, funding is always an issue. The Pathways Advisory Committee developed a funding model that includes local sponsors, membership fees, paid programming, and an annual fundraising event. The college is providing seed money to launch the new initiative and space for the offices with the goal to make the program self-supporting in the future. To date, four gold sponsors – contributing $10,000 annually in cash or in-kind services – are in place, including Munroe Regional Medical Center, On Top of the World Communities, the *Star Banner* and CFCC's Senior Institute. The institute, created to provide lifelong learning opportunities for older residents, donated funds to the Pathways program derived from its annual programming surplus. Additional gold sponsors are being sought.

The benefits of the program to CFCC and the community are worth the college's small investment. As a result of new programs for older residents, a larger percentage of the community has become engaged with the college, some for the first time. Through service leadership, the college has expanded the supply of volunteers serving in the community. Employers are identifying additional staff to meet their needs. Sponsors receive ongoing national and local recognition through their involvement in the initiative.

Margaret Spontak is Executive Director of Corporate Training and Continuing Education at Central Florida Community College in Ocala.

7. Adapting a Workforce Development Project to Meet a Utility Company's Needs

Jim Willis

Context

In the mid-1980s, a local utility company contacted a two-year technical college in a major city in the South, requesting assistance in meeting its needs for electrical distribution technicians, or what are simply called linemen. This college had consolidated with a community college to form a new comprehensive community college in July 2000.

Linemen must be not only technically educated to the equivalent of a first-year college-level electrical technician trainee, but also rather rugged outdoor types. They must operate effectively while suspended on a utility pole some 15 to 45 feet in the air – gaffs firmly embedded into a wooden utility pole, body arched against a strong leather strap, power lines immediately overhead pulsing with extremely high levels of electrical energy – and still be able to perform technical tasks competently and safely in all-weather conditions (*i.e.*, rain, strong wind gusts, hail storms, electrical storms, snow, icing, bitter cold, sweltering heat).

The company had historically hired individuals from the general public to meet its lineman needs. However, it frequently found that those hired seldom fit the demands of the on-the-job four-year apprenticeship required for them to become journeyman linemen. Many were unable to focus on working safely under hazardous conditions. Whether or not an individual is physically and mentally suitable for this kind of job is not readily apparent under typical job-readiness analysis, but usually becomes evident within the early part of the four years of the apprenticeship process. Unfortunately, this fitness is not normally determined during the first six months of probation in the apprenticeship. It was a difficult situation for both the company and the apprentice.

Several individuals hired to fill those positions were not successful in the apprenticeship. In addition to adding unassigned individuals to the company's payroll, this failure also adversely affected the dignity of the new apprentice. Termination was the most economically feasible action for the company, but it was not in the best interest of the apprentice. The company had a great reputation for being a compassionate employer, choosing to use alternative placement strategies rather than dismissal in cases where a new hire did not fit the job of lineman. There were limits to this strategy, however.

Representatives from the company's safety training department asked the college for assistance in finding a better method to identify candidates. This new method should result in a higher probability of hiring linemen who could successfully complete the training. In the discussions that followed, the company and the college decided to develop a series of six courses requiring 237.5 clock hours of classroom instruction and 75 clock hours of laboratory work, conducted over two semesters; 12.5 clock hours of classroom instruction or 37.5 clock hours of laboratory performance were considered to be one college credit hour; therefore, the 312.5 clock hours were equivalent to 21 college semester credit hours or, with CEUs converted at one for every 10 hours, it would yield about 31 CEUs. These courses served as a pre-apprenticeship training program and included all of the fundamental tasks of the apprenticeship program (*e.g.*, climbing poles under all-weather conditions, exhibiting the physical and emotional abilities to work high on a pole focusing on the job in a safe manner, exhibiting technical competence). The courses would screen out applicants unqualified for the lineman apprenticeship program.

This series of courses required an aspiring lineman to perform under conditions similar to those of the apprenticeship, but with a clear understanding that these actions were performed as a student prior to eligibility for the lineman apprenticeship program. Additionally, with a pre-apprenticeship training approach, less technically qualified candidates had an opportunity to enter the prospective applicant pool by gaining the necessary technical knowledge and skills that could be gained in the pre-apprenticeship program.

To keep workforce training affordable, the company and the college desired to have these courses count toward college credit. If they were developed as noncredit courses, the fees paid for the training by the participant or some other source outside the college must cover the entire expense of the training. Minimum cost for noncredit courses is 125 percent of the cost for the comparable credit course, and it was even higher in this case. Likewise, regional accreditation standards required that college credit courses not stand alone, but be part of an authorized academic program of the college taught by appropriate academically credentialed faculty.

Summary of the Case

The college received an appeal from a local utility company that needed assistance in training personnel for the relatively highly technical, physically demanding, and rather hazardous job of electrical utility company lineman. The company wanted to avoid hiring large numbers of individuals to participate in a four-year apprenticeship that required them to perform demanding tasks that they may not be adept at technically, physically, or emotionally. Although physical conditions (*i.e.*, strength, stamina, ability to adjust readily to all-weather conditions) of an apprentice may show up within the first six months of training, the mental disposition of the apprentice (*i.e.*, ability to withstand long periods of work under adverse weather conditions, ability to ignore dangers caused by working in close proximity to high voltage while suspended high above the ground, the need to move up and down poles in precarious regions such as swamps or rugged terrain) may not reveal a weakness until well after the first six months have passed, but long before the four-year apprenticeship has been completed. Where this situation existed, it caused difficulties for company leaders and for the apprentice.

The company requested the college find an affordable way to screen potential candidates for the lineman apprentice program. The company and the college jointly proposed a pre-apprenticeship program that required approximately 312 clock hours of instruction and laboratory performance over a couple of semesters divided into six courses, three in the first semester and three in the second semester. If the courses could be structured as credit courses, they would be less costly for the participant. Regional accreditation standards also had to be met.

Questions to Consider

1. Should the college develop credit or noncredit courses to meet this need? Why?
2. Is cost for participants a legitimate consideration when choosing to make courses credit, since the cost for noncredit courses in this particular state is required to be at least 125 percent more than the cost for the same credit courses? If it should be, why? If it should not be, why?
3. If credit courses are developed, must the college hire at least one full-time faculty member to serve as lead faculty for the program? Why, or why not?
4. If credit courses are developed, can they be included with courses in existing programs if the new courses legitimately belong to the discipline in which they are being grouped? Explain.

Thoughts and Analysis

The chief academic officer for most public and private community colleges prefers the development of credit courses when these courses are to be part of a designed program of study, whether it is for transfer credit or part of a business, career, or technical-studies curriculum that prepares the program completer for the labor market. This requires a curriculum development protocol strictly controlled by a full-time member of the faculty who possesses the appropriate academic credentials to lead the effort. However, in some cases it is advisable to develop a series of new courses as noncredit if they do not readily align with an existing academic program and if they are designed primarily to prepare individuals to enter the labor force in a relatively short time with less than an associate degree.

Credit courses establish a better pathway for the student to enter a degree program at some point in his or her educational pursuits than does a noncredit approach, particularly as it applies to the inclusion of any general education components. The cost factor is a nice side effect in the case of public two-year colleges wherein some amount of subsidy is provided through tax dollars for the credit courses but not for the noncredit courses. This may be a moot point, however, in private two-year colleges.

Generally, a full-time faculty with appropriate academic credentials must lead any credit program that has an academic outcome of an associate degree, and in many cases, an outcome of a certificate that is a subset of an associate degree program. However, that full-time faculty may be part of an existing program when other programs are added to the college's menu.

A first step in developing a new set of credit courses is to determine if these new courses fit into an existing program or if they are part of a new program that does not currently exist in the college's inventory of credit programs. If the new courses can, they should be added to the program that has that same category of courses. This reduces the need for hiring new faculty to lead start-up efforts for this set of new courses.

Outcomes

When approached by representatives of the utility company, the college's continuing education and economic development (CEED) unit was engaged in the original discussions. The CEED representatives at the college sought assistance from faculty in the appropriate units of the college. Along with technical representatives from the utility company, the faculty developed a series of six courses to meet the needs of the company. They determined that it would be in the best interest of all concerned to make these credit courses. Many of the utility company's technical experts served as adjunct faculty to teach these courses. No full-time faculty from the college were assigned to any of the courses, even though they were listed under the course numbers that indicated the academic unit of the college to which these courses were related.

This model existed under the administration of the technical college's leadership for several years and was even cited by visitors from the regional accreditation association as an exemplary model. This model continued to be used until the consolidation of the technical college with the local community college to form a new comprehensive community college.

The new college was required to pursue reaffirmation of accreditation because of the substantive-change rule. Upon review by the accreditation association, it was noted that the six courses that were being taught as part of a pre-apprenticeship program as college credit courses were not appropriately administered under an academic unit of the college. Upon review by the appropriate academic unit leaders, it was determined that the academic credentials of the adjunct faculty were relatively low, although the adjuncts were experientially well qualified. Yet while operating under a relatively short time line to gain reaffirmation of accreditation, the college determined that in order to retain the services of these adjunct faculty without risking concerns about accreditation, these courses must be moved to noncredit status.

No sooner had this change to noncredit occurred than the college discovered that cost for the courses created a major challenge for many of the potential students who had typically been attracted to this particular type of workforce development program. This generated a new set of problems for the utility company that were similar in effect to those that had existed when individuals were being hired directly from the general population and the burden of training these individuals fell primarily on the company's shoulders. It was back to the proverbial drawing board.

In a more recent review, it was determined that these courses needed to grouped into a technical certificate category and tied into one of the academic industrial electrical programs. This would place the program in a specific academic unit with a program chair who would oversee all activities in the pre-apprenticeship program. So the credit courses were resurrected, packaged into a technical certificate program, and placed under the control of the appropriate academic unit of the college. This model now satisfies all concerns pertaining to meeting needs of the utility company with an affordable program while adequately addressing the pedagogical concerns of both the college and the regional accreditation association.

Jim Willis is Vice President for Workforce Development and Continuing Education at Southwest Tennessee Community College in Memphis.